RE-MAKING
THE
AMERICAN
DREAM

CHANGE FROM VALUES

DAVID VAUGHT

ISBN 978-1-959182-94-8 (paperback)
ISBN 978-1-959182-95-5 (hardcover)
ISBN 978-1-959182-96-2 (digital)

Re-Making the American Dream
david@dhvaught.com

Printed in the United States of America

This book is dedicated to the memory of my father, Harry Vaught, Jr., a leader in the Greatest Generation.

PREFACE

Living on the Hudson River in a refurbished railroad barge while studying law at New York University School of Law, my roommate, Lucian Truscott IV began to write about our experiences at West Point. We had been roommates there too in 1968 and had begun an administrative challenge to the requirement that all cadets attend compulsory chapel services every Sunday.

Our main protagonist there, then Colonel Alexander Haig, the Deputy Commandant, counseled us against making such a challenge. As we persisted, Haig did his best to bring the full panoply of unpleasantness West Point and the Army had to offer down on us to deter, dissuade and stop us.

After our graduation, other midshipmen at the U S Naval Academy challenged the compulsory chapel requirement in federal court. As a direct witness to the futility of any administrative remedy within West Point and on the merits of religious freedom, I testified twice in that litigation in Washington, D. C.

Out of the Army and a reporter in New York, Lucian had succeeded in gaining a book contract and financial advance to tell this non-fiction story. He wrote at night, while I studied law books and prepared for classes the next day at NYU. We discussed this controversy and our role in it exhaustively over dinners we prepared on the barge where we lived that winter.

Such a direct and obvious violation of the First Amendment by Army officers sworn to uphold the Constitution of the United

States troubled us no end. Their use of their own power to prevent any challenge being raised in the first place, to tamp it down as the challenge arose, and to mislead the court considering the legal challenge disturbed us. If this was how our country's ideals played out in real life, to us it spelled big trouble.

After weeks of writing every night and putting words to paper on over 100 pages, Lucian wasn't ready to finish his book. It was too painful and too soon. He returned the financial advance and re-considered. A few years later, he took it up again and wrote the novel and TV mini-series, *Dress Gray*, based indirectly on our challenge at West Point. Spelling out the big trouble in a different way, his novel was banned at the West Point book store but was a best seller nationwide.

Decades later, I now put my story down in non-fiction, as a memoir and part essay on what drove us in 1968 to mount such a successful challenge. The successful legal challenge lasted until 1972. How a country boy from southern Illinois, raised in the Liberty Baptist Church in Burnt Prairie, Illinois, confronted entering the required doors of the Cadet Chapel at West Point is a longer story.

I found the answer to that question in the American Dream itself, that often misunderstood aggregation of ideals that both influences our culture, while it morphs forward to re-define itself. Its core idea is based in the freedom of religion, whose broader implications create and foster freedom of thought.

In this book, I trace those roots through my own father, a World War II veteran, farmer, and deacon in the Liberty Baptist Church while also exploring in greater detail the history and legal foundation of not just religious toleration but true religious freedom as our founding fathers implemented it.

As the American Dream endures over time, its ideals weather storms of change, while inspiring new approaches to its core. That process changes us as well as we stand for its principles and seek their implementation and improvement going forward.

This book traces those changes from the initial challenges of 1968 into the follow-on through my participation in the reform campaign for Governor of Dan Walker and through his term of office that ended in 1976.

The conflicts of reform and change in a political system still dominated by an older generation of power seekers led to an exploration of disagreement within the key political advisors of Governor Walker. Those who sought political alliances with the aspiring Speaker of the Illinois House, Clyde Choate, had to face the logical and progressive follow on steps to their successful campaign ideals of reform. The book ends there at the conclusion of the successful defeat of the Clyde Choate speakership.

The walk through these events is personal, but the issues of Re-Making the American Dream run deeper. They are steeped in the transmission of values from generation to generation as new experiences and thoughts challenge us to move forward. How we do that creates an American Dream anew.

EPILOGUE

T he new Epilogue updates these ideas currently. It adds new examples of how the values of the American Dream shape our society and culture and spring from many experiences through the current day. The Epilogue begins with a consideration of Governor Dan Walker's advice after he lost the 1976 Democratic primary for Governor. It continues as Pat Quinn clashed with the Illinois political and governmental establishment over the use of citizen initiative powers to advocate reforms in ethics and governance in Illinois. As I worked with my friend Pat over the decades, he asked that I join him in government when he was Treasurer and then as his role as Lieutenant Governor transitioned to Governor of Illinois when Governor Blagojevich was removed from office mid-term in 2009.

Two main examples on the fiscal crisis our state faced during Governor Quinn's term are described in the Epilogue. First the controversy over raising revenues illustrates the difficulties over timing, amount, building public consensus and the political courage required to propose and enact a large tax increase. Then, once revenues are fixed by that action, the difficult clash over reducing spending to live within those revenues is related. Both depend not just on politics but on the values that sustain our system of government. A longer history of Governor Quinn's six years as Governor is not included in this book but can be found in the Abraham Lincoln Presidential Library's oral history project at https://presidentlincoln.illinois.gov/learn/scholars-researchers/research-divisions/oral-history/collection/governor-pat-quinn-project/Governor-Pat-Quinn-Project/interviews.

Finally the Epilogue considers how the values of the American Dream affect, not just government and politics, but business, law and the efficiencies of our economic and investment system. It closes with examples of how the freedom of religion has helped lead my life to implementing Christ's teaching.

ACKNOWLEDGMENT

Those who encouraged me to write are many. While we were cadets at West Point, Lucian Truscott encouraged me to write letters to the editor. Later, Diane Fisher, the Riffs column editor at the Village Voice, encouraged me to write about country music and its culture. Governor Dan Walker, in the practice of law, encouraged me to refine and sharpen my legal brief writing. Larry McMurtry wrote that those who read must also write to answer back. Governor Pat Quinn, long before he became Governor, encouraged me to write and edit constitutional amendment drafts and legislative proposals. Mary Roberts, as a fellow school board member, encouraged me to write and explain proposals to improve our schools and helped inspire writing this book through her own book writing. Kelly Kraft, as my co-worker as Director of the Governor's Office of Management and Budget in Illinois, helped show me how a professional reporter writes with clarity and with the understanding of the reader in mind. One by one, these people contributed to my desire to write and bolstered my own confidence in doing so.

As I undertook to write this book, many more family and friends stepped forward with encouragement and help, including Taylor Pensoneau and Kathy Wright. All those who are characters in this story remain an inspiration because they too stood up and were counted to remake the American Dream.

A Memoir on Change in the American Dream (1968-1976):

From Freedom of Religion in Burnt Prairie, to the End of Compulsory Religious Services at West Point, to the 82nd Airborne Division and the moral challenges of the Vietnam War era, to the Dan Walker for Governor reform campaign, and the defeat of Clyde Choate's campaign to become Speaker of the Illinois House.

TABLE OF CONTENTS

INTRODUCTION

From the Winter of 1944 to Burnt Prairie

The Saverne Gap reminded me of the Delaware Water Gap, without the water. Not quite as high as the Appalachians, the Vosges Mountains were green, impressive and steep. I was driving through the gap from Strasbourg to Luneville to retrace my father's footsteps in World War II. The 7th Army used this gap to break through to the plains of Strasbourg and become the first Allied army to reach the Rhine in November, 1944.

I wanted to see the actual terrain, as it is called in the military, and consider what it was actually like for my father's unit, the 44th Infantry Division, to take on the German Army in these mountains. Hitler believed his Army could defend the Vosges until the spring of 1945, before falling back to their next strong defensive positions along the Rhine. German generals knew that no army in history had successfully attacked through the Vosges. Since Roman times, they always just went around. Hitler was wrong, and 7th Army went straight through in a month.

My father joined the fight in October, 1944, near Nancy and Luneville, where we were headed next, through the rolling farm country and villages west of the Vosges. The 44th Infantry Division was new to Europe and joined 7th Army on the front to the left of the veteran 45th Infantry Division. The rolling countryside near Luneville reminded me of the rolling farm country in western Iowa, not far from where the 44th had trained in its preparation for the fight.

To me, the American Dream, and its changing nature, begins in Luneville, where my father came straight from the depression in Burnt Prairie, Illinois. He and his generation forged the transformation from a world of dictators, fascists and thugs, to the Western world of parliamentary democracies, open trade and growing economies. I wanted to trace that change from then into the future, when my travel companions, my father's children and grandchildren, would continue to remake the American Dream.

He remembered Nancy, in his talks to me about the war, mainly because it was the last peaceful stopover before sleeping in a foxhole for the winter. He was a corporal and gunner on his 105 mm howitzer in an artillery battery in the 44th Infantry Division. The division was augmented from a skeleton National Guard Division by filling it with draftees. It was equipped and trained to join the buildup of forces in southern France who were headed for the Rhine in the fall of 1944.

My daughters, Amanda and Erica, accompanied me on the trip, along with Amanda's two year old Eloise, and her father Keith. Along with my sister, Dixie, they had all volunteered to join me on this trek, though they were already tiring of military words and concepts. It just looked like farmland and pretty villages to them, not "terrain."

We found a great little café in Nancy for lunch, one with a half dozen tables and two friendly young waitresses who were not afraid to speak a little English with us.

My father saw firsthand the ruins and devastation we only know from pictures of World War II. We were in Alsace-Lorraine, a part of France that is peaceful and prosperous. Strasbourg, fought over for centuries between French and German soldiers who sought to claim and dominate this region, now is the seat of the European Parliament in a more unified Europe. Border crossings are less intrusive than tollbooths. Large Turkish communities and refugees from Syria are in much abundance, changing the cuisine of France to include kebobs at the numerous new take-out restaurants scattered through the neighborhoods of Strasbourg. I am sure that my father saw a very different Alsace-Lorraine during that fall and winter of 1944-45.

These apparent changes are global. In my mind, they, too, are part of the success of the American Dream. Closer to home, though, how did this transition from a worldwide Great Depression to the much greater postwar economic boom occur? The Pax Americana of NATO, the United Nations, and the four freedoms were shaped by these greatest generation veterans, including my father.

How does this remarkable turnabout continue into succeeding generations? How will it be shaped by my granddaughter, Eloise, who was sitting with us in that café in Nancy, sucking down the French lemonade, eating croissants, and quickly picking up a few French words in her growing vocabulary. When Eloise would say "merci" to the young French waitresses, they loved it and broke out in friendly smiles.

To begin exploring that question of generational continuity and change, we'll have to travel back to where my father started in Burnt Prairie, Illinois. But first, we are headed from Nancy up to Sarreguemines.

The 7th Army had great success in the fall of 1944. They invaded from the Mediterranean in August, 1944, before my father's division came over in October to reinforce its front for the assault on the Vosges Mountains. With the French First Army on its southern flank, it attacked through St. Die and the Saverne pass going directly at the Germans, mountains or not. By November, its troops were pursuing the German Army in retreat across the Strasbourg plains. After being knocked out of strong defensive positions in the mountains, the German Army sought the security of the Rhine for its next defensive line. The French motored into Strasbourg, which was their second greatest objective after Paris, because of the centuries-long rivalry with the Germans over its control.

The 7th Army was at the Rhine, the first to get there, fueled by strong supply lines from the Mediterranean, good generals with sound tactical plans, and that can-do determination of American troops not long from the dust of the Great Depression. General George Patton was stuck at Metz.

General Devers, commanding the Army Group that included 7th Army and the French, sent his scouts and engineers north of Strasbourg to reconnoiter the Rhine for crossing. His general orders required his armies to attack the Germans and drive them back across Germany. He didn't intend to let a lightly defended river with quickly prepared defenses slow him down. He moved troops to the river and ordered a crossing in mid-November.

The day before the scheduled river crossing, General Devers had a visitor. General Eisenhower himself arrived and saw the preparations to cross the Rhine firsthand. He was aghast. His other troops up north weren't ready to cross the Rhine. Patton was stalled by a strong defense at Metz and their supplies were lagging through the weak temporary channel ports. Eisenhower didn't want a piecemeal attack into the German rear. General Devers, who was Ike's predecessor as Supreme Commander in Europe, argued for his plan using the 6th Army Group in the south, the large unit General Marshall insisted he command after being replaced by Ike as Supreme Commander before D-Day at Normandy. Devers believed that getting across the Rhine and behind the Germans would help Patton and the others get to and across the Rhine while the Germans were in disarray with a large Army wreaking havoc from their rear. Eisenhower, in what some critics call his biggest mistake of the war, still said, "No." The 7th Army held west of the Rhine.[1]

Late December brought the Battle of the Bulge further north. This serious counter-attack in winter caused responses all along the front. Patton moved his troops north to attack the southern flank of the Bulge. Eisenhower ordered 7th Army to pull back to a stronger defensive position in the Vosges Mountains. He wanted no second bulge in the south. The French were incensed. They simply refused to move back from Strasbourg, telling Eisenhower they weren't going to risk its destruction by the Germans and then have to retake it. So

Patch bent his lines east of the Vosges Mountains from Strasbourg to Sarreguemines, defending along the Blies River instead of backing into the Vosges Mountains.

My father spent the coldest winter in 50 years, sleeping in a foxhole by his howitzer near Sarreguemines. We drove through town down into the valley to the river because I wanted to show my fellow travelers how the 44th Infantry Division used the river to defend against the German counter-attack. Operation Nordwind was the German secondary attack in the south in support of the Bulge.[2] I pulled into a vacant industrial parking lot along the canal, but Erica disliked it immediately and spotted a rest area along the bike path that now parallels the canal. It was filled with pleasure boats like a Kentucky Lake marina, not a hostile defensive position ready to take the brunt of a German assault.

We found a good table at the rest area right next to the canal, joining a couple of French bikers enjoying a break in the sunshine at an adjoining picnic table. I pulled out my sister's Michelin tourist map and unfolded it on the picnic table, ready to explain the military defense of the Blies River. Wordy military lectures at this pretty summer rest area, where Eloise wanted to run along the canal and others wanted to take pictures of the scenery, were a bit much, but the adults slowly began to listen.

I described on the map how the advance through the Saverne gap had proceeded with the 44th Infantry Division on the north end of 7th Army's front. As they later moved back into this defensive position where we stood, the line rotated with the 44th remaining on the left of a now East-West defensive line along the river. Then Panzer Lehr, a feared and capable spearhead of tanks with much prior success in the war, came right at my father's unit. It was the toughest battle he faced in that cold December of 1944 and January of 1945. And unlike the surprise attack and breakthrough up in the Bulge, the 44th Infantry Division, in just its second month on the front line, held back Panzer Lehr. Eisenhower's fears of a second bulge in the south were allayed.

They spent that winter near Bitche, waiting for spring to cross the Rhine. The Bulge had to be cleaned up and the Armies well supplied and ready for the push into Germany. I mostly heard about that winter in family visits to Burwell, Nebraska, in the 1950s. We went there to see Bill Beat, who spent that winter sharing a cold foxhole with my father. My father was the gunner and Bill the assistant gunner on their 105. One set the deflection; the other the elevation. They worked side by side facing each other across the gun sights throughout the whole war. At night, they just tried to stay warm sharing a foxhole wrapped up in a couple of Army blankets. It was the only way to keep each other warm through the night.

Once they woke up startled looking each other in the face and outside, above the foxhole. Quickly they realized that they were 6 feet in the air, so high that it was going to hurt when they landed on the frozen ground. To their complete surprise, the concussion of a 500 pound bomb, dropped by a Messerschmitt trying to destroy their howitzer, had blown them out of their foxhole. The bomb missed, and no one on their gun section was hurt, except for some ringing ears and bruises from landing back on the hard earth.

It was one of their favorite stories, and we heard it over and over in Burwell between trips to swim in the Loup River or watch the bareback riders be thrown at the Burwell rodeo. The rodeo was great. I had never seen anything like it. Casey Tibbs and all the best bronco riders and bull riders made it on the circuit, and the action never stopped.

But we weren't there just for a rodeo. We were there so two foxhole mates who survived one of the deadliest wars in history could re-connect, celebrate their freedom from war, and tell stories. Their favorite story, which I heard many times over the years in Burwell and on Bill Beats visits to Burnt Prairie, started with an inspection from their own chain of command. Headquarters big shots in armies always like to go down and see the real troops in the foxholes from time to time. These were not the lieutenants and captains who were usually down in the foxholes themselves, but the real headquarters types, back in camouflaged tents or buildings away from the front, plotting on maps the next maneuver or the next artillery barrage.

My father was a corporal on a 105 mm howitzer, crewed by five or six enlisted men as one of the six howitzers in his artillery firing battery. Because they fired indirectly up and over the front line infantry a couple miles to the front, they were a little better off day to day than the troops under direct rifle and machine gun fire.

Still, they suffered from the feared German 88's, high-powered artillery that doubled as anti-aircraft pieces that fired high-velocity explosive shells with

Corporal Harry Vaught, Jr.

less arc in their trajectory. The Germans loved to aim those shells for detonation in the trees above the troops or opposing gun emplacements, sending showers of shrapnel down from the treetops into the foxholes and exposed positions on the ground. Everyone in my father's artillery unit hated hearing screeching sounds of the 88's as they approached, and the rain of hot steel on them. They were far worse than an occasional 500 pound bomb from a Messerschmitt trying to knock out a gun, and both the infantry and artillery units suffered from the 88's.

The artillery units were far enough in the rear that they were able to receive hot food delivered to their guns, providing bits of relief from the cold K rations that kept most solders alive. The headquarters Colonel asked the usual question: "How's your morale soldier?" Good positive answers snapped back in return. And then the follow-up: "How's the chow?" My father didn't snap back what was expected at all, instead giving the honest answer: "The beans are usually cold, sir." The pause from the brass made clear that answer didn't go over well with his battery commander, or the other officers along from his battalion. They knew what it took to get hot food prepared in the field mess hall and distributed up front to the troops in winter. They expected all the soldiers to appreciate that effort of the mess sergeant to provide hot food on a cold battle line. The officers simply didn't want to hear otherwise. They turned to Bill Beat for a better answer: "How's your food, soldier?" Bill was quick to respond: "Well, sir, not only are the beans cold, you'd think they could serve more than a single slice of bread with the beans."

At that point in the story, my father and Bill used to laugh and slap their legs when Bill gave his punch line, each playing their own part in delivering their farm boy lines to the brass. Then they would get more serious when they said: "Of course, when they sent us up on the front line with the forward observer team the next day, rifles in our hands, we didn't get any cold beans or bread at all up with the infantry guys." I learned a lot about the Army while listening to my father and Bill in Burwell.

I learned what made the Greatest Generation click as well. That "aw shucks," we were just doing our job and having a little fun attitude was endemic with them.[3] They'd come from the Great Depression, where hot beans were a treat, and a lot better than cold baloney. They hadn't grown up with spending cash in their pockets or much time to go to town for shopping or entertainment. They simply didn't have the money. They had lived where they were born and had fun where they stood.

Their matter-of-fact attitude included accepting what they had to do, whether it was baling hay for the cattle in a hot August sun or enduring 88's in a cold winter in Alsace-Lorraine.

They didn't just tell war stories, though. Surviving the Great Depression and the war left them happy to be home and free. They were more than ready for what came next and determined to play a role in it, just as they had in the victory in the war. Bill went to work for the phone company and was active in development efforts to strengthen the small counties of western Nebraska out by the

Sand Hills. They considered it beautiful country for beef but also for tourism and wanted to attract people to the Loup River and the western skies. For years, they lobbied to build a lake up on the Loup, and Calamus River State Recreation Area, just west of Burwell, stands as a testament to that effort.

Burwell had grown through the Depression to a population of 1,413 in the 1950 census. It's 1,210 today and mostly stable. Burnt Prairie, along with most of rural Illinois, was part of a population peak in 1910, as people continued to move west or to cities and as grain-producing agriculture became less of a subsistence way of life and more of an industrial enterprise.

Returning to Burnt Prairie on the gravel road from Mill Shoals we didn't see any population sign like we did most other places. My sister, Donna, and I were curious, so she got out a school tablet, and we began to write down the names of all the kids we knew. We knew them all, name by name, and when we added in their parents and counted them all up, the Burnt Prairie population by our count was 92.

How does the American Dream work in small rural counties with barely stable or declining populations? What is the American Dream anyway? Is it just about economics or rising family living standards? Or is it something more, created and framed by the aspirations and hard work of ordinary Americans, like those who survived the Depression and won World War II? That's the question I want to explore as I consider how my father's generation transitioned over the years since World War II to mine and on to his grandchildren's. I think the answers are in the story of people as the big tidal waves of changing factors in economics, politics, law, religion, and business play out in their day-to-day lives. That's what makes the American Dream about a whole lot more than living standards or incomes.

CHAPTER 1

FROM BURNT PRAIRIE TO WEST POINT

I went to school in Burnt Prairie, as my father had done, in a big white two-story frame building with a tubular metal fire escape slide extending out from the second floor. There were no playgrounds with slides back then, and we all wanted to sneak a slide down the fire escape, but we never did.

Burnt Prairie School

When I started first grade, the upstairs was empty, with first through fourth grades in one room downstairs and grade five through eight in the other. We had a big metal coal stove in the back of the room by the coat rack and rows of connected desks where the seats folded down from the writing desk behind them.

My father attended there for 11 years, because at the time the upstairs was the Burnt Prairie three-year high school. They could give no diplomas because they didn't have a fourth year, and most students quit school after eighth grade back then and went to work on the farm. My grandmother arranged for my father to live for a year in the county seat of Wayne County, and he graduated from high school there.

Two doors down was the Liberty Baptist Church. My grandmother, Marie Vaught, was a founding member when she was a teenager.

At the homecoming reunion at the church each year I heard her name as they read the minutes of that first church meeting, where a dozen or so Baptists met in a home to begin a new church, arranging to hire their own preacher and build a church. The Presbyterian Church was the only other church in town. We attended both churches in the summer as each had a Vacation Bible School for children. My out of town cousins would even come and attend with us.

Burnt Prairie is in that part of the Bible Belt that stretches from Arkansas, through the Ozarks, into southern Illinois and Kentucky and Tennessee and up along the Ohio River. This is old time religion country, and as the song goes: "It's good enough for me." My father became a Deacon in the Baptist Church. I remember him being anxious about the process of choosing a Deacon. It involved an open questioning session by all the members of the church, followed by a church vote. Anything in his conduct or background was fair game, and he expected their hardest questioning might be about his cigarette habit. He had begun smoking Camels from the rations in World War II, and as a child I couldn't understand how he was so worried about this flaw in his life.

My grandmother, Marie, was a teetotaler and active member of the Women's Christian Temperance Union. She very much disapproved of his hanging out with the veterans at the American

Marie Vaught is pictured here in the third row in the middle, just under the two women with the hats. Beulah Phillips, my Sunday School teacher and neighbor, is on the far right in the same third row.

Legion, where beer flowed pretty freely. She would inspect our refrigerator from time to time to make sure no beer made it home, something he thought she overdid. Because of this relationship with his mother, whose views were well known in the church, no one was going to challenge Marie's son on alcohol. He wasn't worried about questions of drinking alcohol, but the smoking still might come up, and it bothered him.

I was present for the open questioning, and it didn't come up, a sign perhaps that Baptist views on such personal conduct were softening a little. Mostly it was an affirmation that in a small town farming community all the members knew our family and didn't have a problem with a young veteran they knew was stepping up to leadership in the church.

The largest challenge the Deacons faced was recruiting preachers. There was no hint of hierarchy, whether from bishops or associations, or any outside influence on the local church. The local church chose its own leadership in open meetings with questions, votes and sometimes disagreement. It was hard to find a good preacher or to afford one in a small church, and most used the fifth Sunday rule to hire a part-time preacher, allowing them to hold another job. They expected considerable time be spent at funerals, weddings and visiting the sick, but if there were five Sundays in the month the preacher got that one off and didn't even have to attend church on the fifth Sunday. We still had Sunday School and church services, of course, just without the preacher.

The Deacons would do the search, interview and recommend a preacher. My father worked hard on this and came up with a good candidate. The preacher had one request. His job was selling furniture for a factory in northern Illinois, and he wanted to be able to sell to church members. That request was readily granted, and the Deacons were the first to place orders, which required payment in advance so the small factory could begin making the furniture.

The new preacher was well received, with good sermons, the flexibility from his sales job to visit the sick, and he was quickly well liked. But after a few months, questions began to arise about the delivery of the furniture most members of the church had ordered, but not received.

The Deacons inquired, and the new preacher quickly admitted that he had kept and spent the money. The factory had no deposits or payment. No furniture was being assembled. He had made the mistake of putting the needs of his family before honesty or the members of the church who placed the orders. In the Baptist way, he readily confessed, sought forgiveness and asked them to pray for him.

The Deacons did pray. Then they told him that, if he would work off the debt and get every piece of furniture delivered over time he could stay. He did just that. I still have some of that furniture in my guest bedroom, including a bookcase headboard to the bed I slept in for years.

The church members believed in some level of humility and acceptance of other people, at least those in the church. In case you didn't remember that, they would occasionally call for what they called "an old-fashioned foot washing." When there were tensions or hard feelings they thought a great way to ameliorate it was to get out the dishpans and fill them with soap and water. Everyone took off their shoes and started singing a hymn. Your first duty was to take one of the dishpans to the person you disliked the most and get down on your knees and wash their feet. As a kid, I was amazed at seeing this, and the singing of the hymn didn't end until everyone got their feet washed.

These backgrounds and religious beliefs and practices form a foundation for the American Dream. It has many flavors and distinctions, and its diversity is grounded in American concepts of freedom of religion. James Truslow Adams, who coined the phrase American Dream, in his 1931 book, "The Epic of America," argued that ideals were its basis, not material goods, saying it is, "a dream of a social order in which each man or woman shall be able to attain to the fullest stature of which they are innately capable, and recognized by others for what they are."[4] Not every religious group washes feet to demonstrate humility, but in America, recognizing others for what they are was a big reason why my father fought in Europe against an ideology that did the opposite.

Adams saw the American Dream arising not just from religion and ideals but from the work ethic of the frontier. Refugees fleeing Europe's aristocratic classes sought not just freedom from religious conflict but also a better economic approach. Many unsuccessful peasant revolts had erupted among their ancestors from time to time against remnants of the feudal system. Adams said it this way:

> It has been a dream of being able to grow to fullest development as man and woman, unhampered by the barriers which had slowly been erected in older civilizations, unrepressed by social orders which had been developed for the benefit of classes rather than for the simple human being of any and every class.[5]

Full religious freedom, not just religious tolerance, leads to freedom of thought, as well as acceptance of the different religions or ideas of others. It implies listening, self-reliance and the freedom to think, along with freedom from the hierarchy of the aristocracy and their organized official religion.

The American colonies and their Revolution combined these concepts leading to a freedom of economic activity not restrained by privilege and the need to maintain or subsidize the higher, non-working classes. Hard work in the wild forests of North America leveled those who believed they were created equal. Its result became the fulfillment of the aspirations of the pursuit of happiness.

The challenges of privilege and subsidy remain today, but the historical frontier spirit and the freedom to pursue its goals formed the foundation of a continuing and developing American Dream.

In my childhood, both the religion and the work ethic ran deep. Burnt Prairie is in deep southern Illinois near where the Skillet Fork, Little Wabash, Wabash and Ohio rivers all come together near Indiana and Kentucky. In the big flood in 1961 more than half of

White County was under water, but in a normal year, the bottom land farming in the black dirt holds moisture and produces well.

Those forested bottoms were cleared after waves of frontier homesteading on easier ground long passed them by. The Swamp Lands Act in the 1850s opened the low lands by providing a funding mechanism for drainage, a practice that today's environmentalists would not allow.[6] Aspiring poor farmers bought swamp land cheap, moved onto it, put up with mosquitoes, floods and humidity, and put their work ethic to the test sweating in the sun with their axes. They cut down the huge hardwoods—oak, pecan and hickory—and began to plant agricultural crops. Their axes, though, were not quite as fast as the interest accruing on their short-term mortgages. Farmer after farmer was foreclosed after a year or two of strenuous effort, losing all their land, hard work and down payments.

Adding to the thwarted accomplishments of others treated harshly by the American legal system, my grandmother Marie's father, Adam Johnston, finally broke through. He was able to plant enough productive bottomland to pay off his mortgage. With a few more years hard work he was able to move away from the swamp land and mosquitoes into town, and in about 1890 built one of the nicest houses in Burnt Prairie. This home on the main gravel road through town is where both my father and I were raised.

When I was young, grandmother Marie still owned the house, as well as the farm. My father farmed the family farm, paying crop share rent to his mother. As a farm family we all worked every day, doing whatever needed to be done. I started feeding and playing with the animals or pulling weeds in the garden. We had chickens, horses, goats, pigs and a growing herd of Black Angus cattle.

For many small farm families, the Depression had not started with the stock market crash in 1929. It started with declining farm prices after the end of World War I. Nearly half of the population in 1920 was rural, and those farmers over-produced as guaranteed prices during the war ended and world production recovered. By 1921, wheat prices were half what they had been during the wartime boom. Rural banks began to fail throughout the 1920s, as farm income dropped by two-thirds, squeezed between input prices that remained constant while commodity prices went lower. By 1927, the farm foreclosure rate had increased from 4 percent in 1920 to 18 percent.[7] This debt crisis peaked on my grandmother's farm in 1927, when the low farm prices were not producing enough cash to pay the interest to the insurance companies financing agriculture at that time. It only got worse as the national Depression deepened. So the gardens for canning vegetables, the eggs from the chickens, or the wild blackberries to be picked all made their contributions to whatever cash could be made. It wasn't simply the patriarch who brought in a paycheck, but every family member added their cents worth to the family till.

My grandmother was fortunate because after a decade of scraping by like everyone else, the pre-war buildup in oil production came to her land. The monthly royalty checks from an oil well or two went straight to repayment of accumulated farm debt. By the end of World War II, recovery from the Great Depression continued. In many ways Burnt Prairie never fully recovered, but for my grandmother, nearly 20 years after that farm depression struck in 1927, the debt was paid, and the oil checks kept coming.

She and my father made a deal to reinvest the oil money in the farm. Every month he would go to the cattle auction at the local sale barns and buy a Black Angus cow, paid for with Marie's monthly oil check. We then fed and cared for the cattle. And the profits, when they came, were split 50-50.

My mother thought it a great boon because she hated smelling hogs. My father converted the hog farm land to cattle and we happily put up hay, fixed fences, improved the pasture, and put in and tended terraces to prevent erosion and ponds to water the cattle. Marie named her cows, but my father was convinced her method mixed them up and confused him. He tagged them with ear tags and neck chains with numbers, keeping track of the calves that came each spring. Feeding and selling those calves brought new cash to buy more cows, and the herd, fueled by profit and oil royalty checks, grew. Black Angus were great cattle, and my father loved to argue with his friend Vic about the relative merits of Black Angus or Hereford cattle.

Vic was from Burnt Prairie, and he had survived the war as a tail gunner in a B-17. Not many tail gunners made it through 25 missions, but Vic did. After the war, Vic and my father finished their college education and double dated two sorority sisters at Southern Illinois University, Betty becoming Vic's wife, and my mother, Darcy, my father's. Because Vic and Betty lived in Illinois we hung out with them, or vacationed on the 4th of July at Kentucky Lake.

Vic's degree was in agriculture, and he worked for the Cooperative Extension Service of the University of Illinois. His arguments about Herefords were substantial. My father had studied agronomy but preferred sports, and he became a vocational instructor for farmers who signed up for farm training under the GI Bill.

Our Burnt Prairie home was two doors down the main gravel road to the church, and another two doors from the school. Life was based on hard work, sports and the church. The bottoms were a mile down the road past Saw Mill Corner. We turned north there, past the long gone saw mill, a mile or so to the county line, then up and over the hill past our 120-acre hill farm with the cattle. The road then descended into the broad flat floodplain along the Little Wabash River. We'd drive down dirt roads, laid out on section lines north-south and east-west, into the heart of the floodplain, far enough from the river to not flood too often, but close enough.

Farm kids worked all year, but especially during planting season in April and May and harvest in the fall. My mother had a strict rule, though: "No son of mine is driving a tractor until he is 10 years old." Many others didn't obey Mom's rule, and some were injured or lost a finger working on the farm. One of my classmates at Burnt Prairie school lost his mother in a tractor accident when a heavy disk climbed the main tractor wheel, crushing her in a fast and too tight turn at the end of the field. I liked the rule because I interpreted it that if the tractor was prohibited, then by implication the pickup truck was authorized. By the time I could see over, or through, the steering wheel, I was out there with 5-gallon buckets hauling seed corn and starter fertilizer bags from the crib to the edge of the field.

Eddie Masterson was our farm hand. My grandmother had spontaneously banned his brother from any of her farms because she caught him out there working on Sunday. My father liked Eddie, who suffered a dwarfism disorder that left him with very short legs that made him stand only 3 or 4 feet tall. He was a hard worker, and with hand operated clutches and hand throttles he could outwork most farm hands. Before he would agree to work each year he required that my father find him an old Ford Model T to drive to the bottoms. Ford stopped making them in 1927, but an old one with a hand throttle was all Eddie wanted to drive.

While Eddie drove his straight rows on the corn planter, I would load small amounts of seed corn into the 5-gallon buckets, making them ready to quickly dump into the planter boxes at the end of Eddie's rounds. I had to endure a steady, profane stream of Eddie's insults and criticism because no one could live up to his own personal work ethic. "Quit playin', damn it to Hell. We're here to Goddam work," he'd incessantly scream at me. He did speed me up. Fertilizer and seed filled, off he'd rush. On a good day we could plant 40 acres, while my father worked the disk out ahead, hoping to prepare more seedbed for Eddie's planter before the next rain called us to a halt.

Rain meant fixing fence on the cattle farm, fixing equipment or cleaning out a barn. Some farm kids missed school during planting season, but I usually missed the early planting because my mother's other rule was that I was going to be in school.

We always got to school early and either played basketball with the taller kids on the outdoor dirt basketball court or played "move up" on the softball field. We loved "move up" because you didn't have to choose up sides and didn't need 18 players. Three or four batters would face a changing fielding team that moved up when the batter made an out. Outfield into the infield, around the horn to first base and then to pitcher and then up to bat. As each batter struck out or grounded out, he moved to the outfield, working slowly back around the field toward the batter's box with each out.

Principal Whetstone would stand on the back step and yell in a very loud voice, "Books! Books! Books!" He meant for us to drop our bats and balls and run quickly into class and get out our books, and we did just that. I started first grade in a room that included second, third and fourth grade with the same teacher. There was no kindergarten but plenty of time after first grade reading class to listen to what the kids in the other grades were doing. By the time you made it to second grade you pretty well knew the whole multi-grade curriculum by heart. My second year the school was consolidated with some one room schools out in the country, and the seventh and eighth grade moved upstairs, where there was a new cafeteria for those who rode the bus. Downstairs became first through third grades in one room and fourth through sixth grades in the other.

Every Friday we had a spelling bee, but the part I loved was the ciphering match that followed. It started with two first graders sent to the blackboard. If you knew no numbers, then you made marks on the board with the chalk. Whoever made the most marks won, and the loser returned to his seat. The next first grader came up to challenge, and he or she got to call the contest. "Subtraction," a girl would say, and the student who could only make marks was quickly defeated. On it went through three column addition, working its way up to multiplication and division. The first graders got wiped out pretty quickly, but by the time I was in second grade I had figured out how to compete with the third graders. First I had to get past Marti Higdon, the smartest student in our grade, but I could sometimes do that. And I could beat most third graders by being fast on multiplication, because speed counted if you beat the competitor to the correct answer. Then I had to deal with Vernon Coale. My second-grade skills were no match for third grader Vernon. That was, until I figured out that multiplication by fives could be turned into multiplication by 25s. I caught him by surprise with that challenge because I was quick on 25 by 25 being 625. I didn't even have to write down the problem, because I did it in my head and simply wrote the answer before Vernon could add his columns. That was my favorite day in school at Burnt Prairie, beating Vernon in the ciphering match. Just once was enough.

My least favorite day came after my parents took us on our first long vacation, to where my maternal grandmother, Inie, liked to go, Florida. Inie loved Florida in the winter and had started going there in 1937 when her husband, Arthur Ackerman came down with Parkinson's disease. She thought the winter exercise was good for him and rode the train with him to Tampa. After his early death a few years later, she began to drive to Fort Myers and joined other farm widows investing their life insurance proceeds in Florida real estate. She had a place there all her life and always wanted her grandchildren or others to join her on the pre-Interstate trip through the south.

I discovered my "Go Button" in Florida and I wanted to go some more. It was worth driving through the unending streets and red lights of Atlanta before Interstates to make it all the way to Florida for the Christmas holiday. I so badly wanted to go back, and I quickly pleaded with my parents for a return trip. Persistence as a little kid so often pays off with a shaken head yes, but combined with a, "But if you had to miss school to go to Florida, how could you do that with all the missed school work?"

I would not take such excuses for a "no" answer. I went to second grade, and while the first and third graders recited, I worked all the way through every workbook we had. By Christmas I had completed all the second-grade work. I proudly announced to my parents that I was ready to go to Florida because I had finished second grade early.

They didn't agree. There was more farm work to be done, more fence to be mended, more debts to be paid, and a few more trips to Kentucky Lake or Burwell, Nebraska before another drive all the way south to Florida.

My whole motivational framework for school was shattered. How were we going to explain this to my teacher? With some arrangement with my teacher I dejectedly got to help out in the classroom and listen over and over to the repetition of the third-grade curriculum. School became less fun. Grandmother Inie eventually rescued me and organized her own trip to Florida, and I got to go along.

Marti Higdon moved to Carmi after third grade, and little did I know I was headed the same way. Our little group of 10 who started first grade had begun to change. I was a farm boy from Burnt Prairie, through and through, and the changes flowing from the American Dream were about to turn what I was accustomed to into a whole new adventure.

The capabilities one gains from an improving educational system are not the same as the foundational behavior well established on the farm. Farming has been around for millennia, and its culture is rich in its established ways. Helping your neighbor is part of it, when they were injured or needed to bring in wheat early as a flood approached. Always having work to do, and getting up every day to engage it, no matter what it is, comes naturally on the farm. Self-training, initiative, belief in nature and watching the corn grow all flow together in a seamless existence that always produces a new crop or spring-time calves to enhance the herd. What you own is what you earned by the sweat of your brow.

That means you get by with what you have and are thankful for it, all while being particularly skeptical of that newer, less refined way of life in the cities. Way up north means Chicago and its corruption. The dark side of life is playing even closer on the radio in the lyrics of country music, and the Cardinals over in St. Louis are everyone's team, but it is a long, dangerous drive through the city to get to their ballpark. Such biases against the different, the changing, and the new runs deeper in the country than some realize.

I knew that my mother was venturing out into it, though, because neighbor Nora Lampe easily convinced her that teaching in the county seat was better. The pay was better than at Mills Prairie High School, where my mother helped teach the 100 or so high school students five different subjects. The students came both from

Mill Shoals and Burnt Prairie to a newly built school exactly halfway between the two towns, and my mother, Darcy, really liked it there.

Nora wanted for them to drive together over non-paved country roads in winter 12 miles to the Carmi Township High School. With 700 students each teacher taught mainly one subject. Nora was such a nice neighbor, and the money was hard to pass up. After a year teaching in Carmi she said to my father, "You have a teaching certificate, too, and you could coach." I think the baseball and basketball won him over quickly. She went on about how they could both earn a salary and, instead of her driving through the winter to Carmi, he could drive back to the farm mostly in better weather, doing his two jobs while hiring more farm help if he needed it.

My parents were open to this, despite both coming from farm families that had never left the farm. My father was on the school board at Mills Prairie, and they both saw the advantages of the higher pay, and, for their children, more qualified teachers and a better curriculum in Carmi. I had seen them argue before, like in the election where my father favored the Democratic Governor of Illinois, Adlai Stevenson, for President, while my mother, coming from a large Republican family, favored Dwight D. Eisenhower. "How could you not vote for a Governor from your own state?" my father would ask. "How could you not vote for your commander in chief in Europe?" my mother would reply. Neither ever convinced the other on that political question, but they quickly agreed that a GI Bill mortgage for a new house in Carmi and two salaries, while maintaining ties to the farm, was the way to go.

The new in change comes easier but giving up the old comes harder. I was not convinced. Before we moved, I was having too much fun with the approach in Burnt Prairie of "Road Day." A big celebration was planned, lots of cousins would come, and we would all celebrate the end of the dusty gravel road through town with a new, safer blacktop. It ran 6 miles from Mill Shoals through Burnt Prairie all the way to Sawmill Corner, while most roads in the country were still gravel, dirt or mud. Gravel roads were dangerous to new teenage drivers who wanted speed, and time and again I heard the story of their crashes because "they hit loose gravel and went in the ditch." We all watched large Caterpillar equipment, earth movers and bulldozers work in front of our house. I was thrilled and wanted no part of moving out of the country.

My cousin Art came to march in the Road Day parade, and we dressed in full Davy Crockett attire—coonskin caps and moccasins—and carried long rifles and led hunting dogs on a leash. Lucky Leroy, the country singer on the Harrisburg TV station, sang from the back of a flat-bed truck along the new road. The biggest celebration I had seen in my life occurred that night, with people dancing on the streets.

Carmi and a new house meant Beulah Phillips, our next-door neighbor and my Sunday School teacher, couldn't come walking in, at all times of the day, to compare notes on the canning or washing occurring around the house. Grandmother Marie would be that much farther away and less able to conduct her refrigerator inspections to make sure there was no alcohol in the house. The horses and ponies wouldn't be ready to ride in the back yard. Everyone in Carmi rode bikes instead. Our long-time, live-in babysitter, Valeda Savage, was getting married, but Margie Manion would move to Carmi to help out around the house.

I showed up to fifth grade at a school having a single one grade in a room, and there were even two fifth grade rooms, plus other fifth grade rooms in schools across town. A classmate had the same name as me, so the teacher declared that I would be "Dave" and he would be "David." This just wasn't for me.

Grandmother Inie was close, and she stopped by every day to see her daughter and grandchildren. She wanted us to spend more time with my uncle Frank and his four children who lived at her old farm place in the Wabash bottoms near Maunie, and we obliged. Little League baseball in an organized league replaced "Move Up." Life adjusted.

I found out too that it wasn't just Marti Higdon and Vernon Coale who challenged me at school. My father was teaching sixth grade in the downtown school, and Marti became one of his students. He reminded me what I already knew, that she was a smart Burnt Prairie kid who could adjust and thrive here, and I could too. She showed me how she used her bike to learn the streets in town so we could know our way around, even in this big town, with 6,000 people, that dwarfed Burnt Prairie and its 92 residents.

Inie, too, had what I came to call a "Go Button." Up in the morning, make the biscuits and a pie, and out in the world went Inie. "Where are we going today?" she would say when she wanted someone to go with her. It didn't matter if it was fishing in the river, shopping across the Wabash in Evansville, Indiana, or visiting relatives in Seymour. Off she went, and we went with her.

I encountered, too, a much greater skepticism and questioning in the local Baptist church. The students in my Sunday School class would argue with the teacher, which had never happened in Burnt Prairie. They had read their Bibles, too, and found it filled with contradictions beyond explanation. Doyle Bean was a local jeweler on Main Street, but also a patient listener to the youth in his Sunday School class. His answers were calm and faith-based. Despite my friends, in my mind, he always prevailed in the religious argument. My traditional Baptist belief from Burnt Prairie was solidified. My grandmother had taught me to always be tolerant of others' differing religious beliefs because their path to truth is often different. Here in Carmi that began to play out before my eyes. There was even a Catholic church in Carmi, and although that seemed completely different to me, the Catholic friends I had at school were friends just the same.

These little steps into the larger world arrived because my father had made even bigger steps in surviving the Great Depression and World War II. His generation had to accept change, difficult change, and they came out of it ready to change for the better. I didn't have to like it, nor did they, but we were off and into it now in a much bigger way.

My junior high principal had parachuted out of a burning B-17 and been captured by the Germans, living out the war in a POW camp. I was scared to death of him, as was nearly every one of his students. He would preach to us in a demanding way: "Do right because it is right." It was that simple, and you better not do wrong. I listened. Veterans were all around us. Most were more quiet about it than our principal. They marched together in the parade at Corn Day, Carmi's more elaborate and annual version of Road Day.

Veterans were taking charge in larger ways. They didn't like the old politics of the political machines. "Fat" Ziegler ran things in the Democratic Party of White County and served as our State Senator. His use of welfare to buy votes and its related patronage was wasteful, unfair and unproductive.

My father's political career started by tacking silver painted sheriff's stars on telephone poles for Woody Proctor when he challenged "Fat's" candidate in the primary. After teaching sixth grade and coaching at the junior high for three years he ran himself in a three-way primary for Circuit Clerk. Mother asked her Republican relatives to cross over and take a Democratic ballot to stand up to "Fat" and help break his grip on the county. They refused, saying instead that "honest" Republicans were needed to do that.

She was completely dismayed that her family wouldn't help out when her husband was on the political front line of reform. Those votes would have been the difference in my father's race, and it took my mother a long time to forgive her own family for resisting this change. She herself began to split her ticket and vote Democratic.

Others were breaking through. Our cousin, "Pud" Williams, took independent Democratic control of the county board and became its chairman. Gene Johns from Marion sought local support to defeat "Fat's" in the primary. The local insurgents joined, and Gene eventually won, breaking the link to "Shoebox" Paul Powell in southern Illinois and the link and alliance with "Boss" Daley in Chicago.

My father journeyed down to Harrisburg to personally see John Kennedy's Presidential campaign speech. Back home, he had greater troubles with his own mother. She made it known around Burnt Prairie that she could not vote for a Catholic for President. My father urged her to be quiet and not discourage other Democratic voters over religion. If she had her own reservations, he told her to use her secret ballot but keep her mouth shut. Their arguments were heated and blunt, and neither one was listening very well to the other.

Grandma Marie didn't drive and would hire a driver to come to the farm. She would stop at Carter's feed store and buy a bag of corn on the ear, putting it in the trunk of her driver's car. The cattle recognized the car coming through the gate, being trained on the corn, and the herd ran up around the car. Breaking up those ears from her open trunk, I threw them to the cattle and became her listening post on her political dilemma. There was no argument from me. I just listened.

She explained her concern about the Pope and a long history of papal interference in governments in Europe. She didn't want religious wars or unification of church and state to impinge her religious freedom. She knew that the early Baptists in Europe had been persecuted. No way did she want anything like that coming into the United States through the President's office.

On the other hand, she had never in her life voted for a Republican. She thought Nixon was dishonest and would say anything to get elected. She couldn't stomach him at all. She saw it as her duty to vote and make a choice, but this choice was no choice for her. She didn't know what to do, and she also wasn't going to keep quiet about it either.

Grandmother and I fed those cattle for weeks in the fall of 1960, and I heard a lot about freedom of religion and politics. I could not foresee then that these attitudes would stick with me and change my own course. John Kennedy, perceiving this problem, made a speech at a Texas Baptist Seminary on September 12, 1960 and is worth quoting, in part, here:

> I believe in an America where the separation of church and state is absolute, where no Catholic prelate would tell the president (should he be Catholic) how to act, and no Protestant minister would tell his parishioners for whom to vote; where no church or church school is granted any public funds or political preference; and where no man is denied public office merely because his religion differs from the president who might appoint him or the people who might elect him.

> I believe in an America that is officially neither Catholic, Protestant nor Jewish; where no public official either requests or accepts instructions on public policy from the Pope, the National Council of Churches or any other ecclesiastical source; where no religious body seeks to impose its will directly or indirectly upon the general populace or the public acts of its officials; and where religious liberty is so indivisible that an act against one church is treated as an act against all.

> For while this year it may be a Catholic against whom the finger of suspicion is pointed, in other years it has been, and may someday be again, a Jew--or a Quaker or a Unitarian or a Baptist. It was Virginia's harassment of Baptist preachers, for example, that helped lead to Jefferson's statute of religious freedom. Today I may be the victim, but tomorrow it may be you—until the whole fabric of our harmonious society is ripped at a time of great national peril.

> Finally, I believe in an America where religious intolerance will someday end; where all men and all churches are treated as equal; where every man has the same right to attend or not attend the church of his choice; where there

is no Catholic vote, no anti-Catholic vote, no bloc voting of any kind; and where Catholics, Protestants and Jews, at both the lay and pastoral level, will refrain from those attitudes of disdain and division which have so often marred their works in the past, and promote instead the American ideal of brotherhood.

That is the kind of America in which I believe. And it represents the kind of presidency in which I believe—a great office that must neither be humbled by making it the instrument of any one religious group, nor tarnished by arbitrarily withholding its occupancy from the members of any one religious group. I believe in a president whose religious views are his own private affair, neither imposed by him upon the nation, or imposed by the nation upon him as a condition to holding that office.

I would not look with favor upon a president working to subvert the First Amendment's guarantees of religious liberty. Nor would our system of checks and balances permit him to do so. And neither do I look with favor upon those who would work to subvert Article VI of the Constitution by requiring a religious test — even by indirection — for it. If they disagree with that safeguard, they should be out openly working to repeal it.

I want a chief executive whose public acts are responsible to all groups and obligated to none; who can attend any ceremony, service or dinner his office may appropriately require of him; and whose fulfillment of his presidential oath is not limited or conditioned by any religious oath, ritual or obligation.

This is the kind of America I believe in, and this is the kind I fought for in the South Pacific, and the kind my brother died for in Europe. No one suggested then that we may have a "divided loyalty," that we did "not believe in liberty," or that we belonged to a disloyal group that threatened the "freedoms for which our forefathers died."

And in fact, this is the kind of America for which our forefathers died, when they fled here to escape religious test oaths that denied office to members of less favored churches; when they fought for the Constitution, the Bill of Rights and the Virginia Statute of Religious Freedom; and when they fought at the shrine I visited today, the Alamo. For side by side with Bowie and Crockett died McCafferty and Bailey and Carey. But no one knows whether they were Catholic or not, for there was no religious test at the Alamo.[8]

Kennedy affirmatively stated he was running to be President of the United States, and that he would take no orders from the Pope. Marie believed him and was greatly relieved, and told all of Burnt Prairie, or anyone else who would listen, that she would be voting for Kennedy for President.

My father had even more to say to me working on the farm. Riding shotgun in an old pickup driving up to the farm, I heard what he thought about work, family and politics. This was a constant refrain, forceful and by example. He was convinced I did not have to relearn what he had already learned the hard way. Growing up in the Depression, living with little, riding horses, keeping your head down in the war, volunteering when the time was right, and not missing the chance to make a difference were all things he had learned. He expected me to pick them up right there in the cab of that pickup.

Religion was part of it, and it was omnipresent growing up in Baptist churches in Burnt Prairie and Carmi, or when I attended the Georgia Baptist Church near Maunie where my grandmother Inie and most of my mother's Ackerman cousins were members. So was politics, and my father's example flowed from his perpetual involvement in it. So was business, since we were working on a family farm all the time.

He took me with him on his search to buy rare coins. He'd find a widow who inherited some old coins and needed cash and go sit with her in her yard looking at what she had. He worked the psychology of patience and trust, bargaining softly, knowing that the good stuff didn't come out until he had bought some mediocre pieces at a reasonable price. He considered building trust with people as a cornerstone that led to communication and long-term friendship.

His sense of timing and speculation on hot pricing also paid off by mail-ordering for the hard to find rarer coins. That led as well to looking for bargains in the stock market, antiques, or how to make some extra cash selling insurance. He had worked hard on the farm when he was younger, leaving him with a painfully bad back, and he loved exploring other ways to understand markets, negotiation and making money work for you.

To him, working multiple jobs was normal, but his favorite job was coaching basketball or baseball. He bought into the world of Stan Musial and had grown up admiring the Cardinal "gashouse gang" and Pepper Martin, and its famous pitchers like Dizzy Dean. They practiced the fundamentals that he wanted all the players he coached to learn and emulate. Playing the game right, win or lose, was the key to winning in the long run. The teamwork learned in team sports mattered.

I wasn't tall enough or fast enough to do great in basketball, and my hitting never was good enough to make the high school baseball team, but I played and learned both sports. In Babe Ruth League I faced the fearsome Carmi pitcher, Ken Winter. His fastball was scary, and most players went to bat knowing that they would either strike out or take a hard one of his wild pitches. I decided I could at least try for a walk. That same kind of determination to find an angle also made me a better baserunner. Not letting any ground balls get through by at least knocking them down earned me a slot playing second base. These ideals of resilience and always finding a way to contribute came directly from my father's coaching and belief in team sports.

Right out of high school Ken Winter signed with the Cardinals, married my cousin, Nancy, and left for the minor leagues in North Carolina. The other pitchers were not scary, and my athletic confidence grew.

My father coached the Hawthorne Hustlers 4-H Club softball team, where you could play until you were 20, and our team always was competitive in the county tournament, winning the right to play in the statewide tournament. That experience was the most fun playing sports I ever had, but my father pushed me more, telling me I should find a sport in which I could letter in high school. He thought maybe I could learn to be a field goal kicker in football, but where I was better was in long-distance running, a sport where determination counted more than most. I could place on the high school cross-country team to earn my high school athletic letter.

Working on the farm was what I wanted to do forever, raising cattle, planting corn in the spring and being part of the easy flow of the seasons. Working on the farm, I didn't really need a driver's license, I'd drive a pickup to Burnt Prairie after school and on weekends during planting season, often arriving before my father came up after baseball practice. By that time, Eddie was driving our John Deere 60, and I'd jump on the John Deere A and work ahead of him, disking to prepare the seedbed. We disked, harrowed and rotary hoed to get the corn and beans in and up. Eddie always worked from six in the morning to six in the evening while refusing to follow daylight savings time. My father would join us and work late into the night, going back to teach school the following morning.

We'd put up hay in the summer for the cattle, and I'd recruit some high school friends to help. My father hired the local baler with his equipment, and my friends and I would cringe when my father argued about the size of the bales. He was paying by the bale and he didn't want them small. We knew we were in trouble when the conversation ended with my father turning the crank to increase the size of the bales.

No one had yet designed a baler that placed the hay on a wagon drawn behind, or one that used forklifts on tractors to move heavy bales. We wore gloves and piled bales on the wagon with strong arms and backs. The strongest farm hand threw them high to stack them up on the wagon. On many trips to the barn we stopped and picked up the high stacks that had tumbled to the road, lifting the bales again then stacking them even higher in a hot, humid and stuffy barn loft.

In the winter, my father paid me to drive the pickup north after school and feed those bales of hay to the cattle, check the fence, chop the ice and generally taking care of the herd. I dreaded those calls from neighbors to my father: "David left the gate open again and your cattle are in my field." It wasn't just Eddie who could unleash harsh words when my work was faulty on the farm.

Politics was constant with my father and many times we were left to work on our own because he had a political visit to make on his way to the farm. They played it like generals in the field in the war, maneuvering the geography to flank the opposition, building the strength of mass in key areas, and re-supplying the faithful troops in the political fray. His political work was winning though, and by the time I was about to graduate high school he was known in the region outside the county and primed to lead President Johnson's war on poverty as the first Executive Director of the five county Wabash Area Office of Economic Opportunity.

Meanwhile, my own competitive nature wasn't just about sports or academics or the 4-H club softball team. Phil Pearce had helped found a local chapter of the Civil Air Patrol. A Marine, Pearce was a key political rival of the local Democrats as a Republican member of the county board. He had led a platoon of Marines on Okinawa and was the highest decorated soldier in White County. His coolness under fire was crucial when the enemy jumped out of caves and surrounded his unit. He successfully led his unit forward to accomplish their mission, earning him the Navy Cross, the highest honor for bravery except for the Congressional Medal of Honor.

Pearce built an airstrip behind his farm house for his Mooney, a fast retractable gear single engine aircraft. Some successful farmers bought nice cars after a good harvest; he bought both a Cadillac and a Mooney. Aerospace education, military leadership and airplanes were what we learned in the weekly CAP meetings so we could help do air searches for downed airplanes if there was a missing aircraft in our region.

Our CAP squadron encouraged us to attend the summer encampment at Chanute Air Force Base, so I signed up. I didn't realize that meant Phil Pearce would fly us up there in his fast Mooney. I was riding in the front right seat as he explained his plane's new postwar navigation systems, called VOR's or visual omni range, along with the airspeed indicator and altimeter and whole range of instruments you don't see in pickup trucks. I was an avid student. I didn't like the encampment much with its military drills and barracks life, but I was happy for that Mooney ride back to Carmi.

It wasn't long before Pearce and five other business people each contributed $25 to create a flying scholarship for someone in the CAP squadron. They saw a need for new pilots since fewer were trained by the military after the war. They waived the $10 monthly dues at the White County Flying Club, and Ed Wood, the instructor from Outland Aviation in Mt. Vernon, agreed to lower his hourly instruction fee from $6 to $5. A private pilot's license, which normally cost about $600, then became about $400. I was netting more than $10 a week feeding cattle, and I had picked up a job as a busboy at the local Elks Club for another $10. With that $20 I could take an hour of instruction at the airport every week and still have $5 left for Saturday night.

I won the competition for the first scholarship and started flying the club's Cessna 150 at age 16, though I couldn't finish a private license until I was 17. Six months later I finished my training and was ready for my private pilot check ride. Something about this was a lot better than just feeding cattle or driving a John Deere tractor chugging back and forth across the black dirt in the river bottoms.

Just past my 17th birthday, I soloed down to Cape Girardeau, Missouri, to meet the FAA examiner for my check ride. I had studied the Jeppesen manual and passed the FAA written test. Ed Wood had worked me through all the maneuvers and I logged the required solo cross countries.

I got lost on my first solo cross-country flight. Flying to Mattoon, Ed told me it was hard to get lost flying directly to a VOR, but he wanted me to turn it off and plot my course back by dead reckoning, using the compass. I took the winds aloft forecast and calculated the groundspeed and crosswind to my course on my hand-held EB-6 circular slide rule and plotted out checkpoints on my sectional map. I got my logbook signed off at Mattoon and headed back south to the airport at Carmi.

We had an old gyro compass that held steadier than the magnetic, but it was driven by a vacuum pump that had to spin up before it became accurate. Making the mistake of setting it while I was taxiing out, I started out on the heading I had calculated ready to look for my first checkpoint. Railroads and highways come together in almost unique ways at each town, but the differences are subtle. My first checkpoint looked okay. Then I noticed I had crossed the Wabash River, meaning I was in Indiana. You don't have to go through Indiana to fly from one town in Illinois to another. How could I be lost so soon? What good now were all my checkpoints and dead reckoning headings? The gyro compass was simply wrong. Why didn't I wait to set the gyro compass later after it was completely spun up? Then it would have held a stable and accurate heading without it precessing off to the wrong heading.

This was precisely what I loved about flying. On my own with my own eyes, growing flying skills, and a bit too much spirit of adventure, I quickly arrived at the solution to the navigational problem. The key is to figure something out quickly and implement it to correct your first mistake. I had read in *Flying* magazine that it often was the second or third sequential mistake that got you in real trouble. Responding well at the first sign of trouble was the best insurance for a young, over-confident student pilot. I followed the Wabash River down the border until I could see a bridge and road that led to Carmi and made it back safe and sound.

The FAA examiner in Cape Girardeau was going to do his best to simulate and test me on such problems before he was willing to sign off on my new private pilot's certificate. He questioned my dead reckoning flight plan, straying off subject into arcane FAA rules, weather forecasts and aircraft maintenance. I knew all that by spending a lot of time at my local airport talking to pilots, and we were soon in the air, starting out going west on the cross country route he had asked that I plan. Then the prop stopped dead.

We were gliding, without engine power, and I quickly trimmed to the best rate of glide speed. "What are you going to do?" he demanded. I immediately knew the answer. We were high enough to glide back to the airport, so I started my turn and said so. "Good job," he said, "and I'll restart the engine for you." He had quietly and out of my sight reached down and closed the fuel line from the tanks to the engine, creating a real engine failure, not like the simulated failures with the engine idling I had learned with Ed Wood. He, of course, undoubtedly violated every FAA safety guideline on how he was supposed to conduct the test, but he had his own higher standard, and that included throwing every curve he could think of to a young pilot.

Having lost track of the name of my examiner, years later I told this story to the line boys at Cape Girardeau when my daughter, Erica, and I were following the Mississippi River flying back from New Orleans. They laughed and knew immediately who my examiner had been. Long ago retired, they said he was tough and always did it his own way.

I passed the check ride and flew back to Carmi a newly minted, and still over-confident FAA licensed private pilot. This was a life changing event. It took me beyond cattle and corn. New possibilities opened up. The fun and independence of it compounded on itself. I knew I would never give up flying.

Maybe I now could become an aeronautical engineer to build and design airplanes. Flying airplanes by its very nature produces a different perspective. Three dimensions are way more than two. Seeing the world from above and navigating in it without a road is such a different experience that it changes your sense of perspective as well as your way of thinking. I didn't understand this yet, but I was soon to find it out.

Inexperience, over-confidence, uncertainty and a spirit of adventure leads you where? Were those youthful attributes what drove the American Dream? Had it been essential to add the idea of improvement to the randomness of events on an under-populated continent? James Truslow Adams, who first coined the phrase, says the American Dream is "of a land in which life should be better and richer and fuller for every man, with opportunity for each, according to his ability or achievement."[9] Was doing better than before a necessary addition to the energy required to survive? Is such change implicit in freedom, or are the ideals of the prior generation just passed on in a continuum going forward?

I didn't know the answer to these questions and had not even formulated them as I approached the end of high school. I just knew that I didn't know exactly what to do next. Clearly though, my grandparents, parents and leaders like Phil Pearce had planted their seeds.

Late one night as my busboy work at the Elks Club dining room began to slow down, Pearce asked me where I was going to college. I told him I didn't know, and he quickly replied that a new pilot should apply to the Air Force Academy. It was something I could do, he said, and he and my father and others in town would try to help me get in. He suggested I send a letter to my Congressman, Ken Gray, and ask for an appointment to the academy.

Just that simply I went home and typed that letter. I didn't mention it to my parents and had no idea what I was getting in to. I trusted Phil Pearce's judgment, and I appreciated that he had led me to join the fraternity of pilots. I was now open to new possibilities, even if I was unclear on what they were.

Carmi was far different in my mind than Burnt Prairie. Most people in Burnt Prairie didn't ever travel farther than the nearest county seat, but in Carmi there were people who went to Florida, or to Washington to lobby, or to other states in the oil business. I was hanging out at the airport one day, like I did whenever I wasn't working, when Hank Fullop breezed in. I was in the fake tower-looking glassed in octagon-shaped airport building with lots of flying magazines laying around and usually a few pilots would say hello while paying for fuel. It was our home for "hangar flying," where we pretended to fly while we were weathered in or our flying budgets were depleted. Hank's flying budget was never depleted, and he flew the nicest airplane at the airport, a twin engine Piper Apache.

"You want to fly with me down to Grenada, Mississippi? I've got an oil lease down there to work out. We'll be back after lunch." It didn't take me long to stand up and help him pull his twin out of the hangar. Fullop was in the oil business like many of the local pilots. Farmers didn't fly as much. He put me in the right seat and told me about the speed, autopilot and two engines of the Apache.

I knew from the scuttlebutt around the airport that his brother had crashed after an engine failure. I also knew Fullop had the reputation for setting his auto-pilot and then crawling into the back seat of his Apache for a nap. I didn't know if that was true, but I knew he was a local character and the biggest tipper at the Elks Club dining room. The waitresses almost ran when he arrived for dinner, and he was not bashful about pulling out a huge money clip filled with fifties when it came time to pay.

I liked him immediately. He was a real pilot and making money doing it in the oil business. It didn't take us long to get to Mississippi. It was only a little further away than Chicago but closer in culture to Carmi in southern Illinois. We had a nice lunch, and the oil lease was signed. As we got into the airplane, he asked if I wanted to fly the

Apache back to Carmi. He said just follow the VOR's, and I'll show you how to land it when we get back.

I had never flown a twin, but he gave me the five-minute lesson, and then, to my surprise, announced he was crawling into the back seat for a nap. "Wake me up when we get close to Carmi," he said. The engines hummed, and I flew it straight and level, flying past Memphis and Paducah, resetting the VOR frequencies as we passed each one. Gas, undercarriage, mixture, pumps, seatbelts, GUMPS for short, is the pre-landing checklist, and Fullop told me the faster approach speed to our landing at Carmi. As we approached our 2,600-foot-long by 50-foot-wide runway, I saw what many would now consider a too narrow, too short runway for a fast twin. There was no crosswind, and the flaps slowed us down. He showed me how to cut the power to drop it in just over the threshold and use the brakes. It didn't seem all that hard because he knew what he was doing.

A larger world was opening up, and it was fun. Or so I thought. My mother was upset with me for not applying to college. Driven by some teenage non-communication mode, I had not told her about the letter to Congressman Gray. She thought I was doing well enough in school to apply to the University of Illinois. Not many from Carmi went there, but she viewed it as top notch, difficult and worth it. Most of my classmates though got married right out of high school and found a job farming or at one of the plants around the area. Some went to local colleges or to Murray State in Kentucky.

I didn't like this college talk. I knew academically I was in the top ten students in my class, and I also knew I could have been higher had I worked a little to compete with the smart, hard-working girls at the top of my class. I had a girlfriend in the country, though, and we liked playing out a bit of our rebellious streak. I had learned mine in Burnt Prairie, where a healthy dose of disdain was common about life in a larger world. When the high school guidance counselor asked me my future plans, I just tried to put him off by saying all I knew was that I wanted to stop after school for a hamburger and French fries at the Dairy Queen on my way to feed the cattle. That's as far as I had it planned.

My mother was patient, knowing from her own background growing up near Maunie how such bad attitudes worked, or didn't work. She taught better things, and she intended to keep me at it. She had the application forms for the University of Illinois, and she made it clear to me that if I didn't fill them out and send them in, she would do so on my behalf. If I didn't get pulled along by common sense from the front, she was ready to kick me from the rear.

One night my father walked into my bedroom with a perplexed look on his face and told me I was wanted on the phone. He said Congressman Ken Gray was calling. I had no idea what to expect, but the Congressman was a funny, friendly, fast-talking politician who everyone liked. He won me over in the first sentence and then let me know that he had already promised his only Air Force Academy appointment to a star basketball player in Mt. Vernon. His father was his friend, and he couldn't back out on that commitment. He could, if I wanted, put my name in an as alternate in case the basketball star failed the admission tests. Maybe the Air Force Academy would find a way to take me, but he doubted it.

On the other hand, the Army had lots of helicopters and even some fixed wing aircraft. I didn't know at the time that Gray was a helicopter pilot himself and had a financial interest in the Bell helicopter dealership at Washington National Airport. I did learn he was enthusiastic about helicopters. He planned to nominate ten applicants to take competitive tests at West Point, and the Army was going to then pick the top three for admission. He thought I had a good chance being in the top three. "What do you want me to do to help you out," he concluded. He wanted an answer then and there.

I bought it hook, line and sinker and told him that I would take the competitive test as part of his ten nominees. I'd try for West Point instead of the Air Force Academy. I had a little explaining to do to my parents about not telling them I had sent him the letter. My mother was relieved that I at least had some plan. My father, the veteran artillery corporal of World War II and now a front line leader in the Democratic war on poverty, was happy to try to make sure the Congressman did what he promised and encouraged me to be ready for the tests.

He took me to Scott Air Force Base for the physical exam and the more important physical fitness tests. Once again, my father's perpetual advice and conversation played out on the road west across southern Illinois. Neither of us knew the components of the physical test, but he reminded me that playing sports had me in good shape, so the key was a positive attitude. Believing in yourself and your ability to face any challenge was part of his makeup. What he expected and believed would work was doing my best and believing in myself no matter what. The physical tests were scored along with my academic record and my leadership score, which considered everything from being a high school class officer to my leadership in the Civil Air Patrol and the Hawthorne Hustlers 4-H Club.

The Wabash Valley Association wanted the federal government to help minimize the flooding of the crops in the river bottoms and regularly sought out Congressman Gray, who had plenty of seniority, to help. He made a speech at one of their meetings in our high school auditorium, and my father told me to attend. To my surprise, a key point in the speech was to announce to the whole town that I had won one of the three appointments to West Point. Little did I know that my private letter to Congressman Gray would turn into a front page headline in the *Carmi Times*, letting the whole town know I was going to West Point.

Suddenly I wasn't just a high school kid hanging out with my girlfriend on Saturday night in my '57 Chevy and flying airplanes at the airport. It seemed everyone now knew me. No one had heard of anyone from our town going to West Point. They supported what I was doing and had high expectations for me to live up to. The attention didn't last long though. I had to report in on July 1, just a very short time after my high school graduation.

CHAPTER 2

FROM THE LIBERTY BAPTIST CHURCH TO THE CADET CHAPEL

West Point defies adequate description in words. Most of what people know comes from propaganda films over-promoting the place or from the exploits of its famous graduates. All uphold the myth but miss most of the reality.

Two recent graduates broke that mold. Lucian Truscott IV's, "Dress Gray,"[10] was so revealing of West Point's foibles and secrets that for years it was banned at the West Point bookstore. Young people, though, read it and then applied to West Point. Susan Spieth's "Gray Girl"[11] series more recently revealed what it was like for women to join the ranks at West Point. As one of the first female graduates, she doesn't pull any punches.

In my opinion as an old grad, West Point's essence is about purpose, and that goes back to its founding on March 16, 1802 when Thomas Jefferson was President. The United States, in its wisdom, did not set up a permanent military class loyal only to a King, a President or a political party. Article VI of the Constitution requires an oath to support the Constitution, a far different allegiance than one to King George, or any other monarch common in European history.

The Constitution's goal for West Point was to create a Corps of Cadets who would lead the Army, being loyal only to the country as a whole. Since its inception, West Point cadets and military officers take an oath to our Constitution, bearing true faith and allegiance to it and swearing to carry out the lawful orders of its civilian controlled military against all enemies, foreign and domestic.

West Point's core value is truth, a necessity to survive in its totalitarian system. That system is wrapped within our national government to effectively project power. When power is concentrated within the institution you are part of, what protects you and makes it function is truth. The Honor Code at West Point teaches that the whole truth, not a half truth or a political ideology, or some manipulation for personal gain, is crucial. If you speak the whole truth and hear it consistently, you are protected in a functional hierarchy that can carry out its duty without diversion.

West Point is a power center of the Army. Its cadets are there to learn and compete, be identified for advancement, and then project that power to provide for the common defense of the country. It is power without money, and an antidote to the abuse of oligarchy, aggression, dictatorship, corruption and treason that runs dangerously rampant in the world.

I entered West Point on July 1, 1965. Beast Barracks, the initial training of West Point cadets, doesn't teach all that, and its introduction to West Point only scratches the surface of a progression to leadership. It levels and tests and weeds out the faint-hearted. For me, surviving its stresses and physical and mental challenges worked by keeping my head down, responding positively to excellent squad leaders, and being encouraged by those letters every day from my high school girlfriend, Alice.

Leveling off the misconceptions, the false elitism of good students, and the athletic arrogance of high school sports stars takes much longer than just an introductory basic training for a few weeks in the summer. I made it to the academic year as part of a group of classmates from all over the country who were successful in their high school world but only beginning to face a new set of unpredictable challenges.

As classes began, I met Tom Swett, my squad leader, and fellow plebe, Mark Kransdorf. Swett was the meanest squad leader in the toughest company in the 3rd Regiment, D-3. The company was proud of its tough reputation. Swett was my squad leader, and each morning I was on his wall, in trouble for special inspection well before reveille. He loved football, but I decided to hate it.

Besides a heavy academic load of nearly 20 semester hours of classes, plus parades, intramurals, fourth class duties, and no spare time, he expected a report from his squad on football practice each day after class. He wanted detail, and I could have cared less about how the football practice was going. It was outside my own priorities for time management. My football reports were seriously deficient. I simply had other key priorities on my plate, but Swett was determined to either make his priorities mine or to extract a price for it.

"Kransdorf," he would scream at reveille, "did you shine your shoes with a Hershey bar again this morning?" I got to hear his biased, anti-Jewish, tirade nearly every morning because it seemed he couldn't stand to look at Mark Kransdorf. It became my salvation. When Tom Swett could not control his anger at Kransdorf, it was not being directed at me. It was a compounding and spreading of bias in its truly subversive form.

At 2130 each night, though, we were free to leave our rooms and visit other classmates before taps. Kransdorf, better than anyone else, remedied my confusion on the calculus topics we all had to face in math class six days a week. We were graded daily on the solution, or lack thereof, of math we didn't understand. His high school in Brooklyn had taught calculus.

Carmi never got close. The differences and strengths in my classmates often reflected their hometowns. Many of us were from poorer areas or the rural south, but the Congressional appointment system spread appointments in those areas, too, even if our preparation was deficient. The cadets from better-funded and better-taught schools had a head start on us in academics, and many came from areas with tougher athletic competition. We were expected to compete to the best of our abilities and, at the same time help our classmates. We all were struggling through a tougher system than most of us ever expected.

Kransdorf could have taught the calculus class. Despite the grief he was getting from Swett and others, he took the time to be helpful, friendly and a mathematical mentor deluxe. Classmates who he helped, like me, would have done anything in our power to protect Kransdorf from Swett, even if it meant diverting his rage our way. The teamwork in our class blossomed from there. This key lesson of teamwork at West Point was driven home.

Our plebe class started with 1,138 in July, and we lost a hundred or so in Beast Barracks. The rest of us were determined to make it through plebe year. We had two big football games away from West Point to look forward to before getting our first leave at Christmas. Our squad leaders were in the last class of the prior system where plebes received no Christmas leave. They implemented their own equalizing system, making us pay back to them for our privileged new Christmas leave status. Such unfair retribution felt brutal in its overbearing, and our squad leaders were anything but sympathetic about it.

When we learned we'd all be riding chartered trains to Chicago for a football game, and had eight hours of free time after the game, we happily counted the days. We had to do that anyway to be able to spout on demand our fourth-class poop, knowing the number of days to every bit of relief in our schedules, especially the graduation of our upperclassmen, the Army-Navy game and a whole list of others. Add this to the menu for the day, and the movies for the weekend, and we had to be a walking calendar, always ready to respond.

Alice and my parents were going to Chicago for the football game, and that eight hours of freedom in the fall was motivation enough for me to survive a few more weeks of Tom Swett. Calculus was another matter. It involved studying a daily lesson in a cheaply printed booklet written by the head of the math department. It set forth the problems we struggled to understand. It was math, and reading it didn't mean understanding it at all. I was frustrated every night. In the morning every one of us in our small classes of 15 cadets would be required to go to the blackboards and completely on our own work out the solution to an assigned problem.

At the command of "cease work," we took our seats, dreading being the first called upon to go to the board and explain our solution, or lack thereof, to our classmates. Usually the weakest solution on the boards was called first, so each of us would go up and stammer around trying to explain how far we got and what stumped us in the problem. Simply going to the board and trying hard to explain what you didn't understand might get you one point eight into the daily grade book. 2.0 was passing, and 3.0 was perfect. As each of our classmates struggled through, a few did better, giving us little insights into what we might next have to try to master. Never were many 3.0s awarded.

The competition by constant grading was intense. It wasn't just math but every subject. Added to that was the importance of physical education in our plebe gauntlet of survival swimming, boxing, wrestling and gymnastics, plus grades on military training and leadership scores from our cadet chain of command and classmates. These numbers went into the computers daily, and every week our academic scores were posted in the sally ports. We were required to write down our scores and keep track of our progress. We knew a single average score below 2.0 at the semester meant attending college somewhere else later that winter. There was no substitute for victory in this academic competition.

Four classes every day, but only two on Saturday, filled the week, with either intramural sports or a parade each afternoon. For the first couple months of plebe year we had a big parade on Saturday before walking punishment tours on the area. Escaping the area was hard because any excess demerits you received during the month had to be walked off on weekends in dress uniform, carrying a rifle. Another area inspection took place as you arrived, before you walked for hours. Demerits from the area inspections compounded on top of others awarded during the month until you got everything so right you had no excess demerits and escaped. It took me a couple months and then that extra five or six hours each weekend were freed up, not that you could leave the post or go anywhere else with your scant free time.

It wasn't prison as there were plenty of goals and little freedoms to look forward to, but it was a total and confining existence. In this blur of stresses, competition came naturally. Some were going to drop off the bottom and be gone. It was a struggle to avoid that. It was just one more step up the ladder to do better. West Point simply demanded that you survive, compete and change.

By the time I marched with my company across the train tracks into Soldier Field in Chicago I knew that my motivation also came from the folks back home. At 17, submerged in a completely new and pernicious environment, the emotional ties back home held us steady. Alice wrote every day, and her letters encouraged me that she was holding onto our emotional tie across the distance.

We had arranged a meeting place after the game, and my parents and Alice and I went to the house of Louis Savage, who had worked for my father on the farm in Burnt Prairie, for dinner. Savage had moved to Chicago and become a bungalow owner with his Teamster pay. Alice and I spent some private time together in Louis' finished basement. By one in the morning, I was back on the train, riding east for the rest of the weekend.

The real break, though, came in summer leave. Recognition marked the end of plebe year and we had 30 days leave. The confidence boost was enormous as I was back in my 1957 Chevy with Alice and flying airplanes with the White County Flying Club. The huge burst of freedom on leave played to the strains of Buck Owens, "Together Again."

Together again
The gray skies are gone
You're back in my arms
Now where you belong

The love that I knew
Is living again
And nothing else matters
We're together again[12]

It felt great to be back with Alice. Letters and support from my high school sweetheart through my distant difficulties were the survival tools of change. Our friends were getting married or were off in the freedom of the civilian college campus. But upon returning from leave at West Point, I knew I had to sign a written statement, on penalty of an honor violation and expulsion, that I was not married. They demanded to change our entire life, but on leave, we could pretend otherwise, at least for a while.

That made the melodies of Buck's steel player, Tom Brumley, all the more powerful as we danced to country music in Shawneetown or rode the blacktops with the radio playing loud. On leave I was still a country farm boy in my mind and actions, while being pulled into and imprisoned in such a different, aspiring world.

Returning to Camp Buckner to begin our second, or yearling year for summer training, drove this home. Real Army field training with weapons qualification, driving tanks, firing artillery and learning basic patrolling skills in Recondo training were all fun. The reality of Vietnam also began to sink in. We were a privileged class, likely to have the opportunity to serve in Vietnam and not sit stateside in boring garrison duty between wars. It was time to begin really getting ready for that. In 1966, President Johnson was ordering ground troops into Vietnam after the Gulf of Tonkin resolution was rubber-stamped through Congress.

I was more gung-ho than most people would have imagined, picking up a Darby award for excelling in summer field training and earning the nickname "Recondo" among my classmates for hard charging through the training. But, artillery is not a shotgun for hunting, tanks are not John Deere tractors and Vietnam is not the farm.

The Communist threat was real, and the domino theory was operative. Our job as West Point cadets was to learn to lead into this maelstrom of limited war under the umbrella of nuclear threats and mutual assured destruction. I understood that our role was to lead where it was tough, doing hard and awful and immoral things in war. To walk that dark side was necessary in my mind, and it demanded our best.

We had experienced plenty of positive leadership as plebes. Not all upperclassmen were like Tom Swett. Off in the distance was first class valedictorian Wesley Clark, and my Beast Barracks platoon leader, the impressive Art Bonifas. Bonifas led by clear and positive example and urged his squad leaders to do the same. During the regular year in D-3 we lived in the barracks with positive leaders like Rich Hood, who quietly but firmly set a good example and walked the walk of a strong leader. These and others earned our respect.

Tragedy would come to both Bonifas and Hood. Bonifas was killed in a DMZ incident in Korea many years later. Hood was killed near Dak To, a year after his graduation.[13] Though we didn't know all the details, word quickly spread that we had lost one from our company. We learned later that his loss in a "victorious battle" was a half-truth, since the brass had inflated its claim of enemy body count to try to make a loss look like a victory. Such contradictions were oozing back to West Point quicker than the liars and manipulators of truth believed.

We could see it, too, in those officers who returned from Vietnam to be our tactical officers and instructors. Their countenance was dimmed by the war, and as young, idealistic cadets we sensed that in their every move and posture.

As yearlings we got to try our hand with the plebes a bit, seeking our own individual brand of firmness and positive leadership. We learned this slowly, but our class also faced the realities that led increasing numbers to decide to leave. The calling of real life on the outside and from girlfriends, who wanted to be with us and not just write letters, collided with the long march of gray days at West Point.

The chorus from the Animals, "We Gotta Get Out of This Place," became our unofficial theme song:

> We gotta get out of this place
> If it's the last thing we ever do
> We gotta get out of this place
> 'Cause, girl, there's a better life for me and you[14]

Attrition from our ranks increased early in yearling year. The discussions and debates raged through our class in the barracks at night as classmates hesitated before heading for the Boarders' Ward on the way out the door. Our class suffered 30 percent attrition from the first day through graduation. The toughest bulk of it took hold after our classmates proved they could make it through plebe year, but then bolted away in reaction to the idea of staying on for good.

I put my head down and tried to refine my competition. Surprised at first by making the dean's list academically and thriving more than I expected in summer training, I was at a stage of acceptance. Summer training and leave in 1967 was my turning point. West Point's third lieutenant program put me in an artillery battery I really liked with the 101st Airborne Division at Fort Campbell, Kentucky, only a couple hours away from Alice and the farm. Through summer leave and Fort Campbell, our intense summer together brought into focus what letter writing and distance failed to do.

I was an aspiring officer at West Point, headed into a larger world that didn't put a farm-based priority on women or family. While charging into the adrenaline and competition of that world, I hesitated to resolve its conflicts with Alice. She knew what she was looking for but realized she hadn't found in me. The shock of her moving on sent me reeling even deeper in the direction West Point sought, and demanded, from all its prisoners.

The American Dream operates a great deal on how families pursue happiness and prosper. Marrying my high school girlfriend could have been part of that. At West Point, the power center's focus on the Communist threat created a distant role from that pursuit.

We were maintaining the military gains of World War II and the resulting free expansion of the international economy. Our cold war competition was in a bipolar world. The struggle between dictatorship and democracy, so hard-fought through the world wars of the early twentieth century, was not over. While the west prospered, the long Cold War ended only when the Communist dictatorships finally collapsed of their own weight as the century closed.

The Berlin Wall, the Korean DMZ and the Vietnam conflict remained part of that reality for decades, with no quick victories but hard-fought, limited proxy wars and stalemates. Would the gains my father's generation made by defeating Hitler and the Japanese be consolidated? Would the Marshall Plan, NATO, the reserve currency strength of the dollar and expanding economies linked by world trade ultimately be made secure by a huge military-industrial complex? Could this foster and contribute to a better chapter of the American Dream? Did the example and strength of the world's leading economy and military power enhance it?

It pulled both ways. European and Japanese economic recovery drove up trade and helped make the United States the center of the world economy, with a soaring standard of living as a result. Then the drag of huge military costs as the world's policemen, amid the divisions of controversial and unsuccessful adventures such as Vietnam divided, fractured and diminished these gains. The positive spirit of post-war America began to wane.

The Army wanted a leading role in this fight with its own expensive bureaucratic expansion into nation-building led by career soldier-leaders who were hardened by war and schooled in international relations. At West Point, "Onward Christian Soldiers" into the fight against godless Communism was the music I heard. Defending, preserving and expanding the American Dream was the message, and the military sought to solidify its role while this tune played on.

We marched in formation everywhere at West Point. From reveille and breakfast formation to an afternoon march out to intramurals, we formed up in ranks, took roll and forward marched by platoons. On Sunday morning, our chapel formation marched up the hill to the Cadet Chapel. Nobody was excused, although a few could attend the Catholic Chapel or the Jewish Chapel.

There was no separate excuse for Baptists. We went to the big chapel on the hill overlooking the plain with everyone else and took our seats in a huge cathedral-like stone building lined with flags and stain-glassed windows. I saw prayer books and hymnals but very few Bibles in sight.

In through the narthex our formations dislodged as we moved through the nave to our seats, observing the brass and Superintendent up front near the transept. Like the aristocracy of medieval Europe, they presided over our assembly in the chapel, displaying their rank. The chaplains arrived in formation to the music of the largest pipe organ in the world, walking down the center aisle in robes with flag bearers, transmitted as high priests into the open sanctuary and raised pulpits above us. The prayer book and cadet prayer were recited in unison, and the message from the pulpit always was one of reassurance of the righteousness of our cause.

This official imprimatur of a state religion in support of the military's shield and fury struck hard and fast. If you didn't stand and participate you could earn demerits as surely as at area inspection. Mandatory chapel was at the heart of the moral foundation of the disciplined cause we had joined.

I didn't take kindly to it from the beginning, but what was I to do. Follow orders and compete, learn to lead and someday you can help remedy the Army's flaws was the message I heard. It wasn't hard to hear the party line; it was drilled in. The tough must lead in the "moral" fight.

Except war is not moral. It defies Christ's biblical teaching that I heard preached and had absorbed in Burnt Prairie since I first could understand the English language:

> Blessed are the peacemakers: for they shall be called the children of God. Matthew 5:9

> But I say unto you, Love your enemies, bless them that curse you, do good to them that hate you, and pray for them which despitefully use you, and persecute you. Matthew 5:44.

> Thou hypocrite, first cast out the beam out of thine own eye; and then shall thou see clearly to cast out the mote out of thy brother's eye. Matthew 7:5.

> And be not conformed to this world; but be ye transformed by the renewing of your mind, that ye may prove what is that good, and acceptable, and perfect, will of God. Romans 12:2.

> Be not overcome of evil, but overcome evil with good. Romans 12:21.

> But the fruit of the Spirit is love, joy, peace, longsuffering, gentleness, goodness, faith, meekness, temperance: against such there is no law. Galatians 5:22-23.[15]

None of this Biblical teaching I had learned at the Liberty Baptist Church was even remotely answered or reconciled. Instead it was simply contradicted by the mandatory state religion of the Army and the Cadet Chapel. The gulf between the two left its prisoners in a moral vacuum, me included.

Such moral dilemmas were playing out throughout the United States as soldiers confronted the violence of napalm, cluster bombs, claymore mines, and artillery on the Vietnamese Army and population. Like me, most didn't understand the distinctions of the "just war doctrine"[15] promulgated by Christendom long ago. Increasingly, though, the draftees did understand what they saw with their own eyes, and it didn't focus the same way their fathers' views had focused in the wars against Hitler and the band of dictators. Even at West Point we didn't just hear the party line on these moral questions at Cadet Chapel, we heard different views from our friends in college and our girlfriends on weekends.

At West Point, the Cadet Prayer was recited claiming its goal of a "religion filled with gladness and our worship of Thee be natural" but in a service compulsory and not freely entered by me at all. Its most commonly cited phrase is "make us to choose the harder right instead of the easier wrong, and never to be content with a half-truth when the whole can be won."[17] Many of my classmates accepted that as a definition of purpose, with its consistency to the honor code by which we all lived.

But I believed religion could provide a coherent whole truth, arrived at individually through the transformation and renewal of the mind called for in scripture. Such a resolution of moral principles, not just reciting someone else's approved beliefs, was a necessary part of religion for me. In the cauldron of activity required to survive West Point, I was missing the time and content necessary to drive such a resolution.

I found the prayer contradictory with its appeal to "loyalty to all that is noble." It also called for standing with "no fear when truth and right are in jeopardy." To me, the loyalty to the nobility in history was an element of Christendom that included burning at the stake as a penalty for advocating different beliefs. That put "truth and right" in conflict for centuries.

The prayer closed with appeals to teamwork and fellowship around the ideals of West Point, not the ideals of religion. It had no mention of peace as a goal, no prayer for your enemies, nor any reference to cleansing one's own faults before casting blame on another. It called for no transforming or renewing of your mind and omits the fruit of the Spirit altogether.

What does it mean in theological terms when prayer asks that we not diminish hatred and since when is hatred of any kind encouraged as a value in prayer? Why "scorn compromise" when the just war doctrine calls on us before we engage in war to show that all other means of putting an end to it must have been shown to be impractical or ineffective? Might not compromise be one of these other means required before engaging in the violence of war?

Did the mandatory services reconcile these contrasting beliefs and premises? Did they confront the moral ambiguities of war? Did one depart from the Cadet Chapel service with a feeling of peace and resolution?

Walking out of the Cadet Chapel onto the open porch just outside the chapel doors into the relative freedom of a Sunday afternoon was to walk into the light and beauty of the Plain and the Hudson River far below. The beauty of this inspiring place relieved that vacuum and promised something more. But what? The answer was to slowly come.

Positive leadership by example is learned by practice. The plebe system, the cadet chain of command, the third lieutenant summer training, and the day-to-day schooling by our tactical officers and instructors set this forth. General Westmoreland was Superintendent at West Point before he commanded in Vietnam. Our Superintendent, Lieutenant General Koster, had commanded the Americal Division in Vietnam and then came to West Point on the well-worn careerist road toward four stars and service as Chief of Staff of the Army, or some other major career culminating post. Often these lead to a likely further transition into more profitable service in the military-industrial complex. The officers we mostly saw in our companies and our classes, though, were the captains and majors.

We knew, too, from our few weekend leaves and forays into New York City, that the rest of our generation was leading a different life, hugely affected by the specter of Vietnam. My classmates and I had little, if any, respect for anti-war demonstrators or draft-card burners. We also heard more compelling and legitimate concerns from our dates or girlfriends on weekends. In some ways, the civilians in our generation were ahead of us in seeing Vietnam's contradictions, and they certainly were ahead of the thinking of many older Americans.

Where we at West Point were ahead of the curve in understanding Vietnam and its contradictions came from what we directly observed in those captains and majors. Returning from Vietnam service, they were changed from what we had observed as plebes. Their talk was less straight, their reservations submerged in rationalization and self-interest. Their medals stacked high on their chest failed to distinguish true heroism from ticket-punching to speedy promotion. Their words weren't ringing true.

Subtle turns from integrity, leadership by example and an inspiring confidence turned to doubt, phony explanations or the strutting postures of a martinet. This direct hit on our well-tuned radars did not go unnoticed. Our young, idealistic motivations as we gleaned and refined the meanings of true leadership turned sour by some we encountered. They crashed on the rocks of disillusionment.

Our new regimental commander, Lieutenant Colonel Al Haig, drove this home. In 1967, he gave a riveting lecture to the entire Corps of Cadets on commanding his battalion defense under attack by North Vietnamese regulars. He had thoroughly prepared his battalion in a dug-in bait-and-bomb tactic to maximize body count with the firepower of grazing fire, machine guns, mortars, foo gas, mines, booby traps, artillery and air strikes with napalm and fragmentation bombs. Real and substantial body count with advanced technological firepower was the primary tactic in a civil war masquerading as an anti-Communist war of attrition. Haig wanted to brag, detailing how this was done.

Haig wasn't content with our marching in step and in tight ranks at parades. He arrived at our formations slapping his gloves in his hands, making his commanding presence loud and clear. He wanted his regiment to stand out, with his signature apparent. It wasn't enough to naturally cup hands at attention while marching with our rifles. Our free hand had to be squared off at the knuckles. He was personally there, screaming into the ranks when he saw a forbidden cupped hand in his regiment. Returning to the barracks after parades, astonished and with cramped hands, we knew we had picked up a phony, whose leadership was not by example but by the intimidation of a true martinet. We put our heads down and went on.

Progressing through classes in military psychology and leadership we learned the West Point history of fire and maneuver in the classic historic battles, and international relations. Math and engineering were at the center, and I advanced into our only four electives wanting to learn organic and physical chemistry. Computers fascinated me, and despite our heavily prescribed academic load, I volunteered to do an overload course in computer programming. I climbed the academic ladder up to a class rank that peaked at about 250 toward the end of my "Cow" or third year.

One course I didn't like was military law. Regulations and tight, enforceable rules in a confusing mix of detail was not my cup of tea. We sat by class rank in each section of fifteen cadets. The first section began with those whose grades were at the very top in our regiment. As the semester progressed, we re-sectioned so our current section and seating assignments continued to reflect our current order of merit in that subject. Throughout the first semester, I was consistently in the bottom section, the thirteenth, in military law.

Then fate struck. The best instructor in military law was Wynne Morriss, a top of his class Harvard graduate drafted away from his Manhattan law firm into the Army. As a draftee, they didn't issue him an M-16 or ask him to do courts-martial at Tan Son Nhat airbase near Saigon; they sent him to West Point instead to teach military law. He didn't look at all like our other instructors with his longer hair and shoes shined with a Hershey bar. Because of his legal brilliance, he always taught the first section.

Then, the head of the law department decided enough was enough, and at the beginning of the second semester Morriss was sent to teach the thirteenth. "The wheels of justice grind exceedingly slowly, but they also grind exceedingly finely," said Captain Morriss. Somehow the light went on. I was inspired by an inspiring figure. We got a fresh start as second semester began, and our grade average began anew. Mine shot up, so high that in the next re-sectioning, I catapulted to the first section of military law, where Wynne Morriss returned. I stayed with him in first section the rest of the year.

Here the influence of my father, Phil Pearce and Wynne Morriss intersect. Lessons learned from my father's example, the war hero and pilot Phil, and now the Harvard intellectual and legal scholar all swirled together as I absorbed the lessons of this new, influential mentor. His appeal was academic, but he also was an advocate of a legal culture that acted on proven merits, as distinguished from different aspects or traditions of military or farm life.

This second semester began after Christmas leave at the beginning of 1968. The tumultuous year Americans were experiencing outside reverberated at West Point. Returning draftees were changing both the Army and society. There was no hiding the truth from them. They humped the bush, took the casualties, and experienced firsthand their own sergeants and lieutenants on the ground. They knew about the majors and colonels in helicopters above them or back in secure base camps enjoying air-conditioning and steak dinners. Their stories and their realities were different than World War II, and their return to the "world" created a second, broader stage of the anti-war movement.

The radicals and draft-card burners had little credibility at first, but when veteran brothers explained the war to their own sisters and girlfriends, family dynamics created a societal upheaval. Women weren't going to put up with this long, and dinner table arguments became intense as the generation gap widened. The light at the end of the tunnel was dim, and the draftees knew it.

President Johnson was under challenge. His domestic war on poverty was colliding with greatly expanded military spending and inflation. My father was on the front line as executive director of the five-county Wabash Area Office of Economic Opportunity. These new governmental entities were designed by Johnson to get around obstacles in the political structure, such as Boss Daley in Chicago or Governors like George Wallace. By sending federal grant money directly to new regional organizations, resistance to direct help to the poor and racial discrimination was bypassed. My father was writing and receiving federal grants for the early forms of Head Start, local beautification projects, summer camps for kids, Meals on Wheels and job training. Coordinating with both local groups and regional federal administrators, he was well tapped into the effort to build programs from the bottom up among rural poor and farm workers with only basic educations and slim prospects.

Those from his generation were supporting Johnson's aggressive agenda to stave off Communist expansion while at the same time helping to reform the bottom of our domestic economy. They sought to slog it on through, just as they had done in World War II, when the war economy lifted the United States out of the Depression.

General Westmoreland's tipping point strategy naturally followed from the failed strategies of the post-colonial world, pacification, strategic hamlets or arming the Montagnards in the central highlands to cut off the Ho Chi Minh trail. North Vietnamese soldiers were pouring down the trail, and Westmoreland thought his tactic of killing more of them than they could send down to reinforce could be successful.

Like General Lee in the Civil War, Westmoreland's military tactics worked. He killed plenty and he delayed the ultimate reckoning, but his strategy was disastrous. Both prolonged a killing machine in a war already lost through defective strategy. In war, military strategy must follow achievable political aims, not turn them on their heads.

Only then do successful military tactics implement a sound strategy to actually win a war.[18]

Excessive body counts and a flawed strategy strengthened the resolve of the North Vietnamese, whose simpler civil war aim was to unify their country and expel the foreigner. In early 1968, their Tet offensive exposed the lies in Westmoreland's sugar-coated reports to Johnson and his war cabinet, breaking the credibility for people like my father who otherwise were staying the course. In a flurry of history, Senator Eugene McCarthy's anti-war presidential campaign ran strong in the early Democratic primary in New Hampshire, the My Lai massacre occurred with its excesses yet to be widely exposed, Martin Luther King was shot and killed on his hotel balcony in Memphis, and the societal glue began to come apart.

Rich Swick and I got weekend leave immediately after King's killing. Following the leadership example of Mayor John Lindsay, we thought it appropriate to walk the streets of New York City to join the non-violent mourning. Dressed in civilian clothes with our military haircuts, we walked 125th Street in the heart of Harlem that Saturday night, listening, watching and being in the moment. New York City was not burning, but cities across the U. S. were. In Harlem, extension cords allowed record players to be set up in the street to play the "I Have a Dream" speech. King's photographs and black bunting were displayed in the storefronts. We joined in, the only white guys in the crowd at the Apollo Theater that night, and listened to the music. As fellow mourners, we were treated with respect, and we sought to do likewise.

Through our visits to New York City, our girlfriends, families and the evening news, we felt the turmoil in Vietnam where we were preparing to lead its military solution. We knew, though, that the military solution was flawed, just like those draftees knew it as well.

Was law a viable solution to this maelstrom of crisis? Wynne Morriss thought so, as he laid out the theory, logic and history of our legal system. The rules, regulations and military traditions were piled onto that sound and broadly defined legal basis, sometimes well and sometimes in conflicting ways. He pointed out those contradictions, as well as the safeguards, not as a military clone but as a thoughtful professor who sought understanding and appreciation of a system that protected us all, especially those with good lawyers.

Flowing from my grandmothers' traditional Baptist religion, my inherited perspectives were being transformed by a renewing of my mind. The scripture from Romans and the renewal of the mind was at play in the changed circumstances of 1968, the Vietnam War and the generation gaps my friends were experiencing as well. This is an American Dream effect, where its values adapt to changed conditions, re-making it in a new, revised and better foundation going forward.

Changing from the competition of math, engineering, fluid mechanics and chemistry to a consideration of how the fundamental logic and precedent of our legal system established the solid ground on which we could progress flowed naturally from my military law class. I switched electives my last semester, dropping physical chemistry and enrolling into a public policy course in the social science department. Our curriculum was based on recent policy studies. First was the Kerner report on a nation divided, and the second a more obscure report, "Rights in Conflict," discussing the 1968 Democratic convention in Chicago and written by Illinois author and corporate lawyer Dan Walker. I began to believe that maybe flying airplanes and leading military units should give way to understanding more about the legal concepts Wynne Morriss had begun to teach me.

CHAPTER 3

FROM GRANDMA VAUGHT'S
CONCEPT OF RELIGIOUS
FREEDOM TO ALEXANDER HAIG

Congress shall make no law respecting an establishment of religion, or prohibiting the free exercise thereof; or abridging the freedom of speech, or of the press; or the right of the people peaceably to assemble, and to petition the Government for a redress of grievances. First Amendment to the United States Constitution, ratified December 15, 1791.

"Cadets lead the Corps," was the theme of our transition to our first-class year. Our fellow civilian classmates would call it being seniors as we went into the final college year in the fall of 1968. Our military officers told us that carrying out our leadership duties as company officers, platoon leaders and sergeants in the cadet chain of command was a key step in refining our leadership skills before graduation.

I started that year as first sergeant of Company H-3. The company commander and platoon leaders ran their formations, and I ran room assignments, intramural teams and organizing plebe duty rosters. The key was intramurals. If our company could post winning records along with some regimental and brigade championships our regiment could score major points in the competition for company awards. With those came extra weekend leaves for everyone in our company, so our motivation was over the top.

Our athletic cadets wanted to play their favorite sports, mostly football and basketball, but we also had to win at wrestling, boxing, volleyball and cross country. All were worth the same points. I saw the key as letting the other companies concentrate their best athletes to win football while we spread our talents to make off with multiple championships. The strategy worked. Rich Swick led the boxers, and I coached the volleyball team to a brigade championship. My father the coach thought that a great accomplishment.

In the fall of 1968, though, we saw greater challenges and opportunities. My grandmothers' and father's and mother's religion taught that standing on solid ground provided a firm foundation. The hymn we had sung at the Liberty Baptist Church, "My Hope is Built on Nothing Less" by Edward Mote,[19] rang true to me.

> When darkness veils His lovely face,
> I rest on His unchanging grace;
> In every high and stormy gale
> My anchor holds within the veil.
> On Christ, the solid Rock, I stand;
> All other ground is sinking sand.

If the base was flawed, so was the result, and one simply sank in the sand. Logic told us the premise was all important, and false premises flowed through to distorted outcomes.

In living color, distortions were staring us in the face. The winds of this storm blew right at us at West Point as Vietnam loomed just over the horizon.

Grandmother Marie was a believing Baptist, accepting the Cross and Resurrection as foundations of her faith. She found truth in the Bible and believed in an individual struggle of faith, with effort required to understand and implement that truth. No church hierarchy or radio preacher led her down her path. She forged her own and then implemented the truth she found in her own life.

She fought the sins of alcohol through the Women's Christian Temperance Union. She spread the gospel through the Women's Missionary Union. She did not tolerate working on Sunday, and she did not keep quiet in the back pew in a church she helped found as a teenager. She taught and led and advocated based on what she believed were the sound premises of her religion.

Her generosity left her with little money. She had a hard time balancing humility with her advocacy, but she believed everyone had to find their own understanding of truth. Along with her concept of free will she respected the religious beliefs of others and knew that religious freedom protected everyone from the dictatorships of hierarchy.

I knew all this from observing her and listening to her own conflicts about it while out feeding cattle. I listened to her frustrations about my father and the farm and her worries about how my employment cleaning tables at the local Elks Club would "teach me to drink." As a teenager, I didn't agree with everything she said, but she was present as my grandmother, and I had absorbed and accepted more of this than I even knew.

What false premise at West Point was doing us harm? West Point was an institution that had worked, since its founding in 1802, to help lead our country forward. It had helped produce great leaders. How did we get from the honor code at West Point to lying about the body count in Vietnam? How did we get from the great World War II strategies of Generals Eisenhower, MacArthur and Marshall to the limited war strategic failures of Westmoreland and McNamara?

What happened to the founding principles of civilian control of the military? Was it sound that an Army bureaucracy, like lobbyists vying for influence, wanted to expand their power over our foreign policy through soldier-leaders from West Point? Did the profitable path from a distinguished military career to the lucrative profits of the military-industrial complex Eisenhower had warned about cloud their judgment? Did anti-communism and the domino theory blend with careerism and promotion to blind the United States into misperceiving a civil war to expel foreigners in Vietnam?

It was natural for young, idealistic future leaders of the Army to raise and discuss such questions among themselves. West Point was internal and intense, with high expectations of its graduates. The turbulence in the country didn't escape us though, and we sensed that at least part of the underlying foundation was somehow amiss. Like many in our generation, as "cadets leading the corps," we accepted our leadership role to try to correct or adjust these contradictions that seemed at the heart of our straying off course.

A path forward into that controversy crystallized during Reorgy Week, which led into the academic year after the Labor Day holiday in the fall of 1968. Compulsory chapel, in defiance of the First Amendment and our oath to support and defend the Constitution, was the fundamental flawed premise of West Point. Should we do our part to urge a course correction? How would we go about it as leaders in the institution at the heart of the Army?

Fellow company member Rob Leslie had questioned the compulsory nature of chapel as a "Yearling," making an official request to the chain of command to excuse himself. He was invited to a discussion with his tactical officer and told no. Lucian Truscott IV joined him a year later in a second request, but again, to no avail.

Truscott and I drove back Labor Day weekend after stopping at the Ackerman Reunion at Big Prairie. We picked up Rick Swick, who had a Methodist background, at his home in Cumberland, Maryland. We returned in the car my father had given me, which I was not supposed to have at West Point until later in our graduation year. We hid it in Highland Falls for quiet use off post on leaves or privileges away from West Point, paying $10 a month rent to a widow with an open garage. As we drove it back from Illinois and talked, we decided it was time for us to devise a more sophisticated strategy for change.

Swick knew the direct request, which Leslie and Truscott had already tried, was easily answered with a "No." We could not defy or disobey the chain of command directly, but we could come at it more indirectly. We knew how to follow orders, and we sought no symbolic protest that would earn us demerits or confinement away from weekend leaves. We would comply, attend chapel, recite the cadet prayer, and continue our duties as soon-to-be graduates of West Point. But we would respectfully, and with determination, ask for change.

We were paid as cadets, half the pay of a second lieutenant. Most of it went to buy uniforms and books that were furnished and deducted from our pay. Using public funds to directly pay for a chapel and religious services for cadets was a bit much even for the power structure at West Point. Instead, they had all cadets "donate" $3 a month from their pay as a "Cadet Chapel Donation." That's what our pay stub called it, and we did not remember agreeing to donate. We were certainly not freely willing to donate after experiencing Cadet Chapel for three years.

We knew our classmates agreed with us. Fred Van Atta, from Company D-3, wrote a paper in our military psychology and leadership class that included a survey on cadet attitudes toward compulsory chapel. H. Michael Gelfand, in his book "Sea Change at Annapolis," relates its result this way:

> Van Atta randomly distributed five hundred questionnaires for a psychology class and asked cadets for their opinions and habits in regard to compulsory chapel. From the 236 responses he received, Van Atta learned that many of the respondents seldom paid attention at chapel, felt that services should not be mandatory, had skipped chapel, and would attend chapel less often if services were not compulsory. Gelfand, at page 100.[20]

Van Atta concluded: "In my opinion the study indicated that the management decision of mandatory chapel was bad. It caused rebellion more than acceptance and habit. In effect they killed God at West Point."[21]

After the discussions that week as classes began, the four of us drafted identical letters to the Commandant asking that our chapel donation be ceased and restored to our net pay. We submitted it to our tactical officer, properly asking the chain of command for official relief. We expected that such an official request would be answered. To that answer at least, we knew we were entitled.

We had enough sense of the law to know that the Commandant would not be happy to put a denial into an official letter, but that's what we were asking for, an official response. Perhaps, though, facing that reluctance would create an opportunity for further consideration of compulsory chapel itself. We believed a new opportunity for real and better moral training by the Army in its official governmental role was there. Such an approach would not flaunt the first amendment ban on compulsory religious services and could be a small step forward for the change we believed was needed.

Our request called for respecting, considering and listening to each individual's religious beliefs instead of lumping us into a mandatory formation to recite prayers drafted for us and written on paper. It would take away the "party line" lectures from the pulpit with their hollow rationalizations about righteous violence. Instead it could focus on resolving individual religious questions or reservations and would lead to stronger and more mature leaders better capable of dealing with the differing views of the soldiers we were to lead.

Such a voluntary approach also might confront and contribute to the resolution of both the Army's and the country's views on how to minimize the immoralities of war while advancing sounder strategies of confronting the Communist threat. This, we believed, was in the interest of the Army and West Point.

In our naïve view, individual relief from the personal oppression of our religious freedom, along with a public policy goal advocated from the bottom up from cadets running the corps, could work for everyone involved.

We also knew that upon official denial of our requests we could face the dilemma of what to do next. First were questions from our classmates. Submitting an official request through our chain of command began with our cadet company commander, who spoke to our cadet battalion and regimental commanders and staff, and then on to Major Bruce Dalgleish, our tactical officer.[22] Some of the cadets in the chain of command visited with us in person.

What we began to hear from them was caution. They saw our letters as hot potatoes which would only make our lives more complicated. Did we really want to take this on? They asked these questions to us face to face, in serious but informal conversation in the barracks, even before they forwarded the letters to Building 720, the office building for tactical officers which stood just up the hill and in sight of our New South Barracks.

We had survived three years of West Point with them, and our mutual respect and common purpose was evident. They had orally informed our tactical officer that the letters were coming. Cadet officers were chosen in part by their capacity to absorb and comply and articulate the standards and norms of those in the chain of command above them. They were skilled listeners and empathetic, but they were not leaders of a crusade for change.

Our cadet officers knew too that we were no Mark Rudd, who had recently led anti-war protests by occupying the administration buildings of Columbia University until the students he led were forcibly removed by police. Columbia then expelled him from the university. We were not seeking civil or uncivil disobedience, but the question of what we would do if the Commandant said "No," still loomed in our cadet discussions. Did we intend to go to the press? Did we intend to resort to lawyers and file something in federal court? Did we have an endgame in mind that could be destructive to West Point or its reputation?

These discussions with our classmates were extremely useful. We were able to make clear that we really had no contingency plan to expand the controversy outside West Point. That discussion, though, cut two ways. It made clear our uncertainty on those questions of next steps, but in those listening to us it subtly raised, in a non-threatening way, broader concerns about our ultimate intentions. Those in a military chain of command do not threaten or confront their superiors. But they may ask a question or make a request respectfully with the implied expectation that they will accept and comply with the commander's response. That concept of leadership at West Point is one we had faithfully absorbed, and we agreed with it.

The legal specter of the First Amendment, along with our oath to support the Constitution, made this chain of command relationship more complex. In this initial stage, it turned into a counseling approach by Major Dalgleish, who urged us to have discussions with the Cadet Chaplain and consider whether raising such questions was appropriate for our junior status as aspiring officers. Instead, should we comply patiently and advance in our own careers up the chain of command to higher command, where we could more appropriately affect such issues.

Treading this fine line between asking for an answer to a respectful question versus confrontation soon became slippery. It began with Colonel Marion Ross, our new regimental commander. Colonel Haig had become deputy commandant, and we knew little of our new regimental commander, though he would go on to a career of substantial responsibility as a general officer in Korea and with the 3d Army.[23] Major Dalgleish had forwarded our letters up to the next level of the chain of command, and Colonel Ross wanted to see us all right away, late that afternoon before supper.

H. Michael Gelfand, in his book, "Sea Change at Annapolis," at pages 86-87, describes the meeting this way:

> During the evening of 29 October 1968, the men met with
> the new regimental commander, Marion Ross. Ross had
> replaced Haig, who had become the deputy commandant.
> As Truscott explained, Haig told Ross to have a meeting

with the four men and 'scare the living piss out of them.'
Leslie, Swick, Truscott, and Vaught, while standing at
attention in the back of Ross's office, informed him that
they wanted to file a complaint with the inspector general
to end mandatory chapel attendance and donations.
Ross asked why they did not resign from West Point and
indicated that his secretary, who had stayed late and was
ready with a typewriter and resignation form, was on
hand to expedite that process. From Truscott's written
transcript of the events, the conversation continued:

> ROSS: 'You came here voluntarily and agreed to
> abide by the regulations.'
>
> TRUSCOTT: 'I haven't broken any regulations, Sir.
> I go to chapel. I have never skipped chapel.'
>
> SWICK: 'I pay attention to sermons, but I see most
> guys sleeping and inattentive—can you see
> them from where you sit, Sir?'
>
> ROSS: 'No, I sit in front and can see very little from
> my point of view.'
>
> ROSS: (TO SWICK AND VAUGHT): 'You might
> not graduate on June 4th.'
>
> SWICK: 'I may not be alive on June 4th, Sir.'
>
> LESLIE: 'That sounds like a threat, Sir.'
>
> ROSS: 'No, I am just stating a fact. I think you
> ought to resign.'
>
> SWICK: 'Why should I give up a career I've worked
> three years to get, Sir?'
>
> ROSS: 'I could care less what you do with your
> career, Mr. Swick.'
>
> TRUSCOTT: 'What is done with other people who
> want to change things? Are they asked to resign
> and threatened with separation, Sir?'
>
> ROSS: 'I am not threatening anyone.'
>
> LESLIE: 'Do you think we get satisfaction out of
> getting discriminated against and time taken
> out of our day, Sir?'
>
> ROSS: 'You are troublemakers.'

SWICK: 'We are not troublemakers, If we were, we would have had this in court a long time ago and we could still have it in court in two days, Sir.'

ROSS: 'Yes, and if you did you could face charges.'

SWICK: 'What do you mean, Sir?'

LESLIE: 'I don't understand, Sir?'

ROSS: 'We will court-martial you.'

LESLIE: 'For what, Sir?'

VAUGHT: 'Do you mean you would arbitrarily do this?'

ROSS: 'It's been done before and we will do it again.'

LESLIE: 'Sir, you would trump up false charges and arbitrarily court-martial and separate us for a perfectly legal lawsuit?'

ROSS: 'Yes.'

TRUSCOTT: 'Sir, if you are doing that, would that be in keeping with the Cadet Prayer and with your duty as a sworn officer to uphold the Constitution?'

ROSS: 'Yes, I don't give a damn if it is in conflict, and neither does anyone else around here, and it won't be any skin off our asses. I seriously doubt if any of you will graduate.'

The conversation then ended, and the four cadets returned to their quarters.

The gloves had come off rather quickly at Haig's command. The dilemma we all knew was probably coming had arrived. In the short span of time from Labor Day to the end of October, our naïve and compliant "improve West Point" approach was not bearing fruit. As the chain of command turned up the pressure on us to back down, our arrogant resolve became clear.

We were standing on the assertion that we have you by the Achilles heel of illegally taking our pay to advance compulsory religion. The chain of command's counseling approach had turned to open threats of resignation, discriminatory disciplinary action and even court-martial. The Constitution and our oath to uphold it be damned.

Our tentative solution was to openly advocate seeing the inspector general of the Army or going to court. Our underlying approach and strategy remained—insisting on getting an official response to our request to refund our chapel "donations."

Truscott's transcript of the conversation had been recommended by Wynne Morriss. We had gone to see him for advice and learned that in addition to being a professor, he had duties as a legal assistance officer. It turned out he was acting in that capacity when we saw him after class in his office. He was happy to inform us that this status created with us attorney-client privilege which remained as long as our legal controversy continued.

By Army regulations and West Point policy, he had become our lawyer. He anticipated some confrontations with higher ranking officers, and he knew they would threaten us. What he wanted us to do was make use of the legal exception to the hearsay rule involving "past recollection recorded" or "present recollection recorded." If we wrote down what was said in those meetings, we might, in the future, be able to use those memoranda to refresh our recollection in court testimony.

Morriss also knew that Colonel Ross had made a mistake taking us on, by himself, with all four of us present. He had no other witness to contradict our recorded recollections of his threatening meeting. We didn't know these things, but had the good fortune in finding Wynne Morriss, who was quickly teaching.

A few officers eventually came forward to counsel or support what we were doing. They had no attorney-client privilege, though, and were either more timid or secretive in their advice or were acting informally against us on behalf of the chain of command.

Lucian Truscott was approached by Major Bob Berry,[24] a part-time reservist who was acting as a visiting professor in the social science department. In reality he was our connection to the larger military-industrial complex, since his job was as a Washington lobbyist for Litton Industries, a major defense contractor at that time.

Litton's founder had followed the career track of Robert NcNamara from a military assignment with McNamara late in World War II, then with him into Ford. He later formed Litton, which built a portfolio of defense contracts while McNamara advanced to Secretary of Defense. Litton is now part of Northrop Grumman. Berry had worked his way up from being senior counsel at Litton's headquarters in Beverly Hills to creating and leading its lobbying office in Washington, D.C.

Berry liked our West Point class and became an honorary classmate, making his apartment in D.C. available to our classmates and throwing parties for them there. Ultimately, he became a connection for our West Point class to advancing careers in the Army, service in political offices and appointments or to more lucrative employment in defense industries. He was a mentor, a political sponsor, and to some, more than a friend. We suspected at the time some quiet, romantic relationships. His teaching assignment was part of his reserve duty, but he sought out Truscott as part of a new "divide and conquer" strategy that West Point threw at us.

Truscott was my roommate in Company H-3. He came from a military family, and both his grandfathers were general officers. His mother's father had served in the Corps of Engineers as a major general. His father's father was the more famous General Lucian Truscott, Jr., who commanded 5th Army in Italy after successfully leading bloody brawls with the Germans in North Africa, Sicily, Anzio and southern France. As a plebe, Truscott IV went on bereavement leave to attend his grandfather's 1965 funeral. He knew his grandfather well and understood his history as a confidante of President Eisenhower and his role in establishing the post-war CIA in Europe.

The brass decided that Lucian the cadet was the leader of the chapel movement that they should isolate, neutralize and knock off first. The rest of us would follow. Bob Berry opened this strategy playing the long card—the grandson of generals can become a general if he punches all his career tickets and works hard to learn and apply the lessons of leadership from West Point. By pursuing that long game, you will achieve greater power to change and help the Army than by fighting with the chain of command as a lowly cadet. Don't sacrifice your future for a fight you cannot win.

Truscott would bring Berry's cajoling back to our room, and we discussed it with Swick and Leslie. The basic hole in Berry's siren song involved a careerism that was misdirected. We took seriously the gap between upholding the Constitution and what the careerist aspirants to power were advocating. They conveniently ignored our most basic document of organic law and could not explain it away with bare ambition.

Wynne Morriss helped with his theories of autonomous bureaucracies and explained their blind spots. Bureaucracies generally are not authorized to define their own mandates. Instead they are subject to supervision by those invested with authority over policy, or by statutes and constitutional provisions that provide safeguards against their abuses. Morriss would laugh at the foolishness of those who practiced the opposite.

Like the aristocracies of old, the blind insularity of autonomous bureaucracies devolved into "cover your ass" approaches to inefficiency and stupidity. Morriss preferred the legal approach and believed the law could grind through the inconsistency and false premises of the autocrats. Morriss was entertained by the foibles of West Point, but he cautioned that we were in danger from them.

We were all too naïve to completely understand that danger, and the brass used our mistakes to step up the pressure on us, and ultimately to retaliate. By the time we neared graduation we all were in jeopardy, not only of losing class rank, but being threatened with expulsion or being required to walk huge numbers of hours on the area.[25]

When Major Dalgleish was too soft in dealing with us, Colonel Ross would send Major Scudder, another tactical officer in our regiment, to join the fray. He would write us up for demerits, or search our rooms, looking for contraband or letters in our desk drawer files from outsiders in New York or elsewhere. They wanted to know what Lucian's father and West Point graduate, Lieutenant Colonel Lucian Truscott III, was saying to his son. Keeping the pressure up to isolate us from outside help was also part of their divide and conquer plan.

Their careerism worked for them. We didn't know that Colonel Ross would go on to become Lieutenant General Ross. He commanded thirteen divisions in Korea as I Corps Group Commander and retired as commanding general of 3rd Army.[26] Berry later headed the Law Department at West Point and served as General Counsel of the Army under President Nixon.[27] Haig became more infamous as the Reagan administration official who publicly declared himself in charge of the White House when President Reagan was wounded by an assassin. He also was the basis for the fictional character, General Hedges, played by Hal Holbrook in Truscott's 1978 novel and 1986 TV miniseries, "Dress Gray." He was next to arrive in West Point's tag team taking on the defense of compulsory chapel.

Haig continued the focus on Truscott, playing both roles in his good cop, bad cop routine. He once called an honor board to accuse Truscott of an honor violation. Such interference in the operation of the Honor Committee was frowned upon because the honor system was run entirely by cadets. Official statements to officers were required to be completely truthful, including the certification of not being married upon return from leave. But open-ended, "Have you violated any regulations today?" inquiries were improper. So was command interference in the procedures of the honor committee. Haig blatantly ignored these precepts and tried to ram a bogus honor violation through on Truscott. The Cadet Honor Committee found that no honor violation had occurred and thwarted Haig's intimidation plan through the Honor System. Integrity and truth won that one.

Haig sent higher level cadet officers to forcefully ask that Truscott back off on compulsory chapel. He repeatedly called

Truscott to his office overlooking central area where he starred in his own dual role in his good cop, bad cop routine. He continued the Berry argument that a career to later power is the way to go but contrasted that with direct threats. He once took our four letters asking for an end to mandatory chapel donations and threw them in his wastebasket, saying he was doing us a favor so we could graduate. Truscott promptly asserted that no, Haig actually was committing a crime by intercepting without authority an official communication directed to the Commandant. The heart of Haig's scheme was to solve the compulsory chapel challenge himself without informing the Commandant, Brigadier General Rogers, that it existed.

It became clear that our request that the Commandant respond in writing to our letters was stalled on Haig's desk, if not in his wastebasket. In addition to these letters, I sent a separate letter requesting that I be allowed to attend alternative off-post services each Sunday morning at a Baptist Church near Highland Falls. That request was promptly denied by an officer on the 3rd Regimental staff.

Stymied, threatened and cajoled, we faced both a great strain on whatever peace of mind we had achieved by becoming first class cadets, along with a steady erosion in our class rank. We learned from Lucian's father, Lieutenant Colonel Lucian Truscott III, that the Army had an informal personnel practice called flagging. In the days of written personnel folders and file tabs, it was easy for the Army to attach a red flag to your file. It was meant to delay, stall or end your military career, and, according to Lieutenant Colonel Truscott, it was difficult to remove. He had graduated from West Point about the same time as Colonel Haig and Brigadier General Rogers and served as an infantry company commander in Korea and as a battalion commander in Vietnam. He believed his own personnel file had been flagged when he resisted abuses of "free fire zones" killing civilians in his battalion area in the Mekong Delta.

Each of us who challenged compulsory chapel intended to graduate and serve in the Army, flagged or not. At the same time, we continued to consider the what to do next question in our chapel challenge. We didn't intend to pass by the glaring constitutional violation in the heart of West Point, but at the same time we faced decisions about our Army careers. Cadets can choose their own initial branch of service and first assignment based on class rank at West Point.

In winter of 1969, our entire class gathered in Thayer Auditorium to stand and make our selections. Cadets were called in order by class rank, and those at the top tended to choose the limited Corps of Engineers slots. Those who aspired to general officer rank stood and loudly called out "Infantry!" I was high enough in class rank to go for the Engineers, but when my name was called, I chose my father's branch as an enlisted man in World War II, the Artillery. My compadres in the chapel challenge all chose Infantry.

All of us knew that after the officer's basic course in our branch, airborne school and ranger school at Fort Benning, we would soon get orders to Vietnam. We could also choose to "volunteer" for Vietnam duty as our first assignment, which aspiring generals precisely did. Or we could choose a first assignment elsewhere, knowing it would be abbreviated so we could join our classmates in Vietnam. The road to Vietnam was pretty direct for us all.

Rob Leslie and Lucian Truscott volunteered for Vietnam, but they had short, interim assignments, Truscott to Fort Carson in the 5th Mechanized Infantry, and Leslie to Fort Bragg to the 82nd Airborne Division. Rich Swick decided that, as a soon to be married father, his duty to family dictated he volunteer for the longest possible assignment before the ultimate transfer to Vietnam. He figured it was Alaska, so he was headed to the cold of Fort Richardson near Anchorage.

I decided that the fairest characterization of the Vietnam War, by this time under President Nixon, was one of waste, now a pointless squandering of resources, time and lives for political posturing. I, like Swick, was in no hurry to go to Vietnam. Waste or not, there were other legitimate assignments in an Army that was deployed to defend our interests worldwide. Defending the United States remained a paramount mission in my mind, so I chose the unit that was on alert as the first line of deployment to any new or different military crisis, the 82nd Airborne Division.

Would serving in these assignments erase the flags that Lieutenant Colonel Truscott thought we had all gained by refusing the demands of Colonels Ross and Haig to withdraw our compulsory chapel complaints? We didn't know, but the responses we received to our complaints convinced us we had already earned that flagged status. Rob Leslie thought service in Vietnam would erase it, and that after the required minimum service in a combat arm he could successfully seek a branch transfer to the Judge Advocate General's Corps and serve as an Army attorney. I didn't overthink it too much and believed our job was to do what was expected of us, put our head down and do our job. The chips would fall under their own gravity.

Legend had it that no cadet in the history of West Point had ever dared to take a complaint to the official annual visit of the Department of the Army Inspector General. West Point was simply too perfect and cadets too compliant to consider such a flagrant and out-of-step move. Upon the official notice that the inspector general's representative was present and open to any and all complaints from the officers, enlisted men and cadets stationed at West Point, we made our formal request to see him. My written complaint asked for an end to compulsory chapel as unconstitutional and "discriminatory to cadets of various religions and harmful to my moral development."

Haig, in the meantime, was tapped for a different assignment, departing West Point in December of 1968 to serve in President Nixon's White House. How much influence he would have with the Commander in Chief was unknown, but this transfer left no doubt that we had been dealing in the political power center of the Army at West Point. If we persisted we would have to continue to deal with the ramifications that flowed from it. By the time President Nixon resigned, Haig had become his Chief of Staff and he went on to serve as NATO Commander and Secretary of State under President

Reagan, then CEO of United Technologies, a defense contractor. Haig would make the switch from an officer in the ranks to a political general in the more profitable power centers of the United States. We didn't forget him, and, unfortunately, from his perch in D.C., he didn't forget us.

CHAPTER 4

FROM CHAPEL DONATIONS TO THE AREA

The Inspector General, a colonel from the Pentagon, personally met with us. He was polite and listened to our concerns. He promised to take them back to the Pentagon. He said he would suggest that this issue be reviewed at the next annual meeting of the superintendents of all five service academies, since Annapolis and others also had compulsory chapel. He doubted any change could come before that regular annual meeting, which would not be held until after we graduated. He counseled patience on our behalf and reassured us that we had been heard.

The fight had worn us down. Every mistake we made was a demerit or was somehow used against us. Much of that is the West Point way of discipline, and we had survived its challenges for three years. Becoming targets of the unfairness of retaliation was a hard burden to bear. Under challenge, we needed to focus on graduating. During my last year at West Point, my class rank declined from near 250 out of 800 at the end of my third year to just over 300. Truscott went one demerit over the annual limit. He faced a Commandant's Board to reconsider the validity of the demerits. If found valid he faced expulsion on the eve of graduation. Truscott and I became members of the "Century Club," the unique group of cadets who walked more than 100 punishment tours on the area during their four years at West Point but survived it to graduate. Swick and Leslie marched punishment tours with us as well.

Normally you walked only five hours a week, but we had so many hours left on the area that we couldn't finish before graduation. We heard rumors that the brass intended to require that we stay into what would have been our 60-day graduation leave and finish on the normal area schedule while delaying our graduation. This would have made our date of rank for all future Army promotions delayed and would have deprived us of the ceremony of graduating with our classmates and in class rank order.

Was this just a threat or an early implementation of the flagging procedure we had heard about? We were hanging by a thread and our four years of work and hardship could be erased by those holding the scissors. After enough pause for us to understand this, our area assignment was changed to six hours daily, six days a week.

Truscott's feet fell apart with serious blisters. The doctors in the hospital wanted to excuse him, but he feared the consequences and they allowed him to walk in combat boots instead. The Commandant then intervened, granting Truscott a reprieve from the area.

I toughed it out as the last of our group on the area, marching six hours a day into June Week. The huge four-year goal of celebration with parents and girlfriends went out the window as I watched from the area as my other classmates celebrated their upcoming graduation on June 4. My parents and grandmother Inie were in town but couldn't see me because I was confined to barracks until I finished my tours on the area. Finally, on June 3, I walked my last punishment tour and was able enjoy a pre-graduation dinner with my parents the night before graduation.

While I was still on the area the superintendent, Lieutenant General Samuel Koster, addressed our entire class from the poop deck overlooking the mess hall. He had advice for them. He cautioned our class to remember what happened to troublemakers in the Army, and he raised his arm and pointed to central area. Our class had seen us marching punishment tours while they celebrated with their family and friends during June Week. You have only to look at the area at West Point to see what happens to troublemakers, Koster said.

In March of 1968, as commanding general of the American Division, then Major General Koster had been in a helicopter in Vietnam over an area the Army called "Pinkville."[28] One of the villages there was My Lai. In the later public outcry over the court-martial of First Lieutenant Calley for his role in the deaths of My Lai's substantial civilian population, many of the public identified that Calley was a scapegoat, asking why those who gave the orders faced no sanction.

Initially the follow-up to the excessive civilian deaths at My Lai was handled within the American Division. No reports of possible war crimes, as required by Army regulations, had been forwarded to higher headquarters in Saigon or Washington, D. C. for investigation. Officers in the division, including Major General Koster, were implicated in this initial cover-up. An official investigation was later handled by Lieutenant General Peers, and its result called for sanctions on Koster.

A few years later, Koster was unceremoniously relieved of his command as Superintendent, retired from military service and reduced in rank. Perhaps he blamed that, too, on "troublemakers," instead of his own conduct as an officer sworn to follow orders and Army regulations. He was caught trying to cover up a war crime that became a national scandal and a black mark on the Army. His black mark was most egregious since it was undeserved by most veterans who served honorably and effectively during the Vietnam War. In the eyes of some, he tarred patriotic and brave soldiers with his own deceit. Through his failure to live up to the ideals of West Point, its honor code and his officer's oath, he did those other good soldiers a great injustice.

I graduated with my class on June 4, 1969, and proudly accepted a commission as a second lieutenant in the United States Army, ready to do whatever duty in defense of my country was required.

CHAPTER 5

FROM DUTY, HONOR, COUNTRY TO DISILLUSIONMENT

Inie was resplendent at the graduation in Michie Stadium, overlooking the beautiful Hudson River valley. Her smile lifted my spirits, and the exuberance of graduating with my class was gripping. My family was proud, relieved and happy to be there.

Called in class rank order, we lined up to the podium and received our diplomas and our promotions to second lieutenant. Having missed June Week at West Point, we loaded my trunks and uniforms and headed to New York City to celebrate. We weren't going to miss our own version of June Week.

My father was known as a teenager for riding his horse all over Burnt Prairie and its surrounding area. We always had horses growing up because he thought them great. He had been to the Kentucky Derby and the Preakness, and now he took advantage of the chance to see the Belmont Stakes on Long Island.

His father had served as a Democratic Precinct Committeeman in Burnt Prairie in 1932, so visiting President Roosevelt's home at Hyde Park on the east side of the Hudson, and just north of West Point, was high on our agenda. Inie and my mother posed in front of the flowering trees and shrubs on the grounds, and we took our time absorbing the place. We missed the wedding ceremony of Rich and Gael Swick in New York City, and soon headed back to Illinois.

Was this the way the American Dream advanced? Families were celebrating graduations, sons and daughters were pursuing the best education they could find and learning the best course forward to define the pursuit of happiness. These activities implement the ideals that are passed from prior generations and learned anew in the challenges the younger generations face.

In the 1960s, the American Dream was under serious challenge. Martin Luther King, in his famous speech at the Lincoln Memorial, called on the American Dream as he re-focused it on broader and even more profound objectives.[29] As race relations exploded after the assassination of Martin Luther King, and the generation gap expanded as the unpleasant truths of Vietnam sunk in, the turmoil of my last year at West Point seemed much more intense. It was somehow related to these broader societal challenges. Leaders at the top influence how the American Dream is carried out, but it is the bottom-up change that sets the stage. Politicians more often follow the lead of their constituents than lead it themselves. The same is true for the American Dream, which arises from ordinary Americans.

Both the civil rights movement and the anti-war movement were working that way, with change seeping through the population like water preparing to break through an earthen dam. Part of the change in the American Dream was upon us, and the reliance on its ideals and values drawn from freedom of religion and expressed in our Constitution were present and in conflict in the Army's power center at West Point. What we had been involved in was as much a part of this bottom-up change that America as a whole also was experiencing, bit by bit and drip by drip.

The normal annual leave in the Army is 30 days. But when you have endured, survived and changed at West Point, it's a well-deserved and needed 60 days graduation leave. I dived into mine with relief. I had flown a Piper Cub in the West Point Flying Club, taking that beautiful flight flying under the airline traffic down the

Hudson to the Statue of Liberty and back, but now I was back in the Cessnas of the White County Flying Club, ready and with the time to go where I pleased.

I still wanted to fly in the Army, but flight school would have to come after my assignment at Fort Bragg and most likely also after a tour in Vietnam. Wynne Morriss had me hooked on the law, but a branch transfer through the Army's excess leave program could only be done after two years in the combat arms. Politics was changing in Illinois, too, and I saw firsthand how my father was implementing the war on poverty.

His favorite programs were Head Start and a summer camping program for children whose parents could not afford to pay summer camp fees. My father always felt people should use their free time to advantage. He had done that in the Army, using sports and boxing competition to earn his promotion to corporal while still in training. I volunteered to serve as a counselor in his camping program and traveled with the campers and other camp counselors into the Shawnee National Forest.

The underlying turmoil from aching joints left over from the area, my mind still troubled by the unresolved compulsory chapel at West Point in defiance of our constitutional liberties, and the cloud of those personnel flags and how to resolve them created more than an underlying mood of unease. In a time of celebration and relief, the psychological burden swirled underneath it all.

As I spent some time on the farm, flew in the three dimensions of the sky that added much to my own perspective and clarity, and had fun at the summer camp, reflection on the events of the last year at West Point didn't clear it up much. Was my preliminary understanding of the First Amendment's freedom of religion clause what really drove me to persist in challenging my chain of command at West Point?

Did I really understand how Colonel Ross's "don't give a damn" statement put the officer's oath to support the Constitution in direct violation with that same Constitution? Did the negative changes I thought I had seen in the officers at West Point really indicate that the premises of loyalty to the chain of command must contradict the freedoms the military defends for us all? Had we been influenced by the growing anti-war sentiment and the political turmoil of the late 1960s enough to feel a need to act where we stood?

Was there an even deeper moral issue at stake? Did my own religious upbringing and beliefs now conflict with the basic military mission of governmentally authorized violence I had sworn to carry out? Was the compulsory chapel challenge simply an opening chapter in a larger personal moral crisis? Did my farm boy mentality of simply putting my head down and doing what next needed to be done provide the survival motivation to keep keeping on? Or was I just a rebel by nature still viewing with disdain the larger complex world I found outside the cattle pastures around Burnt Prairie?

I had not yet even clearly formulated these questions, but I know they unconsciously were at issue. In the meantime, I was ready for what came next. It turned out Oklahoma was a comfortable place for me. Fort Sill is deep in the southwestern part of Oklahoma, near where the Comanches fought their last stand in the 1870s. Its dry, rolling country was a fun place to learn to shoot artillery.

I bought a used motorcycle from a sergeant whose tour was up and rode it all over the state on weekends. Many in the oil patch contingent back in White County had come from Oklahoma, and I got to visit the places I had heard them talk about. I joined the Fort Sill flying club and came close to finishing my commercial license, cut short before I could arrange the final check ride when I had to move on to Fort Benning.

I liked the field duty on the guns or adjusting fire in forward observer training. We got to do aerial adjustment from the back seat of a Cessna flown by an Army fixed-wing pilot. I learned the differences between high explosive, white phosphorus and timed delay fusing of artillery shells. We studied recoil systems and how to maintain and clean the howitzers. I witnessed firsthand how they accurately fired shells for miles with an accuracy driven by the skill of the forward observer calling in fire missions. Through field duty and classroom instruction for the three months at Fort Sill I learned the basics of firepower and how it contributed to the fire and maneuver the infantry and armor were leading on the combined arms battlefield. Like Recondo at Camp Buckner, I absorbed it all with enough enthusiasm to prepare to use it in the combat that was coming across the Pacific, or wherever the 82nd Airborne was ordered to go into harm's way.

The freedom from the confines of West Point also presented many opportunities to be part of the larger population. A camp counselor working in my father's camping program became a girlfriend visiting me in Oklahoma. On Labor Day, just two weeks after Woodstock, we drove to the Dallas International Pop Festival where 100,000 of my generation gathered to hear the same bands that had played at Woodstock and listen to Wavy Gravy tell us what was going on. Spending Labor Day weekend sleeping on the ground in Texas and listening to BB King, Janis Joplin, Jimi Hendrix (an 82nd Airborne Division veteran), Crosby Stills and Nash, the Grateful Dead and Led Zeppelin, to name just a few, was a great holiday for us.

The *Dallas Morning News* thought otherwise and described it this way:

> Young people assembling to hear music is one thing. Young people assembling in unspeakable costumes, half-naked, barefooted, defying propriety and scorning morality is another. Who and where are their parents? Where do these young people get the money to loaf around the country in their smelly regalia?[30]

The country was split, culturally, politically and generationally. That was obvious spending the holiday weekend on the warm dirt of Texas.

Don Randolph, my classmate in the 3rd Regiment at West Point, later became an attorney in California after leaving the Army as a

Captain in 1973 as a conscientious objector. He invited me to join him in his new Corvette and drive to Oklahoma City on October 15, 1969, the first of many nationwide protests in the moratorium against the war. We heard the speakers and talked with those we stood next to in the crowd. The next day we were both back in fatigues calling in artillery fire on the Fort Sill artillery range.

One Saturday morning, as I was putting on my helmet to ride free on my motorcycle, Cornelius Cooper, another classmate in the 3rd Regiment at West Point, walked up and wanted to talk. Cooper was known as a student who always asked questions, sometimes too many in the mind of some other classmates. I liked his questions, and we knew each other well enough for him to know that. He also knew that I had done a good bit of questioning myself in asking the West Point chain of command to end compulsory chapel.

"Have you ever heard of Martin Buber?" he asked. I didn't see any connection between this question and putting gas in my motorcycle. I was just anxious to get out of Fort Sill for the weekend. "I and thou," he said and seemed perplexed that I had not heard of Buber's book. I told him he was going to have to explain, and he did. What I heard was that he was quite troubled with how Buber's religious concepts made sense to him but made no sense at all while learning to fire high explosive or white phosphorus shells at enemy soldiers. I listened but was soon out on the blacktop heading east from Fort Sill toward the Quachita Mountains in southeastern Oklahoma.

Airborne School at Fort Benning followed the basic course, and Ranger School was scheduled for January. The sergeants ran Airborne School, and they were tough. Reveille was early, but John Clapper, Don Randolph, Hugh Stirts and I rented a house in Columbus so we could get away at night and cook our own food. We got the very short haircuts required of airborne troopers and did pushups and pullups on demand. We dealt daily with the requirement to do eight pullups whenever a sergeant ordered it. If we failed to do all eight at any time, we could be re-cycled back to repeat that week of airborne training.

It was clear that the sergeants were in charge, and our second lieutenant bars meant virtually nothing. We advanced to the swing landing trainer, where the sergeant holding the rope controlled the pulley above us to drop us unceremoniously into a saw dust pit. We did this over and over until we learned to fall with an excellent side, forward and rear PLF, or parachute landing fall. Bruises or knots on our heads from slamming our steel pots onto the ground in a poorly executed PLF didn't help, but we soon advanced to the scarier 34-foot tower. After we learned a proper exit out the fake aircraft door up at 34 feet above the ground, another set of cables and pulleys caught us mid-air, breaking our fall while we were staring straight at the ground.

Looming above us for the first two weeks of airborne training was the 250-foot tower, where they attached you to an open parachute and quickly hauled you up to the top where the parachute automatically was set free and you descended in a real free parachute to again practice your PLF.

I thought the training was great and was looking forward to the final week at the airport where we would board the seemingly ancient C-119 Flying Boxcars that noisily creaked and jolted through the air making it feel a relief to go out the door above the drop zone. We lined up on each side of the aircraft, an officer at each end of what was called a stick of airborne troopers. Our role was either to lead or push any reluctant troopers in our stick out the door. Standing in the door with your toes in the breeze and your hands holding the outside skin of the plane was the way a lieutenant was to lead his stick forward.

I learned from the sergeants that I was not a "midnight jumper," those who immediately and beyond their control closed their eyes tightly going out the door, unable to tell if they were jumping during daylight or at midnight. I was a daylight jumper and enjoyed every second of floating outside that aircraft door, with the earth on the horizon slowly turning and twisting a little until my parachute opened. Five jumps that week qualified us as officially Airborne, with the last jump from a turbine powered C-141 jet.

My father shared my glee at Airborne School and came down and pinned my airborne wings on my uniform in the closing ceremony. That made this graduation, preceded by the airborne jumps, a counterpoint to June Week. A happy and unspoiled graduation with my father felt even better than the one I had experienced at West Point just a few months before.

CHAPTER 6

FROM AIRBORNE SCHOOL TO FEDERAL DISTRICT COURT: *ANDERSON V. LAIRD*, 316 F. SUPP. 1081 (D.D.C. 1970)

We were are all still a little beat up and sore from the parachute landing falls (PLF's) and landings in some stiff December breezes on the Fryar Drop Zone. Fryar was named for an airborne soldier awarded the Medal of Honor for saving his platoon leader and platoon during an enemy attack early in the war in the Philippines. It wasn't lost on us that airborne soldiers had earned their reputation for toughness, bravery and heroism. I was proud to join their ranks.

My roommates, though, were less enthusiastic about the upcoming winter Ranger School, which was our next assignment at Fort Benning. They wanted at least a medical delay until a little warmer weather. The day after airborne graduation they headed over to the hospital on sick call to see if their injuries could justify a delay. I just wanted to plow ahead and get it over, but they persuaded all four roommates to go on sick call with them before we left for Christmas leave.

The roommates who convinced us to seek a temporary medical profile were told no by the doctors. The other two, me included, who were less concerned, received an official three week temporary medical profile delaying our entry into Ranger School until our sore knees and hips could recover. My injured hip, which had acted up from too much repetitive stress during many hours on the West Point area concrete earlier that year, had been aggravated on the swing landing trainer.

The doctor called it bursitis and told me that when inflammation flares up it is better to ease it back under control than to keep irritating it and injuring it further. All of us who graduated from West Point had some bum knees from football or other intramurals and were used to nursing them through. That's what I thought I'd do in Ranger School, but an Army doctor convinced me otherwise.

I headed back to Illinois for Christmas leave, ready to report back to January Ranger knowing that my entry into that tough school would be delayed a few weeks to a later class.

In early January 1970, I processed in at Ranger School to serve as an aggressor working against my classmates on night patrols because of my medical profile and then to begin Ranger School with the next class in three weeks.

From our morning formation, I saw the Ranger Sergeants use rakes to remove a thin layer of ice from a swimming pool in the Ranger encampment. Then with packs, rifles and steel pots they ordered all my classmates in the Ranger class to jump in the pool, and then simply get back out. About half my classmates did so promptly, but the other half had trouble getting out of the pool in the cold.

The cold water quickly caused cramping and the beginning of hypothermia, and the weight of the packs, rifles and steel pots was just too much. My classmates called to the sergeants to help get them out, but they barked back that they were our classmates and to go in and help them ourselves. In they went again, and soon more than half the Ranger class was having difficulty getting out of the pool.

Classmates began to improvise, helping those stranded in the pool. From the pool deck, hands and stray materials found around the pool were extended. Once all were out of the freezing water and into the freezing air they formed up in wet uniforms and headed for an obstacle course, off into the challenges and physical torture of the toughest combat simulation school the Army had to offer. Most of Ranger School was spent in the cold with little sleep.

Seeing this and hearing about it from my Infantry classmates still at Fort Benning who had completed Ranger earlier, I knew what I was in for later in January. As aggressors, we formed up at reveille at the Ranger camp to receive our daily assignments. There was plenty of hurry up and wait time. A week or so in, we were ordered to wait in building 700 something. All 30 of us on medical profiles went in to find it empty with no chairs and no heat, so we stood in the cold patiently waiting for what was next. "Attention!" In walked the post commander, Major General Sid Berry.

Berry was not happy. More specifically, he was not happy with us, all West Point graduates on medical profiles delaying our entry into Ranger School. He berated us. Then he insulted us. Then he got all worked up and did it again. "What were we doing seeking medical excuses on sick call?" "Is that what they taught our disgraceful class at West Point?"

He said he was going to correct the record and make sure we got to do Ranger School in the winter like we were ordered to do. We would all report promptly to the hospital on Fort Benning. He had ordered medical boards with three Army doctors examining each of us to eliminate those medical profiles. We were dismissed.

Major General Berry went on to have a distinguished military career later serving as Superintendent at West Point and as a Corps commander in Europe, but he had not seen the movie, "The Horse Soldiers."[31] William Holden played the military doctor in that movie loosely based on a Civil War raid deep into Mississippi. The commander, John Wayne, wanted no part of his doctor's limits on what any of his troops could do or try to do.

It turned out the doctors in the medical boards at Fort Benning were more like the Holden character than John Wayne. They apparently resented Major General Berry's interference in their sphere and upheld all 30 medical profiles. In my case, they even extended it to six weeks.

Colonel Geraci was the meanest looking Ranger commander I could imagine. He looked like a combination boxer/football lineman whose shoulders were so broad and strong that his head was just perched on them like he had no neck. Here's how David Hackworth described him:

> Colonel John P. Geraci was Ranger, Airborne, Special Forces and a grizzly, all-animal fighter. His radio call sign was "Mal Hombre," loosely translated, "mean motherfucker." During the Tet Offensive, his 1/506th Airborne "Centurion" Battalion had racked up 1,294 VC KIA in exchange for eleven of his rock-hard centurions.[32]

He lined us against the wall in his Ranger Director's office a few at a time, like we were as plebes at West Point. His tongue lashing was even more severe than the one we had already heard from Sid Berry. His message was clear. Our extended profiles had cost us the opportunity to serve as Rangers, and we would forever regret it. Then he told us to get out of his office and report to our next duty assignment.

My new orders provided a little leave time before reporting in to the 82nd Airborne Division at Fort Bragg, so I headed to Illinois. My mother had taken a leave of absence from teaching at the Carmi High School when I became a student there. Even as a high school teacher, or maybe because of that, she thought it more important to spend time with her children. Every day in high school, my cousin, Art Ackerman, and I would have lunch she prepared in her kitchen.

We were sitting at that same kitchen table after supper when the phone rang. It was Wynne Morriss trying to find me. He quickly said that I was the only one of the four challengers of compulsory chapel at West Point who was available. I needed to drop what I was doing and immediately fly to Washington, D.C. to testify in the federal court case filed to end compulsory chapel.

I didn't know a case had been filed, but he had been following the chapel controversy since our graduation. Michael Anderson, a midshipman at the Naval Academy, believed the First Amendment gave him the right to go straight to court to end compulsory chapel at the academies. He drove to Washington, D.C. and sought out the American Civil Liberties Union (ACLU), not knowing their board of directors had assigned the inevitable service academy chapel case to Marvin Karpatkin in New York. Internal politics within the ACLU had caused the Washington office, whose purpose was mainly lobbying, not litigation, to file the case itself. Morriss was irritated at their legal haste because they forgot one key legal doctrine, the exhaustion of administrative remedies.

As a key component of the broader standing doctrine that limits the jurisdiction of federal courts, it requires that a plaintiff must first exhaust all available administrative remedies before filing in federal court. The U.S. Attorney defending the service academies had quickly filed a preliminary motion to dispose of Anderson's case on these grounds without it ever being heard on its merits.

Morriss, though, knew the exception to this rule, and my testimony would be the key to it. If the administrative remedy is unavailable, or has been shown to be futile, a plaintiff can proceed directly to court. The court was hearing the motion the next morning at 1000 hours. Without my testimony that the administrative remedy was futile, it would be granted and the case would be over before it really began.

Wynne wanted to know if I could catch a plane right away and be there. I did not hesitate to say yes. He told me how to get in touch with the plaintiffs' trial attorney, Warren Kaplan, so I could arrive at the correct courtroom.

My parents were skeptical but supportive. They had been at West Point to miss June Week while other parents around them celebrated with their cadets. From their perspective, if a few letters and meetings with senior officers about compulsory chapel led to the kind of retaliation they had personally seen, what would voluntarily participating in a federal court challenge bring?

They knew I would go but urged some caution. I didn't completely understand the reason I immediately said yes, but I felt I had a duty to the court to factually say what happened. The same chain of command that had used every underhanded power handle to retaliate against us for raising a question at West Point now was using a technicality to prevent the courts from considering the case. The considered application of such a key constitutional provision to a particular denial of religious freedom clearly seemed more important to me than the procedural technicality.

I had no inherent power as a second lieutenant to even the score with West Point for coming down on me the year before, but I did know how to tell the truth and trust the system to work it out. Playing a small role in what Wynne Morriss had taught by allowing the wheels of justice to grind exceedingly slowly, but also exceedingly finely, appealed to me as right and fair.

It was snowing in the Midwest, and no flights from Evansville, Indiana, would get me to Washington, D.C. in the morning, let alone by 1000 hours. I found a flight, though, from Indianapolis, that left early enough to have a shot. It would take a four-hour drive through the snow at night to make it to Indianapolis on time for the only flight.

My father volunteered that he would go with me because I might need the help. Mainly he was curious about Warren Kaplan and the whole group seeking to upend a long-held religious tradition at West Point. As a deacon at the Liberty Baptist Church, he was not unfamiliar with the underlying issues at stake. His understanding of religious liberty, and that of my grandmothers, and where it came from were silently coming into play. Both his action in coming along and what I had learned or absorbed in Burnt Prairie were coming to the fore in that drive through the February snow storm.

We made the flight, and I traveled in uniform, including the shined combat boots worn in the 82d Airborne Division with its dress uniform. At about 1015 hours, I opened the large wooden doors of the correct federal courtroom to the universal stares of everyone in the front who turned to see me, including the judge.

They had been waiting impatiently because Warren Kaplan had informed the judge that he had a witness whose testimony would dispose of the motion. Judge Corcoran listened to the defense attorneys' objections because they had no prior notice of this witness or development. I walked on down the aisle and heard Warren Kaplan ask for a recess to confer with his new witness, who he had never met. The judge allowed 15 minutes.

I had never testified in court, even on a small matter. Walking down that aisle, I saw the imbalance between Warren at one table and a whole host of attorneys from the government at the other table. I had no idea what their cross-examination would be like. Fifteen minutes to prepare a new witness is not nearly enough. My sense of apprehension was real.

Fortunately, Wynne Morriss had already prepared Warren Kaplan with the facts of our administrative challenge, so Kaplan was mainly concerned about the basics of testimony: "Answer the questions. Be patient and try to be responsive to the other attorney's questions. Stick with the facts. Don't editorialize. The judge will decide the law. Just give them the facts, and you'll be fine." That I was prepared to do.

Sworn as a witness and onto the stand next to the judge, I could not help but notice the irritation from defense counsel. The Assistant U. S. Attorney, Joseph Hannon,[33] cross-examining me acted intimidating and snarled at me a bit, but he had no basis for questioning my explicit testimony. I had first-hand knowledge of how the administrative remedy at West Point did not work and only caused deeper personal trouble and discouragement. Everyone at the defense table was from the Pentagon or the U. S. Attorney's office and took notes.

They knew who I was now, and my testimony was clear enough that the judge soon denied their motion.

In his published order, entered later after a complete hearing on the merits, he described it this way:

> The Court first took testimony and heard argument on whether the plaintiffs had exhausted their administrative remedies within the Academies before filing suit. The Court ruled that adequate and effective administrative remedies were not available and hence that the exhaustion doctrine was not available as a defense. Thereafter the Court completed testimony on the merits and took the case under advisement. *Anderson v. Laird*, 316 F. Supp. 1081 (D.D.C. 1970) at 1083.

I was relieved to be away from such a hostile gaggle of lawyers as I left the courtroom. My father had seen it all. Standing alone with me confronting such hostility, he was impressed with Warren Kaplan.

After the hearing, Kaplan asked where we were staying the night, and when we stated we had no plans, invited us to stay in his guest bedroom in Washington. He was a Harvard graduate and civil rights attorney, who also volunteered to handle cases for the ACLU. I hadn't known many attorneys personally growing up. In White County they did real estate for farmers or banks or were local politicians. Adding Warren Kaplan and Wynne Morriss to the list I knew impressed me greatly.

The short hearing I had participated in was just preliminary. The full evidentiary hearing on the case would come later, so I completed my leave and headed on to Fort Bragg. There I was assigned to a field artillery battalion in the 82nd Airborne Division, a unit filled with recent Vietnam returnees and draftees, all Airborne volunteers. I liked the sergeants the best, most of whom were from poor areas of the United States and building up their service so they could retire after 20 years as an E6 or E7 (staff sergeant or sergeant first class), or even higher.

Some officers were Vietnam returnees, but most were Officers Candidate School graduates getting ready to go. They all tended to drink too much at the various battalion drinking parties throughout the week. Some suffered from the combat stresses of their prior tours in Vietnam, yet many volunteered to return for successive tours in Vietnam. The combination of alcohol and firepower in Vietnam was new to me. The current approach to the effects of combat stresses were not well established then, but the consequences of a long, intense war were playing out before our eyes. It was a different Army than I expected. We ran our physical training in the morning, did maintenance on our vehicles in the motor pool, hung out around the mess hall and sometimes went to the field on exercises.

I was assigned as an escort officer for Brass Strike, an ongoing firepower demonstration for rotating groups of visiting newspaper reporters, civic leaders and other VIPs. The artillery would pound the firing range with coordinated barrages and air bursts and then the Air Force Phantoms would add their napalm in a fierce display. The Army narrator would explain the explosive tumult and confirm the invincibility of firepower. The civilians in attendance were duly impressed and not hard to please. President Nixon called them his silent majority, and the Army was doing its best to keep them on board.

During one time on target a shell impacted to the side a bit, not in the tight cluster of fire for effect. The civilians in the bleachers didn't even notice. Back at the barracks I learned that the guns had been frozen for inspection after the gun fired out. In the inspection of the guns, the incorrect deflection entered on the gun sight had been revealed. The section chief, one of the sergeants I liked, reaching for his retirement pay, had not found and corrected the error of his gunner, who entered the incorrect settings. The battalion commander ordered him busted from E6 to E1 (staff sergeant to private). The man was a private once again.

Such a complete over-reaction had the effect of permanently reducing his upcoming retirement pay, which he had earned in more than 17 years of service, including combat tours in Vietnam. There was simply no way, under the promotion regulations and timetables, he could advance back to E6 in the three years he had left before his retirement at 20 years of service. The Army's draftee culture included many such harsh results.

On post housing was not available for junior officers, and Rob Leslie, who was assigned to brigade headquarters just across the street from my artillery battalion, steered me to a cheaper but better area of rentals near downtown. We wanted no part of what we called the "grad barracks" with our other classmates in new, more-expensive rentals near the post. Living just down the street from Leslie, his wife Jo and their young daughter Lorna, I spent considerable free time with them.

Jo was upset that her husband was soon to depart for Vietnam and berated him for volunteering. Before their marriage she had been a reporter for the *Cleveland Plain Dealer* and had reported from Washington, D.C. as well. She was informed, believed that facts were facts, openly opposed the war and knew the details of its wasteful excesses. Leslie was painting his rental place to get cheaper rent, and Jo would fix nice dinners. We all enjoyed talking most evenings.

Leslie was jumping at the bit about my testimony in the federal court. He was upset he had been in a field exercise, beyond the reach of Morriss's phone call, but would have been with me if available. We began to plan how he could to testify on the merits before departing for Vietnam.

This was an active shift in attitude, from more naively making a request of our chain of command at West Point or responding when needed by Wynne Morriss. Now we were joining the fray in a new, more purposeful way, and Jo wholeheartedly approved and urged us on. We now knew the counter-fire to expect in this battle against the autocrats fighting against the Constitution, and we were going to maneuver around and against them with greater determination and skill.

I called Warren Kaplan and told him of Leslie's knowledge about how compulsory chapel really worked, including his history of seeking exemption from it over three separate years as a cadet. Warren told me the hearing date in April, but said getting us subpoenaed would be almost impossible because we were outside the district of the federal court in Washington. They would have to get the subpoena transferred for service by the U. S. Marshall into our district in North Carolina. In the meantime, the government would object, and undoubtedly the Army would try to make sure we were unavailable at Fort Bragg.

He didn't have an immediate answer to this problem. Leslie, though, researched the Army regulations himself and came up with a solution. We were voluntarily testifying, but needed some excuse from duty at Fort Bragg to make the trip to Washington. We asked Kaplan to type up the subpoena on the official form without filing or processing it with the court, and mail it to us with a letter requesting our attendance in court. The lawyer was helping us implement our tactic. We were amateurs becoming veterans.

Leslie spoke with the warrant officers in the 82nd Airborne Division personnel office, asking them what to do about this subpoena because he was hesitant to ask his Brigade Commander, but felt obligated to comply. The warrant officers understood that concern and were willing to use their authority to issue routine orders from division personnel for temporary duty at no expense to the government. Leslie was going TDY (temporary duty) to Washington federal court.

I was more audacious. I found a regulation about required court appearances by soldiers. I typed up an administrative leave blank, walked into the battalion commander's office, saluted, and asked that he sign to approve my leave, waving my subpoena form so he could see it. He growled about me wasting time and signed it. I was going on free leave to Washington federal court.

Our determination to slay the beast of constitutional violation was firm. Leslie thought it was an advantage that the Department of Defense lawyers didn't know who he was or what his testimony would be. He entered the court room in uniform, with his nametag removed. A judge advocate general colonel quickly approached him and asked who he was and what he was doing there. To both mine and the colonel's astonishment, Leslie told him that was for him alone to know and yours to find out.

When the colonel reminded him that he had a right to know the identity of prospective witnesses, Leslie retorted that it was improper for counsel to speak directly to opposing witnesses, and his question should be properly made to plaintiff's counsel, not directly to the witness. Leslie was, of course, right about that, and standing in that court room within a month of his scheduled departure for his voluntary tour in Vietnam, he was in no mood to be polite. Our budding relationship with the chain of command was not getting any friendlier.

Leslie testified in great detail about cadets sleeping in chapel services, how they resented forced religion, and he cited the Van Atta survey on cadet attitudes about compulsory chapel from his research project in a leadership class at West Point. He pointed out that if a cadet failed to stand and recite the prayers and codes, he could be written up for that offense and walk the area. He made the point of chapel's ineffectiveness at any potentially valid training purpose, leaving its only purpose to require a religious participation in worship despite any cadet objections.

Second Lieutenant Leslie's testimony, and mine that day as well, was contradicted by officers of much higher rank. Admiral Moorer, Chairman of the Joint Chiefs of Staff, took time away from his duties running the Pentagon and providing for the country's defense to personally contradict us. We witnessed his concocted testimony with its argument that the military, as part of the executive branch of government, had its own authority for training future officers who would lead the military in ways that achieved its purposes. It did not need either Constitutional guidance or restraint.

There was no forced religion in the military, according to Admiral Moorer. His testimony was based as well on Article I, Section 8 of the Constitution, providing that Congress could "make rules for the government and regulation of land and naval forces." He said the military was carrying out that authorization with no religious purpose.

Judge Corcoran, in his decision later, quoted Admiral Moorer this way:

> The purpose, of course, is to enhance his leadership and command ability by putting him in a position where he can get a feel, an understanding of the impact of religion on the various types of individuals and so he can see this in operation; and, consequently, as he acts as a leader in later years, he will appreciate this impact that religion will have on so many people.

> [T]hat is the sole purpose. We are in the process of developing leaders and this is a vital part of the overall leadership package; and that is the sole purpose. *Anderson v. Laird*, 316 F. Supp. 1081 (D.D.C. 1970) at 1089.

The Assistant Secretary of Defense for Manpower and Reserve Affairs, Roger Kelly, also left his Pentagon office to add to Admiral Moorer's testimony, as did Vice Admiral James Calvert, Superintendent of the Naval Academy. Judge Corcoran also quoted Secretary Kelly:

> The institutional judgment of the Department of Defense as to the primary effect of required chapel attendance is to develop in those required to attend chapel an understanding of the religious beliefs and the spiritual value systems of other midshipmen and cadets. * * *

It meant primary effect of requiring attendance at chapel
is to instill in a midshipman the understanding of the
religious beliefs of others. *Anderson v. Laird*, 316 F. Supp.
1081 (D.D.C. 1970) at 1090.

Their party line was clear, and as I heard it live in the courtroom,
I was most astonished at how untruthful it was. It is understandable
that two sides in litigation will have different views, but facts are facts
and without a clear and truthful factual base, justice becomes much
harder. I understood later that their testimony was rehearsed to make
a point so that the purpose and effect tests of legal precedent could
be called upon to skirt a more plain or literal application of the First
Amendment.

They were resting on their power, not their truth, and like
Colonel Ross, they didn't give a damn what the Constitution said
about religious freedom in our country.

I was truly shocked and horrified. I didn't know then the long-
held legal adage, when you are weak on the facts, argue the law. But
in this case, the government was weak on both the law and the facts.
They relied on the law by lying about the facts.

It is one thing for an aberrant Colonel, irritated at cadets under
his command for causing trouble in his unit, to go overboard. It
is quite another for the highest officers in the Pentagon to depart
from truth in a federal courtroom. From the second row behind the
attorneys' tables, live and in person, I felt the hostility directed right
at us. I could plainly see the power unhinged, and it was like trying
to dodge a lightning bolt at close range. I was spinning in place
by witnessing a manipulation of truth in the defense of raw power
unrestrained by constitutional law.

This was not the American Dream. It was coercion and abuse
of power. It stepped back toward the unification of church and state
that existed for centuries in Europe. It ignored the breakthroughs
toward religious freedom achieved in the American Revolution. It
corrupted the ideals that made us free.

Others did stand up on behalf of the First Amendment's freedom of religion clause. I was relieved and proud that groups such as the Baptist Joint Committee were stepping forward and writing *amicus* briefs in support of religious freedom. The military chaplains' organization and every major religious group all stepped up. These groups relied on the legal history of religious freedom in our country, one of our founding principles and practices. They also reinforced the argument that religion itself is voluntary by its nature, dependent on each individual's approaches to it.

There was, however, one great religious exception. We met Bob Timberg that day, a Naval Academy graduate and Marine veteran in Vietnam, and the only newspaper reporter covering the case in the courtroom. He had spoken to Billy Graham at a recent chapel service at Annapolis and expected different fireworks from him.[34] To Timberg's routine question about the chapel case at Annapolis, Graham had exploded with criticism of those of us questioning the practice. Graham questioned the religious convictions of those involved in the suit, saying: "What kind of religious convictions? Communism is a religion, too." He went on to characterize the chapel case as an attack to force all chaplains out of the military, and according to Timberg: "The nation's best known (and probably best-loved) religious leader had literally portrayed seven service academy men in good standing as little more than Communist dupes conspiring to rid the armed forces of its chaplains."[35]

We learned from Timberg that Graham was that very day spending the night in the family quarters of the White House with Richard Nixon. The next morning he walked out by the portico of the White House and repeated his Communist charge to the press at the White House.

I was encouraged by what I had heard from religious leaders in court, especially by the almost universal support of religious freedom by the country's various religious groups. My Baptist roots were shaken, though, by the minority religious view of the well-known preacher, Billy Graham. If his public criticism was so harsh, what opinion had he privately expressed to the Commander in Chief in the privacy of the White House family quarters? With Billy Graham and Alexander Haig both in the White House expressing such views, I knew I could not expect much kindness from the chain of command.

One of the traditional hymns at the Liberty Baptist Church in Burnt Prairie was "Trust and Obey." Its last verse says this:

> Then in fellowship sweet we will
> sit at His feet.
> Or we'll walk by His side in the
> way.
> What He says we will do, where
> He sends, we will go;
> Never fear, only trust and obey.
> Trust and obey, for there's no
> other way
> To be happy in Jesus, but to
> trust and obey.[36]

I never heard this song at the Cadet Chapel, but I am convinced Billy Graham and many others I knew approved its message. It does not call, however, for following or obeying Billy Graham. As Martin Luther so clearly pointed out in the Reformation, it also does not call for following or obeying the Pope. I also did not interpret that it called for me to trust and obey my military chain of command in matters of religion. Its standard bearer is much higher, and those who distort its meaning to justify obedience in a different sense are missing the point.

Billy Graham, though, was well respected in Burnt Prairie. So was the military and its chain of command. How did it affect the American Dream that I was now challenging both? Is it rigid in support of inherited truth from family or organized religion? Or are its values re-applied as we learn and adapt, renewing our minds?

The American Dream at this time in history was under great challenge, and I was engaged in a minor part of that challenge.

The Dream had faced greater challenges before, in the American Revolution, the Civil War, the Great Depression, the Civil Rights Movement and in World War II. Through all of these, religion, and the freedom of individuals to embrace it in their own ways, based on their own free will, played significant roles. The ideals of the American Dream were largely based on religion and its free exercise, and the freedom of thought and action that flow from it.

Before the founding fathers expressed it in the Constitution and Bill of Rights, immigrants sought it, escaping the religious wars, persecution and religious tests imposed by European governments, unified with approved religion. For centuries in Europe, kings ruled by the divine right of kings, and their princes before them unified their regions with the sword under the banner of a prescribed religion.[37]

The Peace of Augsburg in 1555 ended a religious war by providing that the prince of each territory would determine which state religion would prevail in his territory, either Lutheran or Catholic. This idea was reaffirmed after the Thirty Years War in the Treaty of Westphalia in 1648. Whole provinces were required to change their religious allegiance if a new prince took the reins demanding obedience both to him and to his religious belief. This system of mandatory religious affiliation persisted a long time. Many who dissented were burned at the stake and others fled this oppressive system. Some of them, like my German ancestors, found their way to religious freedom in Virginia or other colonies in North America.

The unification of church and state begin in earnest with Christendom. In the fifth century, Emperor Constantine shifted from Roman persecution of early Christians, and instead embraced Christianity as a means to achieve stability in the Roman Empire. The Imperial religion had been one of religion, war, victory and peace, a phrase somewhat reminiscent of the peace through strength justification of current military spending in the United States. Its religion was emperor worship as a deity, and public affirmations of that deity were required of all Romans.

As Christianity became the state religion, the theologians and political leaders of the Roman state and provinces began to share responsibilities for attaining domestic peace within the sprawling Roman Empire at its peak. The mandatory nature of Roman religion remained and was applied to Christianity to create Christendom, where Roman Catholic bishops and the Pope set the moral tone of the domestic peace enforced by the Emperor and his legions.

Dealing with religious factions, splinter groups and heresies were much apparent in the writings of Augustine, the Bishop of Herro, and the freedom of Jews to continue their beliefs and practices created the seed of the idea of religious tolerance.

As the Roman Empire declined, replaced by kings and princes throughout its former vast territories, Christendom remained with princes, kings and bishops sharing, but often disagreeing over their roles, in a unified religious state. By the time of the Papal Revolution in the 11th century, the power and authority of the Pope to name bishops was made clear. Pope Gregory VII in his Decree on Investiture said:

> We decree that no one of the clergy shall receive the investiture with a bishopric or abbey or church from the hand of an emperor or king or any lay person, male or female. But if he shall presume to do so, he shall clearly know that such investiture is bereft of apostolic authority, and that he himself shall lie under excommunication until fitting satisfaction shall be rendered.[38]

In the dispute over appointments of church officials that followed, the Holy Roman Emperor invaded from the north and occupied Rome, only to be repelled by the Pope's armies in his alliance with the Norman rulers of southern Italy. This controversy of control continued past this war until the Concordat of Worms in 1122, where the relative powers of the state versus its religious allies were clarified, coinciding with the growth of law schools and a legal profession that could help resolve such jurisdictional issues peaceably in debate between theologians and princely authorities.

No doubt remained in the basic fabric of Christendom, which required both allegiance to the bishops of the church and the princes of the state. Each supported and reinforced a state religion of public duty and fealty. Dissent or heresies resulted in excommunication by the Pope, enforced by state sanctions that included burning at the stake and death. Many suffered this fate until Martin Luther withstood his challenge to papal authority and the corruption of indulgences in the church's fundraising.[39]

Luther's theology in the 16th century replaced the necessary intervention of priests in personal salvation with faith alone, freeing individual believers from the burdens and control of the church hierarchy of Christendom. He supported his new ideas in disputations with bishops and open written debate made possible by the invention of the Gutenberg printing press, which spread his reforms faster than the bureaucracies of church and state could respond.

The resulting Reformation's rejection of hierarchy and state control solidly opened the door to religious toleration and freedom, which continued in a bloody path of religious wars, persecutions, and emigrations that spread its new paradigms into the colonies of North America, beginning in the 17th century.

Luther survived, though, despite his excommunication by the Pope and his banishment by the Holy Roman Emperor. Unlike other dissenters from Christendom who were burned at the stake, Luther was protected by his prince, Frederick the Wise. As both nobles and lay people accepted Luther's teaching, the religious grip of the Roman Catholic hierarchy and its princely allies was weakened but offset by a counter-vailing power of princes who allied with the Lutherans. The unification of church and state was weakened but not ended.

Luther's writings were extensive and widely circulated in printed form. They included his two kingdoms theory, distinguishing the heavenly kingdom of faith from the earthly kingdom which provided the existing political order. The heavenly kingdom of faith was dependent on no hierarchy on earth but by faith alone. This grain of religious liberty operated within an official state religion, which was protected by princely rulers on Earth, while an individual's faith was his own.

Some went further than Luther in the break from the power structure and led peasant revolts against the aristocracy as well, seeking to redefine economic freedom, as well as religious belief. A confusing tumult of local and regional wars resulted as religious belief and tolerance of other beliefs played out over the next few centuries in Europe. Economic dislocation led refugees to seek new homes in principalities in line with their beliefs or to flee Europe altogether for North America.

John Calvin and others arose as well with different protestant views creating new strains of Christian belief blossoming into new and different denominations that also sought freedom to live their beliefs. This additional branch of Protestantism was recognized with Lutheran and Catholic religions in the October 24, 1648 Treaty of Westphalia as long as the province followed the prince in religious affiliation.

From the early colonies in North America, a religious diversity further emerged. Some clung to state sanctioned religious orthodoxy in their region, following the protestant strain established in the Church of England. Others used the distance from Europe to pursue more independent forms of religious belief. This blending of ideals while still part of the British Empire played out in the colonies as elected legislatures sparred with Royal Governors appointed by the King.[40]

Some of my ancestors arrived in colonial Virginia, where one of the fundamental legal doctrines of religious freedom emerged. The Virginia Declaration of Rights, which hangs on my office wall today, set this out as follows:

> That religion, or the duty we owe to our Creator, and the manner of discharging it, can be directed only by reason

and conviction, not by force or violence, and therefore, all men are equally entitled to the free exercise of religion, according to the dictates of conscience and that, it is the mutual duty of all to practice Christian forbearance, love and charity towards each other. Virginia Declaration of Rights, Article XVI.[41]

This fundamental statement of religious liberty, based on natural law, adopted in June of 1776 predates the Declaration of Independence and the First Amendment to the U. S. Constitution. It influenced both.

It also reflects clearly to me my grandmother's view of religion and liberty. How did such concepts come to rest in me, the grandson of German immigrants who left the religious turmoil of Germany for Virginia? How did these attitudes survive from long before I was born through the migration of generations down the Ohio River to southern Illinois?

In the 1760s the Episcopal clergy sought to persecute Baptist religious dissenters. Using statutes prohibiting disturbances of the peace, vagrancy and "strolling," this effort led to the jailing of five Baptist preachers in Spotsylvania County in 1768. They had been preaching without the authority of the local magistrates. Other Baptists were arrested for preaching in other counties. An establishment church, supported by government action, was seeking its foothold in colonial America. James Madison, then a student at Princeton, wrote against this practice, seeking "liberty of conscience for all." This advocacy, and support from Baptists in Virginia, led to his election to office, where he teamed with Thomas Jefferson to establish the initial legal framework for freedom of religion in early American law.[42]

These inherent ideals of the American Dream were my underlying motivation to challenge compulsory chapel and endure grief from the chain of command in the Army for my testimony in court to abolish it. Only later did my curiosity lead me to more fully understand the details of that history and legal precedent. In reality, the controversy surrounding my seat-of-the-pants inclination to join in this challenge of freedom drove me forward into that more rigorous understanding.

By this mechanism the American Dream is both realized and updated. It derives from the sum total of such experiences, influences and changes, maintaining much of its basis by inheritance and custom but subject to revision and adaptation as individual Americans change and influence events as they unfold.

CHAPTER 7

FROM ANDERSON V. LAIRD TO RETALIATION

I t didn't take long after Vietnam volunteer "Airborne" Leslie and I arrived back at Fort Bragg to hear our summons to report. We got word that division headquarters wanted to see us both right away. Together, we were scheduled to see the 82nd Airborne Division Staff Judge Advocate at headquarters.

"What were you doing?" was his incredulous sounding question. "Why didn't you consult with me, your division's attorney?" We knew someone at the Pentagon was giving him a hard time that we had slipped away without an alert from him. We also knew that this very prompt meeting was a very bad sign.

He put us on notice that if there were any more testimonies or developments he expected to hear it first from us. We were dismissed.

Leslie's departure to Vietnam was just weeks away. Quickly he was deployed, but not long after his arrival he was wounded with a U.S.-made grenade thrown by North Vietnamese Army regulars while he was leading his platoon up a hill near the Demilitarized Zone. He was medevaced to a hospital in Japan to recover from serious injuries and Jo was beside herself.

Not scheduled for Vietnam orders for another 10 months, I was ready to face the full negative response I expected. We had testified in Washington in April. Along with my class, promotions to First Lieutenant were automatically entered one year after graduation. It took affirmative paperwork from the chain of command to stop it.

Stop it they did. On June 4, 1970, one year after graduation, while all my classmates were changing their gold lieutenant bars to silver, I was transferred to another artillery battalion in the 82nd, still as a second lieutenant. I considered it pure retaliation. My date of rank, a key measure of advancement in a professional military, had plummeted from the top third of my West Point class to the bottom, and then on below all the other lieutenants commissioned after college in 1969 who were automatically promoted to first lieutenant in June. I appealed this discriminatory action directly to the Secretary of the Army under Article 138 of the Uniform Code of Military Justice. I didn't expect much relief.

I was a regular officer in the Army who graduated high enough in my class at West Point to know I could take anything they threw at me. I was ready and willing to carry out whatever difficult duty the Army assigned, and I then wanted to get into flight school at Fort Rucker to fly helicopters wherever the Army sent me.

By the time of my testimony in April, though, it had already sunk in with me that the conduct of Colonel Ross, Major Berry, Colonel Haig and now Admiral Moorer had precipitated a change in my outlook. I was becoming a dissenting political actor within the Army, a role somehow out of place but changed by the events themselves. Power before principle, lies before truth, and career advancement at all costs was the piercing response I felt for upholding the First Amendment in the compulsory chapel challenge.

Dodging the merits of issues that arise does not advance the American Dream, but it did steer me in a different direction. I researched the Army regulations and found the application to the Army's excess leave program to go to law school. I was eligible after two years in the artillery, and it was time to apply. If I was then admitted to a law school to begin next year, the Army would put me on unpaid leave for three years and expect that I would return to serve in the Judge Advocate Generals Corps in the Army when I was admitted to the bar.

As the decade of the 1960s came to a close, the country faced similar difficult challenges. Individual power first, lying and the supremacy of political considerations were shredding the American Dream nationwide. The unresolved issues and divisions over the Vietnam War, Civil Rights, political corruption and the environment remained. I was not just on a slippery slope, I was accelerating on a steep water slide into a muddy and less hopeful world.

I had seen a new perspective, though, in the law and in political action. Now I would do my time in the Army, and as soon as I could, either branch transfer to service as an Army lawyer, or one outside into the civilian world. The examples of Wynne Morriss and Warren Kaplan laid down a positive marker for a better direction than the examples of my superior officers in my chain of command.

I was no longer only a farm boy wanting to fly airplanes. This was a huge attitude change that had crystallized in April in Washington listening to Admiral Moorer, Roger Kelley and Billy Graham. Sometimes you learn clearly what you are by seeing firsthand what you are not.

Payday was always fun for me in the 82nd Airborne. Underpaid enlistees lined up after reveille, physical training and breakfast to receive their pay in a pay line manned by the junior officers and a few sergeants of their unit. Each of us working the line got a document signed, counted out cash for net pay directly into the hands of the soldiers, or helped meet our battery's participation quota for charitable contributions or memberships from soldiers' pay. Army Emergency Relief or the United Way got their mandatory donations from the underpaid troops, and one of us made sure each soldier was signed up to make a payroll deduction monthly for U.S. savings bonds.

All the quotas were 100 percent. Every trooper got to voluntarily participate. If they hesitated, they only slowed the pay line for everyone else while they were counseled in place. There was a 100 percent quota, too, for membership in the Association of the

United States Army, or AUSA. Unit quotas and results were shown on bulletin boards throughout the division, and it was our duty as officers to make sure they were met.

At the end of the pay line, the troops were usually freed from duty, cash in hand, off to make car payments, repay short-term loans, or drink it away on the strip from the gates at Fort Bragg down into Fayetteville. Base pay for a private first class was $167.70 monthly, but airborne soldiers were cash rich compared to most since they received $55 a month extra for jumping out of airplanes. I was paid $417.60 base pay plus $110 for airborne. Some sent money home or used it to support unpaid Army wives and a baby, but most returned to barracks the next morning just as broke as they were the day before, ready to eat chow in the mess hall for another month until the next payday.

Membership in the AUSA was just a few dollars, but its large membership base of soldiers and retirees, combined with the funding power of defense industries, made it the perfect political power machine in Washington. It could lobby for better pay for the troops at the same time it sought more procurement for weapons systems, jeeps and every other contract available to support an Army troop strength which peaked in excess of 1.5 million in the late 1960s, compared to 470,000-plus active duty Army personnel today.[43]

AUSA's agenda included "worldwide deployment" of Army forces, and it supported the concept of soldier diplomats influencing foreign policy and national defense. Modernization of tanks, artillery systems and helicopters to enable possible multiple simultaneous wars in Europe and Asia required huge spending on training and readiness to make sure the Army was strong and ready, not depleted and hollow.[44]

These budgetary priorities conflicted with every other need of the country in its federal budget. President Johnson's war on poverty was under fiscal strain, and needs for domestic infrastructure, education, health and safety also clamored for funding. This budgetary battle, as inflation grew under the strains of the Vietnam War, made AUSA's platform extremely political.

Although its membership has declined, AUSA today has in excess of 60,000 members in 125 chapters with an annual operating budget of more than $30 million.[45]

The federal Act to Prevent Pernicious Political Activities, commonly known as the Hatch Act, was enacted in 1939. It applies throughout the federal government but not to the military, which regulates and limits political conduct through its own regulations. AUSA is not a candidate for office, so its activities would be subject to restrictions only if it were a political "cause" as defined in those regulations. Official use of government facilities for political purposes is restricted and raising funds for political "causes" is included in these restrictions. The trend of the law since 1939 was not to crack down on such political activities among employees of the government but to extend First Amendment protections and expand federal employees and military personnel's rights to engage in some political activities.

Given what I saw in military pay lines, I thought AUSA's activities, and the official coercion involved in gaining members, crossed the line and should be restricted, or at least moderated. Freedom to participate in political or lobbying activities includes the right not to participate. My own failure to join the AUSA caused my unit not to meet its quota, and in the view of my chain of command, that was a bad thing for me to do.

They saw it as even worse when I raised my complaints about coercive recruitment of AUSA members in the 82nd Airborne Division in an Article 138 complaint to the Secretary of the Army. Article 138 is actually a law and part of the Uniform Code of Military Justice:

> Any member of the <u>armed forces</u> who believes himself wronged by his <u>commanding officer</u>, and who, upon due application to that <u>commanding officer</u>, is refused redress, may complain to any <u>superior commissioned officer</u>, who shall forward the complaint to the officer

> exercising general court-martial jurisdiction over the
> officer against whom it is made. The officer exercising
> general court-martial jurisdiction shall examine into the
> complaint and take proper measures for redressing the
> wrong complained of; and he shall, as soon as possible,
> send to the Secretary concerned a true statement of that
> complaint, with the proceedings had thereon. 10 US
> Code § 938.

Complaining formally in writing to the chain of command
using a provision that required a report to the Secretary of the Army
concerning that complaint was not something any officers I knew
ever did. But when my chain of command, with official action,
reporting and use of government funds to carry out this activity,
required soldiers of a free country in the barracks pay line to join the
AUSA, I believed this was abusive. I thought it time to raise what
was in reality a political complaint against the Army and indirectly
the lobbyist group that supported its budget and spending. My
protestations were, of course, noticed but essentially ignored, and the
AUSA continued to gain members and lobbying strength.

I knew at the time that my drafting and submission of an
official complaint about lobbying in Washington and its funding
and support was not a normal duty of a junior officer in the Army. It
was a political act that went beyond putting my toe into controversial
political waters.

Anderson v. Laird was decided in the district court on July 31,
1970. Judge Corcoran ruled for the government, a disappointment,
but it was expected that no matter his ruling, both sides would appeal.
What was factually new in the judge's findings is that the April 1969
Superintendent's Conference of all the service academies had issued a
new policy statement on excusing cadets from the compulsory chapel
requirement. Quoted in Judge Corcoran's opinion, it provided:

> It is understood that intelligent provisions must be made
> for bona fide cases where attendance would be in conflict

with sincerely held convictions of individual cadets or midshipmen. Thus when the effect on the individual cadet is opposite to that intended, i. e., when he becomes incapable of observing, assimilating or becoming involved with an understanding of the religious beliefs of men and finds himself turning away from an understanding of what their religious belief and value systems are, then he is relieved from the attendance requirement. 316 F. Supp 1081, at 1084-85.

The judge made no reference to my unsuccessful attempt my last year at West Point to attend Baptist services in Highland Falls, New York, immediately south and adjacent to West Point. I was allowed under my first class privileges to go off post on weekends, and my request had been to expand that to allow attendance at Baptist services in a convenient location instead of compulsory chapel services. Judge Corcoran's order incorrectly stated that "there is no town nearby to provide other alternatives." 316 F. Supp 1081 at 1084. My request was based on free exercise of my own religion. Though I believe it was "based on a conflict with sincerely held convictions," I did not claim I was incapable of understanding the religious beliefs of others as the April 1969 policy now required.

In my mind, Judge Corcoran's ruling was unconvincing and merely followed the testimony and briefs of the government. He simply deferred to military judgment without giving due regard to the Constitutional rights of cadets, which they do not surrender upon taking an oath to defend the country.

CHAPTER 8

FROM CARRYING A RIFLE AND BINOCULARS AS A FORWARD OBSERVER TO POLITICAL RESISTANCE

Events and people I knew began to drive the path of political resistance. Cornelius Cooper was serving in the artillery battalion next door. I saw him around the division artillery area on Ardennes Street where both our battalions had barracks and headquarters. He was living just south of Fort Bragg, in what we called the "grad barracks," while Airborne Leslie and I found cheaper rentals near downtown Fayetteville. Cooper came down to visit on weekends, and we asked why he didn't find better housing where we lived and spent our weekends.

He liked the idea since his month-to-month lease cost more than $140 compared to our rentals at $85 a month, and he began to look for a place to move. Fifty dollars a month more when you are netting less than $500 is quite a dent in your budget. That was about half a monthly car payment on the new cars we bought upon graduation from West Point. Cooper didn't move, though, and I asked him why. He said nothing was available.

I knew from driving around the neighborhood that there were plenty of "For Rent" signs up, and military officers were always good for their rent, which was reimbursed up to about $80 in a monthly housing allowance. Cooper tried to find a place but had no success. The reality gradually dawned on us as he related stories of what it meant to be a young Black man trying to rent an apartment in North Carolina.

The federal open housing law had just passed in 1968, and the idea of racial integration in housing was new in Fayetteville. One landlord referred Cooper to a place he said was available, but when he arrived at the location he found it on a dirt dead end street in a city of mostly paved streets. Every porch was occupied by Black folks who lived on that unpaved and muddy street.

Cornelius Cooper came from California, graduated from West Point high in his class, had a new car, steady pay and wanted to live in a cheaper but better part of town. I decided I needed to help so I volunteered to follow after him a few hours and see if I could rent the apartments he was told were not available. Without exception I was welcomed and offered the rental at each place I went where he had been turned away.

Cornelius Cooper complained to the Fort Bragg housing office. It had the power to enforce the federal fair housing act by denying an Army housing allowance to any soldier who rented from a discriminatory landlord. If a soldier lost his housing allowance, he would have no real choice but to move. Losing all your Army renters where the Army was the main industry, such as in Fayetteville, would doom your rental business. Cooper's fair housing complaint did not result in the application of such a powerful remedy.

Instead he heard lots of talk from high ranking officers responding to his complaint and received plenty of encouragement that the Army would be fair to him. But there was no action taken on his complaint. He did learn that the commanding general at Fort Bragg had a close relative in the realtor's association in Fayetteville. His family ties, though, were little help to Cooper. I advised my friend Cooper to describe his housing experience in a complaint under Article 138. He joined in this political act in criticism of the Army's response to housing discrimination against its soldiers to the chain of command. The Army was watching, and they were tiring of such complaints.[46]

CHAPTER 9

FROM AN ALERT TO FIRST LIEUTENANT CORNELIUS COOPER, WEST POINT'S FIRST CONSCIENTIOUS OBJECTOR

T wo events accelerated the change at Fort Bragg. First, Syria invaded U.S. ally, Jordan, with 300 Soviet tanks and 16,000 soldiers advancing to within 45 miles of its capital, Amman. Second, the 82nd Airborne Division was placed on alert and began to move and load units on transport aircraft at Pope Air Force Base in preparation to airlift and defend the airport at Amman. We were going to stop those tanks and defend our ally, King Hussein.[40]

My unit was issued ammunition to load in our M16 clips, local maps to plot artillery concentrations around the Amman airport, and LAWs, or light anti-tank weapons, to fire at Syrian tanks. We made ready to transport our 105 mm howitzers that could fire both indirect and direct fire at tanks. Those LAWs, though, had an effective range of only a couple hundred meters, while tank machine guns and main guns had effective ranges of more than 1,000 meters. Our mission was to secure the airport so other troops could reinforce King Hussein's capital city to insure the tanks did not advance. We made our equipment ready and waited for further orders to deploy.

This was why I had volunteered for the 82nd Airborne Division, to be in the first line of defense of the nation's interests. Responding to an invasion of an ally that was led by Soviet-made tanks was a clear, positive purpose for the use of military force and so different than the quagmire in Vietnam. I was ready to go.

First Lieutenant Cooper showed up in my office with a different story. He quickly told me that his study of Martin Buber and his own religious beliefs had changed his view of warfare. He said he had become a conscientious objector. His unit was on alert and he hadn't submitted an application to recognize his conscientious objector status. Worse than that, he had just told his battery commander that he was not going to the airport on the alert since he was a conscientious objector.

Suddenly, without going to law school or being admitted to the bar, I became in effect Cooper's interim attorney. I grabbed the Army regulations off the shelf and looked up the procedure. I readily ascertained that a verbal claim was insufficient and would probably get Cooper court-martialed for refusing to go on alert. His battery commander had told Cooper he didn't have time for this, to get out of his office and report to the battalion commander. He stopped by my office on the way.

I guessed the lawyers would be waiting for him when he got there, if not the military police. I helped him by typing up his official application for conscientious objector status right then and there in my office. We followed the paragraphs required in the regulation and then inserted in the reasons paragraph that they were being drafted with assistance of counsel and would be submitted after review by Cooper's attorney. I urged Cooper to walk in, salute and hand that signed application to the battalion commander immediately. The regulation then said he would surrender his rifle and bayonet and be placed on administrative, non-combat duties until his claim could be adjudicated.

I immediately called Marvin Karpatkin in New York City and told him I had a new client for him, who he readily accepted, asking that we drive to New York at our first opportunity. Cooper walked into his battalion commander's office, saw that the 82nd Airborne Division staff judge advocate was in the room, saluted and filed his signed application. The battalion commander asked the lawyer what happens now, and he advised that Cooper should turn in his rifle and bayonet and serve administrative non-combat duties until his case was heard.

The alert ended when President Nixon acted aggressively with the preparations of naval and land forces before calling Leonid Brezhnev on the Russian hotline. He reminded Brezhnev that he had furnished those tanks to the Syrians, and President Nixon expected his help in withdrawing them. Brezhnev agreed, in one of the very few successful uses of the hotline. Jordan's effective military defenses, backed up by a threatened U.S. response, had blunted the Syrian offensive. The Syrian/Russian tanks withdrew to Syria.

That action freed Cornelius Cooper and I to drive to New York to meet with Marvin Karpatkin. I had heard of Karpatkin from Wynne Morriss when he was figuring out why Anderson v Laird got filed in Washington, D.C., instead of New York. The ACLU had wanted Karpatkin to file the service academy chapel case whenever it arose but had been cut off at the pass by the Washington ACLU office instead.

We drove to New York City the next weekend, and Cooper had long conversations with Karpatkin about his moral views on war. Karpatkin sent him to the Union Theological Seminary to talk to Roger Shinn, a theologian who had commanded an infantry company in World War II. Shinn had studied with Dietrich Bonhoeffer, the famous German Lutheran theologian who had consistently stood up to Hitler on religious grounds and was executed in a concentration camp in 1945. Shinn believed that God provided "courage in the struggle for justice and peace." Awarded the Silver Star for Valor in the Battle of the Bulge, he was not a conscientious objector but understood the doctrine and sincerely held religious beliefs. The author of 15 books, in his leadership of the United Church of Christ,

Shinn called for Christians to "resist the powers of evil." He served as a public member of President Eisenhower's Commission on Religion in America and would become the key religious witness in Cooper's upcoming conscientious objection hearing at Fort Bragg.[48]

Conscientious objection usually arises at the draft board level, when those who morally oppose war ask for draft deferments from military service or for alternative service as a medic or in another non-combat role. During the Vietnam War, conscientious objector applications skyrocketed, as did draft card burning. Karpatkin had represented clients before the U.S. Supreme Court on both these issues.

He also had handled conscientious objection cases for soldiers who had already entered military service but had a change of moral views on the use of deadly force in war. Upon the "crystallization" of these new religious views, they were allowed to promptly file to have their conscientious objection status recognized during their service in the military.[49] Cooper fell into this class but his long period of preparation and study of war at West Point, completion of Airborne and Ranger schools, and volunteering to serve in the 82nd Airborne Division, with its first line of response duties, made his case seem more difficult. The Army clearly did not want the publicity of West Point officers objecting to the Vietnam War at a time the country was politically divided on the issue.

Karpatkin also had unsuccessfully represented another West Point Lieutenant, Louis Font, in claiming conscientious objection status based on a selective war model. Font did not morally object to all wars and would have fought to oppose dictators such as Hitler. Font said in his official application:

> My religious beliefs compel me to regard the Vietnam war [as] immoral and unjust and I cannot contribute in any capacity to an immoral war. Quoted in Font v. Laird, 318 F. Supp. 891 (1970).

The Army clearly did not want its soldiers to be able to pick and choose their wars. More importantly, the case law on conscientious objection ruled consistently that the right to object was based on sincerely held moral beliefs but those were only recognized because Congress had provided for it in its statutes. Freedom of thought, conscience or religion under the First Amendment was not broad enough in our constitutional system for recognition beyond what the statute provided.

Under that legal standard, political, sociological or economic justifications to oppose a war were not sufficient. The courts viewed selective objection, even when based on sincerely held religious beliefs mostly political, but more importantly outside the statute which required moral objections to all wars or to any war at any time.

My view at this time certainly led to political objection to the Vietnam War as wasteful, not in our national interest, and continuing only based on falsehoods advanced for political purposes by our elected leaders. Despite that political objection, I continued to see it as my duty to serve in Vietnam, if so ordered. Others did not, and I respected their different views.

Lucian Truscott IV had his own basis for objection. The grandson of two generals, he saw Vietnam as a military waste of good enlisted soldiers. In his writing for publication, he was required to submit articles through Army channels to be cleared for security reasons. He contended in one of these submissions that if he were ordered to Vietnam he would carry a rifle and fight as infantry, but he would refuse to command troops in combat. To do so, he maintained, would violate his duty to protect the resources under his command. In other words, he would not submit the lives of his soldiers to a wasteful and, at that point, useless military exercise that no longer advanced the legitimate interests of the country. The Army did not want the public to hear that opinion from a West Point graduate bearing the name of his famous, hard-fighting grandfather, General Lucian Truscott of World War II fame. They began separation charges against him in the interest of national security, and he was discharged from the Army.

I became fascinated with these legal issues, though I was much more like Roger Shinn in my own moral beliefs than Louis Font, Cornelius Cooper or Lucian Truscott IV. I was prepared to help Cornelius Cooper in what I saw as a personally risky stance against powerful interests. I felt their retaliation to my activities. I believed Cooper had much more to face and needed all the help he could get as he sought to be the first West Point graduate in history to be recognized as a conscientious objector under the protection of our law.

I knew that Karpatkin expected a long fight in federal court after the Army would deny Cooper's claim in its administrative hearing. Making a good record in that administrative hearing would be important in sustaining that appeal. I agreed to testify personally in that hearing, affirming the sincerity of Cooper's beliefs and urging the Army to recognize his religious dissent from their use of effective and powerful lethal force in war.

How did this idea of religious dissent from the state's monopoly on the use of violence arise? Violence was very much a part of Christian persecution by the Roman Empire in the first centuries of Christianity. As state and religion merged into Christendom, this history of religious violence was re-directed by Christians to suppress religious heretics and dissenters. The Crusades turned religious violence into religious war. After the Reformation, religious violence and territorial wars combined for centuries of religious warfare and strife. Just a few hundred years ago in Europe people were burned at the stake, beheaded, or drawn and quartered for much less than standing up to a powerful military power to dissent from its conduct of war.

Some religious groups, though, began to gain some forms of religious tolerance. Among these the Quaker and Anabaptists were most opposed to the use of violence in either religious persecution or war. It was well known in the American Revolution that Quakers opposed war but instead of official recognition, used provisions to buy out of military service or in other non-violent ways supported the revolutionary cause.

In the first official draft law in the United States, these buy-out provisions continued in the Civil War. Official procedures for conscientious objection recognition, without the buying out method, developed in both world wars, with some objectors performing alternative service as medics, farm workers or fire fighters.[50]

As the country changed in the political tumult of the 1960s, opposition to the Vietnam War drove draft card burning protests and more numerous draft exemptions through an educational exemption or conscientious objector status. Some fled the country to Canada or Europe. The Supreme Court expanded conscientious objection eligibility by revising the moral requirement from one based in particular religions with a history of opposing all wars to sincerely held moral beliefs even if not grounded in those particular religious groups.[51]

Still, no West Point graduate had successfully changed course after graduation, crystallizing new moral objections after being committed through the rigors of West Point to defending the country with violence.

In the meantime, our alert for Jordan had not gone well. Unit readiness had deteriorated as Vietnam draftees who were "short," and just waiting a few months to be discharged, responded with contempt to their remaining service. New enlistees served in the 82nd for a short time before being ordered to Vietnam, creating much turnover of newly trained soldiers. Officers, too, were rotating at a rapid rate. We knew that drug addiction problems abounded in the Vietnam era Army, but what wasn't yet known was that a major drug smuggling ring, led primarily by Army sergeants, was moving drugs from Vietnam to Fort Bragg and other bases in Air Force transport aircraft and on into the domestic pipeline up and down the EastCoast.[52] Organized crime had moved into the ranks with devastating effect. As jeeps and other vehicles proceeded to Pope Air

Force Base for loading, many arrived without their radios, which had been stolen and sold onto the black market for cash. It was not a pretty sight and was seen all the way to the Pentagon.[53]

We learned we had a new division commander, sent to restore the 82nd Airborne back to an effective first line of defense. No longer would soldiers be rotated in and immediately rotated out to Vietnam. Instead they would all stay for a three-year tour as the division was re-trained and made effective again. Therefore, those of us expecting orders to Vietnam in a few months now had a permanent assignment stateside. Our units at Fort Bragg would also become the prototype for the new "Volunteer Army," free of draftees.

The Pentagon, and Congress, began to listen to our division chaplain, Lieutenant Colonel John P. McCullagh, who was leading an effort to have the drug problem recognized with real and effective responses instead of courts-martial and bad discharges.[54] This transformation was only beginning after the Vietnam War's deleterious effects on the Army were made clear by the Jordan alert, and led to the rebuilding of the Army after Vietnam. Many of my classmates led these efforts in their units and deserve great credit for restoring the greatest Army in the world from this low point in the early 1970s to its more successful days in the 1980s and decades beyond.

Those of us still in conflict with the Army and its Vietnam War had challenges to face. Cooper's conscientious objector application required a fact-finding hearing and decision by a hearing officer chosen by the Army. They picked a captain staff judge advocate who had attended divinity school and as such knew both religion and law. Cooper's father came from California to testify for his son. The Reverend Dr. Roger Shinn was there in person.

We looked up the Army regulation on the use of staff cars and requested, on the prescribed form, that the division motor pool send a staff car to the Fayetteville airport to pick up the official participants in the hearing. Marvin Karpatkin, an attorney who had fought the military in court over draft card burning and conscientious objection,[55] was amazed that we could do him this courtesy as counsel for First Lieutenant Cooper. His enlisted driver arrived at the Fayetteville airport in uniform, driving a green-painted staff car with the appropriate military markings and delivered him to the hearing site on Fort Bragg without incident.

As I had been with all legal proceedings since Wynne Morriss aroused my interest in the law, I was fascinated at the hearing. Marvin Karpatkin was treated with respect and listened to. The hearing officer asked good and penetrating questions of Roger Shinn and the other witnesses, of whom I was one. Cooper testified in his own behalf and made his moral objections to any and all wars at any time clear. The legal procedures required by the Army regulations were followed, and it was not the kangaroo court I had feared.

Despite Karpatkin's preparation to appeal to the federal courts, the Army instead used this administrative hearing process to recognize Cooper's status as a conscientious objector and, in due time, he was honorably discharged.

The *New York Times* covered Cooper's case. In the February 13, 1971 paper, Cooper said to them that as a Black man serving in the military, "I am caused to be more than usually sensitive to the fact of violence in life and the effect of violence on men's lives." He indicated in the following day's paper that he wanted to pursue medicine as "something of social value."

What carried the day, in my opinion, was Cooper's deep exploration of moral issues through the study of Martin Buber, while comparing that to his training in the Army and at Ranger School.

Cornelius Cooper

Roger Shinn, a combat veteran, understood the basis for the moral conflict this created and with credibility laid it out well in his hearing testimony. The Army decided to cut its losses on Cornelius Cooper and let him move on.

My route away from the Army was different. I was reassigned to a G-2 intelligence section in XVIII Airborne Corps Artillery. I was required to sit at a desk next to a Top Secret safe and prepare intelligence assessments for upcoming military exercises. I was promptly ordered to apply for a Top Secret security clearance.[56] The application form was long, and I checked the Army regulation that authorized it. If I refused to fill it out, separation proceedings in the interest of national security would lead me along the Truscott route. If I filled it out incompletely or with deception, it would only get worse, since the form was attested under penalties of perjury.

In reality it was a simple ruse to help the Army decide what to do with me by investigating and digging into my background and motivations. Soon after submitting a long, complete and thorough questionnaire, I got a call from my father. Neighbors, local political officials and friends were calling him with the same question: "Why was the FBI here asking me about David?"

Soon after this I got word to report to Building 4528 on the other side of the post. I drove up at my appointed time to see a building with only a number. Unsure which door to enter, I knocked and entered the nearest door, only to be screamed at by soldiers with their 45's drawn. I had entered a top secret secure area through the wrong, but unlocked, door.

This was quickly cleared up since I was an officer in uniform with a name tag and at the right building for my appointment. I was taken to a private room with an obvious, but partially hidden microphone protruding from a boom box on the desk, and interviewed for hours. Much of it was based on my answers to the questionnaire, but the scary new issue raised implied that I had some knowledge of a midwestern drug smuggling ring. I made it clear that I knew nothing about that. I answered all the questions truthfully and fully. I felt it important to resist some minor questions claiming a right of privacy and First Amendment protection not to speak about my private views on some subjects. This did not go over well with the military intelligence officer conducting the interview. I am convinced, though, that my overall willingness to be frank and forthcoming, along with my agreement with the necessity of our country's overall military purposes and preparedness, caused my performance in the "Top Secret" investigation to be helpful.

I was certainly hopeful that the Army would be willing to approve my application for branch transfer to the staff judge advocate corps after my required two years of service in the artillery. Not long after the interview the colonel in command of XVIII Airborne Corps Artillery asked that I report to his office. Sitting in the waiting room, another officer suddenly called everyone to attention, as the colonel came out from his office and stood at attention near his doorway. Other officers simultaneously appeared from other doorways. "Attention to orders!" said the adjutant. He then read my promotion orders to first lieutenant, and the colonel stepped forward immediately to pin on my silver bars. This was like a surprise ambush, and they were not giving me any opportunity to think about or possibly refuse the promotion. I didn't even know you could refuse a promotion, but I later learned there was a regulation on that too, and they were avoiding that possibility with their surprise ambush plan. These senior officers were nice, congratulatory, and seemed more welcoming than I was accustomed to, both at the promotion ceremony and afterwards. The colonel asked me to come in next week for a chat with him in his office.

It was fatherly advice he had to offer. He commiserated about my rough start to my service as an officer but advised that I needed to decide what I wanted to do next. Other doors were open was his message. He wanted to talk to me about what those were. I explained that I had already begun the process to apply for a branch transfer and wanted to go to law school and continue to serve in the Army as a lawyer. I had not spent four years at West Point to lose that kind of expectation, no matter what I had learned about the darker side of power in the Army. The Colonel said he would talk to his contacts, who were inquiring about me in the Pentagon, and get back to me.

It wasn't long before he sent me to see the G1 personnel officer at XVIII Airborne Corps headquarters. The three-star general who had mishandled Cooper's housing complaint had his office in this most imposing building on the post. The G1 also was a colonel, and like my commander, a friendly, helpful officer with a father-like demeanor. He wanted to help, and thought my plan to go to law school was a good one.

But he had a twist in his questions: "Would I be willing to simply attend law school out of the Army and not return to active duty?" In other words, if I simply submitted a resignation of my commission, perhaps it could be accepted honorably, and I could use the GI bill to attend law school. He was testing the idea of a somewhat friendly parting of the ways. He told me to think about it and let my commanding officer know my response.

When back to my colonel at XVIII Airborne Corps Artillery for another fatherly counseling session, I informed him I could agree to the G1's approach. Once again, he said he would check with his contacts in the Pentagon and get back to me. I began to feel a sense of freedom and relief. Unlike Airborne Leslie or Rich Swick, who were being accepted for branch transfer and law school, or unlike Lucian Truscott IV in his continual head-butting sessions with the Army over the nature of his discharge, I was on a path more like Cornelius Cooper, honorably going forth to study medicine or law in the civilian world to pursue a different "social value." I thought of Wynne Morriss again saying that the wheels of justice grind exceedingly slowly, but also exceedingly finely.

I also thought of Phil Pearce and other folks back home who had encouraged and supported me in learning to fly and taking on the challenges of West Point. I was confident that it was time for a new direction, but I was also sure many of my old friends would not approve. This unease was part of the disillusionment I felt about the military. Its power and my father's generation had helped expand the American Dream throughout much of the world.

Was my intellectual support of these positive developments reflected in my actions? I had learned the painful lesson that its abuses of power had also restrained, and in my opinion, done harm to the American Dream as the closing days of the Vietnam War negatively impacted the culture and politics of the United States as a whole. I had played my own small, unique role in that history, and like many others torn by this larger historical contradiction, it was time for me to continue my own path forward in a new and positive way.

CHAPTER 10

FROM THE ARMY TO LAW SCHOOL

I got my applications in to law school and began the process of resignation of my commission and processing out of the Army. Just after the Christmas holidays, I visited my friend and former roommate at West Point, Lucian Truscott, who was working as a reporter in New York City where I planned to attend law school. Truscott had freelanced for the *Village Voice* during his graduation leave and was writing for them regularly after leaving the Army.

His path out of the Army had been rocky, and he was concerned there were yet blind curves ahead for me as well. Major General Rogers, the division commander of the 5th Mechanized Division and former Commandant at West Point, had conversations with Truscott similar to those I had with the colonels in XVIII Airborne Corps. He had submitted his article about refusing to command troops in Vietnam, which the Army did not like. They initiated military intelligence and security procedures to begin discharge proceedings, at first leading him to believe those would end with an honorable discharge but changed course along the way to an other than honorable discharge.

I wanted no part of such a thing and believed quite strongly that I had done my duty in following orders as an officer, but also by telling the truth in federal court in the chapel case. I expected no harsh retaliation for standing up in legal ways for changes that needed to be made. I intended to use the GI Bill, just as Cornelius Cooper planned to do, to pursue some other "social value." West Point graduates' sense of duty extends far beyond military service after graduation, and I expected the Army to recognize that, even if they disagreed with the policy stands I had taken at West Point and in the Army.

Truscott was quite skeptical and believed the degradation of integrity in the Army during Vietnam was a danger to the country as a whole and to me in particular. The extent and breadth of these concerns would remain at issue with us for some time. On New Year's Day we were interrupted by a call from Illinois that my father had suffered a heart attack and was in intensive care in the hospital in Evansville, Indiana. Truscott took off and helped me drive through the winter weather from New York to see my father.

I had never been in an intensive care room at a hospital, and it was shocking. During our 10 minutes of visitation an hour my father was in and out of consciousness, appearing weak and helpless with oxygen and wires and monitors everywhere. The ominous reports from doctors about disability and the low likelihood of an even lower quality of life going forward were clear. They did not foster any pleasant and hopeful conversation with my mother as she faced the tragedy of her husband's weakened and failing heart.

Then, on January 4, 1971, he passed away. He survived a couple days in intensive care but his heart failed rapidly with little opportunity to talk about it or say goodbye. Nothing in my experience had prepared me for this finality on short notice.

His first heart attack had been at age 38, a heart attack after he played hard in a fundraising basketball game against a student team at school. His favorite type of fund-raising game was donkey basketball, where you had to be on the donkey to make a basket. The donkeys were totally uncooperative, and the crowd found the whole scene funny as expert horsemen and teachers alike were thrown, kicked or bitten trying to ride the donkeys with a basketball in hand.

I had been there as a young high school student for that first heart attack, which occurred in the days before trauma centers when paramedic interventions were rare in downstate Illinois. As his pain and inability to rest caused him to roll back and forth on his bed back home, I was asked to call his doctor. Dr. Harrell's instructions were clear: "Rest and come in to the office in the morning." Then he asked if I knew how to make a hot toddy. I said no, and he instructed me to heat water on the stove, dissolve as much sugar into it as I could, and then add a stiff dose of whiskey. He advised that drinking it should help my father relax and get some sleep.

I considered my father a delayed casualty of the war because of the addictive nicotine in the Camel cigarettes he had been smoking. He first became addicted to them in his Army rations and that greatly hurt his cardiovascular health over the years. He was otherwise athletic and in good physical condition, but the cigarettes and inadequate treatment for high blood pressure took their toll. Under the care of a cardiologist in Evansville, Indiana he lived nine years after his first heart attack.

He was omnipresent in my life as I grew up in Burnt Prairie. One of his old friends told me years later that she always remembered seeing him walking from his home two doors down to the Liberty Baptist Church carrying his Bible. To me, that story symbolized my father confronting truth. Truth, when you find it, is often experienced as it crashes through misconceptions, excuses and self-deception. When his joking response to the brass in the winter of 1944 about cold beans turned into an assignment on the front line, he confronted the truth of war. When my mother's family would not support him in a primary election because they "always voted Republican," he confronted the hard truth of slow political change. When he saw me volunteering to testify against the Army in the chapel case, without hesitation he confronted the truth of religious freedom by getting on that airliner with me to Washington.

He was very much himself in his last letter[50] to me, giving me good advice knowing full-well that the Army was taking a toll on me personally. He closed it with advice to pursue enjoyable outside interests in my spare time, like sports, education, church and friends, to make "life much better." He reminded me of my mother's birthday, told me how to get my absentee ballot in for the election and updated me on what he was doing in the election campaigns.

He included a long story about how he was helping my mother's cousin, Frank Barbre, get the Carmi High School Vocational Center established. To maximize its receipt of state and federal funds, and to serve the most students in an efficient way, it needed to consolidate vocational programs with other school districts in the county that were prejudiced against and wanted no part of consolidation of anything with Carmi, the county seat. One of the school boards, though, was split, and he related how personal grievances and disagreements created an opportunity for the enemies of your political enemies to turn the tide. He worked those personal divisions to line up the necessary votes at the school board just before Barbre was to seek their approval in his personal presentation to the board. With a vote that night, the vocational program was consolidated. He thought this example would help me in finding allies in the Army bureaucracy. Always helpful, always giving advice, always being supportive, this final conversation by letter was like so many all while I was growing up and is what I still remember about my father.

What my family and I now faced was the uncertainty and pain from the loss of our father and husband. We now confronted that truth. Instead of returning to visit in Illinois before law school with the support, perspective and advice I was accustomed to receive from my father, now I faced alone the disillusionment from my experiences in the Army. What I had to do was help set a new course for dealing with his affairs on the family farm amidst the grief of his loss. The American Dream moves on. How changes are confronted by its people across time forms it and shapes it as it is refined or eroded by the actions of everyday people as they confront its truth.

My sister, Donna, was in a cave on a college trip to Mexico and couldn't be reached when father died. The funeral proceeded while Congressman Ken Gray tried to help us reach her through the embassy, or at the border on her return. My father's friends came forward to help. Grandmother Inie went into deep grieving. She had lost her husband to Parkinson's Disease at a young age, and she now compounded that grief for her daughter and grandchildren. She was beside herself in what I saw as old-fashioned, desperate and vocal despair. At the cemetery in Burnt Prairie, she turned for the worse. My mother and Inie's son, Frank Ackerman, were in the back seat of the car with her. Just as we were pulling away from the cemetery, she cried out and grabbed the back of her neck. "Oh, I'm having a stroke," she said. Uncle Frank tried to calm her, and we took her back home and put her to bed.

The next morning she seemed better and got up to have lunch with the family at her dinner table where she had served our family homemade biscuits, fried chicken, all kinds of pies and many good times for as long as I could remember. She said hello to everyone, looked around, and then asked: "Where's Arthur? I don't see Ted." Uncle Frank recognized who she was asking for, and we all heard him respond that Ted had died decades ago and wouldn't be here. Arthur was her husband who had died 20 years before. Her sense of time was confused by her stroke though she strangely seemed alert and with us. That afternoon the doctor admitted her to the hospital where she lapsed into a coma. She spent the next eight months in a nursing home with a feeding tube, never saying another word or responding at all before her death in August of 1971.

My mother and others in her family visited Inie every day, in the false hope that she would respond or recover. Charlie Kirk went with me to pick up my sister at the St. Louis airport after Ken Gray relayed the news of her father's death as she crossed the border coming back from Mexico. My emergency leave was quickly up, and I traveled back to Fort Bragg to process out of the Army, which took a few more weeks.

My father had no will, so upon my final return from Fort Bragg we had to deal with the problems of estate and inheritance taxes and banks and insurance companies. He owed a substantial sum on 40 acres he had bought in White County, and the bank called the note, demanding immediate payment. He had applied for an insurance policy shortly before his death but the company had returned the application by mistake and refused to pay.

My mother went back to work at her high school the day after my father's funeral. She liked her students, and they kept her going until she left school for the Wilmar Restorium to see Inie every afternoon. Beyond that, she didn't open her mail for months and lived daily through her grief. I helped her with the attorney and set out to deal with things one at a time.

To our dismay, our attorney agreed with the insurance company that they had not accepted my father's offer to buy an insurance policy. The offer and acceptance sounded right to me in theory, but it didn't pass the smell test. Our attorney was no help on that one, but our insurance agent, Sam Endicott, did help. We persisted, we pleaded, and we asked for help for this group policy offered as a benefit for veterans by the American Legion until we were heard. The $10,000 check finally arrived.

We scrounged up the cash to pay off the bank in full from other sources, and our attorney gave them a hard time for being so anxious to make demands after an unexpected tragedy. We filed and paid the estate and inheritance taxes, which back then kicked in at just over $60,000 in value. We kept up the farm arrangements my father had put in place with Dan Masterson and Dutch Williams when he moved off the farm from Burnt Prairie. We strengthened our relationship with those good farmers as they, too, mourned the passing of my father.

CHAPTER 11

FROM FORT BRAGG
TO PUD'S FARM

The cattle farms were vacant of cattle, and we found out that Pud Williams was interested in buying one of them. My father had worked hard to restore a hundred-acre farm south of Burnt Prairie that had been farmed out, its topsoil depleted and eroded during the Great Depression. He planted legumes, grazed cattle on improved pasture, applied lots of manure, planted Timothy, improved fence, fertilized, cleared brush and scrub trees and built a new barn, complete with a concrete floor for storing hay and feed. He taught me learned lessons of agronomy there, and I fed the cattle all through high school, moving hay and feed and chopping ice with an ax so the cattle could drink, all while trying to keep the gates closed. We fixed fence with Eddie Masterson and with high school friends cleaned manure from the barn and spread it over the farm. We tended the cattle, often loading them into Allen Carter's truck for sale. When the pasture began to be over grazed, we'd recruit a group of my high school friends to help and drive them down the roads to the hill farm over on the Wayne County border. We kept two ponies there, and I rode them over every inch of that farm.

Pud Williams was a distant cousin, since his grandmother and my grandfather were brother and sister. We had traded beef quarters for pork which Williams raised for years, and as a member of the county board, he had supported my father's hiring to lead the multi-county poverty agency they started under President Johnson. When my father moved to the regional planning agency, he used federal money to study the feasibility of adding an unplanned interchange to Interstate 64 at Burnt Prairie. The study showed that an interchange was key to local economic growth and necessary for continued oil and coal development in the area. As chairman of the White County Board Williams worked with my father, other regional officials and Congressman Ken Gray to get that done. Today, due to Williams' daughter Nancy's lobbying of the Illinois General Assembly, that interchange is officially called the Robert J. "Pud" Williams Memorial Exit with a big, brown official sign for everyone to see.

Pud Williams also was a big farmer and buying additional acres was part of his plan. We worked out a contract for deed with him, and my mother enjoyed holding his feet to the fire over

The Pud Williams interchange
at Burnt Prairie on I-64

its terms in the negotiation. Pud and his wife Dorothy had played bridge regularly with my parents for years, and he was always good for a smile and a joke. My mother found it fun to make him live up to his every exaggerated word, and it was always good to see him drive up in his pickup to our otherwise quiet abode.

One day in the spring of 1971 Pud mentioned that his good farm hand had suffered a hernia and could no longer drive a tractor which was delaying his planting season. I told him I was waiting to go to New York for law school while working with our lawyer on estate matters, so I had some time to help. I had driven tractors on the farm since I was 10, and I could fill in for his injured farm hand. Ready for some help, I told him I had one condition--I was only agreeing to work on the tractors in the field to move along the planting of his corn and soybean crops. I was not staying around when it was too wet to work the fields after a rain to fix fence or clean manure out of barns. I would work cheap as a farm hand to help him out, but only to a point.

Groaning about my condition, he put me to work the next day. Dorothy fixed lunch for us all, farm style, with more than plenty to eat, and we worked from when the sun came up until dark, working the field cultivators ahead of Pud planting corn. His tractors were all diesel and International Harvester red, not like the gasoline-powered John Deere my father had used. They were more powerful, with Hydro control of the transmission, better brakes and the many improvements that industrial agriculture was undertaking to compete and make bigger farmers more efficient.

They didn't yet have a cab, or air-conditioning, but out in the dust and diesel smoke they did have a sturdy tractor radio mounted on the main tire fender, blasting away loud country music into my right ear. WMCL over in McLeansboro played plenty of it, and I later wrote a music review on what it was like to hear "After the Fire is Gone" by Conway Twitty and Loretta Lynn while out there in the dirt and sun and incessant bouncing in the tractor seat.

> The hard pulling diesels roared and chugged while Conway and Loretta's chorus became a shouting contest. "Love is where you find it when you find no love at home, And there's nothing cold as ashes after the fire is gone," became a phrase of competition as the radio, mounted by my right ear, brought Conway, Loretta, the steel guitar, the roaring diesel, and the jerking of the field cultivator shovels into conflict under the early morning sun. Loretta won. She was the loudest by far.[58]

Country music in the context of working on a farm in rural America was a great place for me to be.

CHAPTER 12

FROM PAUL SIMON TO DAN WALKER

Pud Williams prodded me and joked about not working after a rain. I told him the very next rain I was driving down to meet the candidate for governor who was walking the state. He laughed and said I was crazy to waste time and gas on that. He planned to see the real next governor at a fundraising dinner in Belleville.

In July, 1971, I read in the Evansville, Indiana paper that Dan Walker had called a press conference. I went down the next day to hear him speak from the steps of the old bank in Old Shawneetown. The old bank had long been closed, and most of the town had moved to New Shawneetown on higher ground after the 1937 Ohio River flood. All that was left of Old Shawneetown were decaying streets and weed-filled empty lots next to what was left of a row of decaying bars along with a Texaco filling station. Upon arriving I saw no TV cameras, no reporters, and no one on the street but me. I bought a Coke at the gas station and asked if anyone knew about a candidate for governor walking into town. They knew not a word about it.

After a while, I saw a small group walking through the weeds toward the old bank. I walked over, looking for someone running for governor. I spotted him and walked up and introduced myself to the candidate.

"No, it's not me. I'm Dick Febuary, Mayor of New Shawneetown. That's him there," he said.

I had approached Febuary because of his short-sleeved white shirt and tie, but the real candidate for governor looked a bit like a displaced farmer, in work boots, khakis, and a distinctive red bandanna wrapped around his neck. "Hi, I'm Dan Walker," he said with his distinctive glaring-blue eyes drilling right through me. He asked if I had seen any press around, and I said no. He suggested we walk over to the gas station and talk a bit.

I met Dan Walker early in his walk across Illinois in 1971

This was no Colonel Alexander Haig I was meeting. Instead Walker was a Naval Academy graduate and corporate lawyer who was taking on Boss Daley in Chicago. I had studied his "Rights in Conflict" report on the 1968 Democratic Convention in the public policy course I took my last semester at West Point. He intended to pry loose the tightly held reins of political power in Illinois.

He had begun his confrontation with Daley in the "Rights in Conflict" report, calling the over-reaction to peace demonstrators at the 1968 Democratic Convention in Chicago a "police riot." On this hot southern Illinois summer day, just three years after the convention and on his fourth day of a 1,137 mile walk the length and breadth of Illinois, he stood talking with me in Old Shawneetown. He was alone out there, asking for help in a quest that most people thought was foolhardy.

It turned out that Dick Febuary was one of only three mayors in the whole state who showed him the courtesy of greeting him as he walked through their towns. He was friendly as he listened to me, and wanted to recruit me to help in his campaign.

I didn't fully realize at the time that I had just met my new mentor, a person worth listening to, and a wise leader to believe in when I had just recently lost mine. His story was simple. The people of Illinois, all of them, had to stand up to the corruption and arrogance of Boss Daley and his cronies. The way to begin that was to take the Governor's office away from him and fight for our state and its future. He wasn't just talking in theory about resisting coercion and abuses of power. He was standing tall and walking forward, asking others to join in. He didn't need to say another word. I signed up.

He invited me to join in and walk with him over to New Shawneetown, a few miles away. I should have done that, but I was already convinced. Many others across the state did just that, walking with Walker so that he could listen to their views and concerns for as long as they could keep up with him. Listen he did, and he just kept walking day by day, becoming a legend with every next step. The press never showed up in Old Shawneetown, but the word of mouth, aided by all those new friends who invited him to stay the night in their homes along his walk, and reinforced by growing local and statewide press along the way, Dan Walker grew into a political movement downstate Illinois hadn't witnessed.

I went back and told Pud I was going to work to elect Dan Walker. Pud asked: "Hold it a bit. You haven't even met the real candidate for Governor. Are you willing to go with me to meet Paul Simon?" I told Pud I would go listen, but I didn't want to hear any kowtowing to the great Boss Daley. From my seat in the huge meeting room at Augustine's in Belleville, I heard just that. I stood up and walked out during Paul Simon's speech. Pud Williams was furious at my discourtesy, but I waited out in the lobby and rode back the two hours to Carmi, arguing with him all the way.

This is what political change is like, friends and neighbors and the gaps of generations arguing their way into new realities. We were headed into a primary election a few months away where I would be for Walkin' Dan and Pud, the Democratic Chairman of the White County Board, would be for the regular party's candidate, Paul Simon.

I started a voter registration drive in White County and sent Dan Walker a letter about it with a $50 contribution enclosed. I wasn't in the Army now, or just a farm boy or a law student. I was all that quickly a novice political organizer in a fight to have a say about our state. Eighteen-year-olds had just won the right to vote, and we focused our voter registration drive on them. They readily signed up. The Vietnam War had made voting by young people much more important. By 1971, most people were for this new political empowerment.

I had experienced obstacles in the military to the continuing development of the American Dream. Could it be that politics led to a truer path? Did implementing those ideals take political action? My father had certainly turned to politics when he returned from World War II. Now it looked like my turn was coming.

CHAPTER 13

FROM NEW YORK CITY TO THE POLITICAL FIELD

Lucian Truscott IV had found a cheap housing alternative for going to law school in New York. Working at the *Village Voice* in Greenwich Village, just up the street from New York University School of Law at Washington Square, he scouted the classified ads at the paper's office before they were published the next day. What he found were people buying and fixing up obsolete, old wooden 19th century Pennsylvania Railroad barges to live in on the Hudson River. He wanted to buy half of one and asked me help him finish it out. The barge already had an enclosed roof and big sliding doors, so we put windows in two by four frames into those openings to provide great views of the river and the Statue of Liberty. We rigged bottle gas to a hot water heater and installed a shower and bathroom. In a junkyard, we found an old potbellied stove to burn coal for heat. We would drive down to Jersey City in the old 1963 red Chevy pickup truck I bought for $400 before my move to New York to begin law school and buy coal by the bag, storing it in a big wooden bin made out of an old crate.

We found old furniture, a gas stove for free and built sheet rock walls to create bedrooms and divide the space with George and Barb next door. This was much cheaper than paying apartment rent in

Manhattan, and it brought with it a whole new group of friends who had speed boats on the Hudson, or who lived on the edge of poverty down by the river. A few neighbors tried to upscale the area with higher-quality improvements and amenities.[59]

George was a soap opera actor, and his pregnant wife, Barb, was British and managing editor at *Skiing* magazine. More prosperous than poor Army vets trying to go to law school on the GI bill, or get established as a low paid reporter, they became good friends with lots of ideas on how to live on the river.

I quickly learned how to take the bus through the Holland tunnel and catch the A train down to NYU. After hours of classes or study in the basement libraries at NYU, I could easily walk over to Truscott's office at the *Village Voice* to grab a sandwich from a deli and listen to the reporters talking about their latest stories in that weekly paper. The anti-war movement was still swirling in Greenwich Village, the women's movement was just gaining traction, and Truscott became famous for writing about the Stonewall riots that ushered in the beginning of the gay rights movement. The *Voice* crew was talented, smart, ambitious and rebellious, charting new territory in how to write for and advocate about what was happening in the world. I learned a lot listening and hanging out at Truscott's desk.

Diane Fisher liked my stories about country music. She edited the *Riffs* column in the paper and asked if I could write something on country music. She was helpful, offered to edit it and help me get it into a form she could add to her music review column, which featured a number of different writers. I put down about 500 words, trying to relate the music to the way country music flows from its rural culture. I thought easterners in general, and New Yorkers especially, were a bit arrogant in their put downs of this stylistic music and its culture which they didn't bother to understand. Fisher's openness to something different reflected a characteristic of that time and place I very much appreciated.[60]

She printed my first column, and the *Village Voice* paid me $50. They gave me a press pass, and Fisher said I could tell the record companies I was writing for the *Riffs* column so they would put me on the list and send me free review copies of their latest albums. Now when I hung out in the *Voice* office I was one of their freelance writers, becoming infamous as the country hick from Burnt Prairie who knew how to spell and liked country music.

Johnny Cash, Jerry Lee Lewis, Kenneth Lovelace, Bill Monroe, Earl Scruggs, Tom T. Hall, Stonewall Jackson, Merle Haggard, Waylon Jennings, Charley Pride, The Chuck Wagon Gang, The Grateful Dead, Ray Price, Carl and Pearl Butler, Loretta Lynn, Conway Twitty, and a whole host of others were featured in my columns as I tried to keep finding themes that tied the music to what was going on back in farm country.

Speeding down the Epworth blacktop with my high school girlfriend in my 1957 Chevy blaring Waylon Jennings' "Brown Eyed Handsome Man," was the kind of scene from my life that fit the tempo, sound and spirit of the music. I had interviewed Waylon backstage at the Fayetteville, North Carolina, municipal auditorium and wrote a column about him long before he was well known in New York City. This time Fisher said I had gone too far. My analogies and comparisons were stretched too far for her readers to understand, she said.

My reaction to such a rejection told me I was becoming attached to writing about country music, and I wanted to take it further. Fisher picked up on my disappointment and told me she'd try to get my column published elsewhere. Before I knew it, she had a commitment at a country music magazine, but told me they would only pay $25. I said go with it, and to my surprise, my story on Waylon Jennings became their cover story that month. Waylon's publicist in New York even called and thanked me for doing that story.

Law school was completely boring, and I was consumed with reading and studying hundreds of pages, and endless hours where professors berated smart new law students who didn't yet have a clue about deeper logical and analytical dissection of cases and voluminous legal writing.

My favorite course was property because it began with a history of a centuries-long battle between nobles and landowners who were seeking ownership rights from their king. This battle formed our legal system. It was history and politics and law all rolled together to form what we know now as property law.

Some days I would drive my red pickup into school for my first class at 1000 hours and park behind the garbage trucks. Usually no parking was available on some streets from 0800 to 1100 to allow for garbage to be picked up. As soon as the trucks completed their pass, cars would line up, following the trucks and peeling into the parking spots as the garbage trucks passed. Once the garbage was picked up, often more than an hour before the 1100 cutoff, no tickets were handed out.

On one exam day the garbage slots were all used up. I orbited the neighborhood hoping to find a spot and not be late for the 1100 exam. To my dismay, a New York City policeman pulled behind me and turned on his flashing lights. I pulled over, and he demanded to know why I was orbiting in the area. I told him about my exam, but he was skeptical about my Illinois plates, and told me to wait in my truck while he called those plates in. I asked how long it would be, and his angry reply was that I was suspected of being the getaway driver for an armed robbery that just occurred, and I had my choice: "Wait quietly and patiently in your truck or come with me to the Tombs for booking on suspicion of armed robbery. Which do you want?" The Tombs was a notorious, dangerous jail at that time, and I took the patience in the truck. When I was finally cleared, I was late for the exam and expected further trouble there. At the Dean's Office I explained my morning and they quickly said: "No problem, we even had a late exam arrival last week because he was mugged at gunpoint on his way here." They set me up for the makeup exam without further question.

I really wasn't ready for law school, psychologically or otherwise, and spent most of my time on the barge and in New York City debating and discussing with Truscott and friends who would visit the many aspects of recovering from our short Army careers and our training at West Point.

John Kerry's sister, Peggy, was a girlfriend of Truscott's at that time, so politics wasn't far from our conversations either. President Nixon was careening his way into his early Watergate mistakes. John Kerry was throwing his Vietnam medals onto the steps of the Capitol and running for Congress. Nixon was out to torpedo him, which he quite successfully did.

Ed Koch was the congressman from Greenwich Village, on his way to being Mayor of New York City, and a frequent visitor at the *Voice* offices. We talked to all comers there as politics degenerated into the Watergate scandal in Washington.

CHAPTER 14

FROM RECOVERY TO A NEW MISSION

I followed the news of Dan Walker's Daley challenge back in Illinois. To everyone's surprise but mine, I learned in March that he snuck up on Paul Simon and defeated him in the biggest upset in Illinois history for the Democratic nomination for governor. The next day, I sent a letter to Walker asking him if his campaign offered any summer jobs more interesting than being a first-year summer law intern in New York.

David Cleverdon soon called asking me to fly to Chicago for an interview at the Dan Walker for Governor campaign headquarters. He offered a prepaid roundtrip airline ticket, but he didn't really need to do much to convince me to come. He knew about my letters and contribution to Dan Walker, and he already had my file card in his campaign box.

Cleverdon was looking for regional campaign directors to work as paid members of the campaign staff. If he could field six good organizers downstate, plus a similar number in the suburbs, and in Chicago, they could consolidate Dan Walker's strengths from the walk and the primary into a ground campaign throughout Illinois. He said if I could sign on to that plan and commit to stay until November they could pay $600 a month salary. I had been making

144

less than $500 as an officer in the Army, and six months of that would send me back to law school after a short leave of absence with a little cash in my pocket. More importantly, I would be on the front line of a challenge not just to Boss Daley but to an incumbent Republican Governor with a well-funded campaign.

Cleverdon sent me in to talk to Barbara O'Connor, who had been working downstate on the phone in the primary, and she gave me a preliminary look at her campaign box of file cards. In the time before computer databases, campaign boxes were little black-and-white speckled hard cardboard boxes with a sliding metal bracket to make the 3- by 5-inch cards stand up. Her box was full of cards, arranged by county, and she showed me the starting point from the primary in the 28 counties in southern Illinois they wanted me to work. My area covered about one fourth of the geographic area of the state with about 5 percent of the population, but Dan Walker had walked through it all and done well there in the primary.

It didn't take me long to apply for a leave of absence from law school and say yes to the offer to join the Dan Walker for Governor campaign. As soon as my law exams were over in late May I headed to Chicago to get started. David Cleverdon was called the Campaign Director and worked directly for the Campaign Manager, Vic deGrazia. They made it clear that they ran things and kept the "candidate" busy out campaigning.

Cleverdon had worked the civil rights movement in Mississippi and then fought the Abner Mikva congressional wars in the Chicago suburbs, a swing district where Mikva would win in the presidential years, only to be defeated in the off year. That cycle repeated for nearly a decade, and Cleverdon ran the ground game in those campaigns, serving as a Mikva Congressional staffer when they won.

Dan Walker had been the 1970 Adlai Stevenson campaign manager in his successful Senate campaign after Senator Dirksen died in office. They wanted to step up those organizing efforts to build an independent statewide political force.

Vic deGrazia had served as one of the developers of Woodlawn Gardens, a low-income housing project in Chicago inspired by Saul Alinsky. He had signed a $9 million mortgage note to develop the project, with assistance from federal housing monies, and that mortgage had just defaulted, having failed to make a payment as the general election campaign began.[61] He and Cleverdon were devotees to the Alinsky organizing approach, and they sought to instill his methods into the campaign staff.

> What follows is for those who want to change the world from what it is to what they believe it should be. *The Prince* was written by Machiavelli for the Haves on how to hold power. *Rules for Radicals* is written for the Have-Nots on how to take it away.[62]

Alinsky died in 1972 as I was starting on the campaign. It became clear to me that Cleverdon and deGrazia were doing their best to apply his community organizing techniques to Walker's campaign, in both poor and middle class communities in urban and rural parts of Illinois.

CHAPTER 15

FROM THE GRASSROOTS TO THE EXECUTIVE MANSION AND MAYOR DALEY

M y first job was to sign up as many Citizen Committee members as possible, pledging by signing a card that they would work to elect Dan Walker. The first rule was that we were going to count each of our organizing activities and report. Cleverdon called weekly morning staff meetings in Chicago, where each of us would report by county or township or ward how many people we had signed up as members of the Dan Walker for Governor Citizens Committee in our ever-growing army of volunteers. He wanted the meetings at 0730, so we could finish quickly and still put in a full day's work organizing. Campaign organizing goes late into the evening. How was I to travel the six or more hours it took to drive to Chicago, spend another six hours returning to southern Illinois and still put in my full day's work?

My answer was the White County Flying Club's Cessna 172. I would schedule it for the staff meeting day, depart at 0500 and land at Meigs Field by about 0700 to take a cab over to the Clark Street campaign headquarters. I could be back in southern Illinois before noon.

I asked my fellow downstate organizers if anyone wanted me to pick them up and fly with me, to save them time and still get in their full day of organizing. Most of them just looked the other way and started talking to someone else. Flying in the dark in a single engine Cessna? Landing in the crosswind off the lake at Meigs Field just after sunrise? None of this came close to their comfort zone. Except there was one who saw the merit of it, and Pat Quinn, organizing near St. Louis in the Metro East, signed on.

I would leave the Carmi airport closer to 0400 hours and hop over to Sparta or Vandalia or Collinsville to pick up Quinn at 0500 hours. Back and forth we went, comparing campaign stories, trying to figure out how much the campaign literature we picked up from the headquarters would weigh to keep the weight and balance of the Cessna in range. We didn't want an unscheduled loss of control landing in Lake Michigan. If we got the weight and balance correct, our takeoff from Meigs would instead be successful. It was hard to keep Quinn and his boxes to the small number we could handle in the weight and balance table. On one takeoff where we had pushed the limit, I yelled out to him on takeoff halfway down the runway at Meigs: "Lean forward, we don't want all that campaign literature to hold down the tail." Pat complied and we climbed out just fine, as if just leaning forward would correct any improper loading outside the center of gravity envelope.

Barbara O'Connor worked me through the cards she already had in the southern Illinois box. One of her favorites was Steve McCurdy, a college student from Pinckneyville. Walker didn't walk through his county, and Steve missed the walk. He called the campaign headquarters in Chicago later to find out where to go see Walker. They told him he missed it, and that Walker was near Peoria, hundreds of miles north of Pinckneyville. Steve headed north toward Peoria and found Dan on the road. He walked with him and signed on to the campaign just a couple weeks before the primary.

O'Connor called McCurdy when she got his card from the walk crew. She offered to ship down a box of campaign literature and asked him to distribute it in his precinct in Pinckneyville with anyone he could get to help. The supply was enough to cover all four precincts in Pinckneyville and was gone in one weekend with help from his friends. He called back and asked for more. She shipped the literature to him on a Greyhound bus, and he and his crew worked all eight precincts in the county seat of DuQuoin. Then they went on to the smaller towns in their county, Tamaroa, Willisville and Cutler, and worked them as well. McCurdy was the only card in the box in Perry County, but when the results came in on primary night Dan Walker carried Perry County, which would be the only county south of Springfield that he carried where he hadn't walked.

Barbara O'Connor told me to go find more Steve McCurdys. There were other key people in the boxes I was to go see. Einar Dyhrkopp had been named Southern Illinois Chairman of the Dan Walker for Governor campaign. Dyhrkopp had met Dan Walker in Shawneetown, early on the walk. Dyhrkopp was close to other area Democratic leaders, such as Clyde Choate, the minority leader of the Illinois House of Representatives, and the late Paul Powell, Illinois Secretary of State. Powell had died suddenly and in his Springfield hotel room closet were stacks of shoe boxes stuffed with about $600,000 in small bills. The shoebox scandal, with its indications of cash as the political lubricant of choice in Illinois politics, was mostly explained by southern Illinois politicians with the whispered phrase: "They only found the hotel shoeboxes. That was just the tip of the iceberg." Powell was known in the rumor mill as the best person to see to buy a patronage job, often for as little as $500 in cash provided you pledged at least 2 percent of your monthly pay to the Powell cash machine for as long as you held the job. From Shawneetown to Powell's hometown in Vienna to Choate's home base in Anna, very few doubted that the pay-for-play patronage system went away with Powell's death.

Paul Simon had a clean reputation as a small-town newspaper publisher in Troy who stood with law enforcement and had crusaded for honesty in government. Comfortable with Boss Daley, he wanted to keep his distance from Dyhrkopp and his Powell friends. To hear Dyhrkopp's friend, Tony Castellano, tell it, Simon tilted his nose in the air and passed them right on by. Snubbed by the holier-than-thou Simon, Dyhrkopp and Castellano were quick to sign on with his opponent, and once loyal, they were in it for the long haul.

Strangely enough, though, Dyhrkopp's wife, Frances, who was the elected State Democratic Committeewoman in the Congressional district, did support Paul Simon, turning the household into a place in the primary with a foot in both camps. After Walker won the primary, the Dyhrkopp's were unified in their support for the Democratic candidate for governor. Dyhrkopp was to play a leading role in his campaign in the territory I was to cover. I couldn't wait to meet him and Frances at their Gold Hill Ranch home just outside of Shawneetown.

On the other side of the volunteer list were people like Betty Ison in Mt. Vernon. Just north of the coal mining center of southern Illinois, Mt. Vernon was the more prosperous banking, insurance and commercial center that considered itself the future of the region. A swing county politically, its business class was divided between rock-ribbed Republicans and conservative Democrats who wanted a more positive and refined approach to economic development for their region. Betty Ison, along with her husband, Troy, had moved from eastern Kentucky to build up a multi-county and prosperous independent gas station chain. They were more interested in Walker's reform credentials and his new approaches to helping southern Illinois economically than any ties he might have to the Powellites of political history. Like many of her contemporaries, Ison was repelled by Simon and Daley supporters from the primary, and she wanted to move the appeal of Democrats forward with a cleaner, more prosperous look.

This contrasting view of how to use politics to advance the American Dream dominated my work to elect a new Governor. The Powellites long history of patronage, personal profit, and local political dominance was met by the post-World War II aspirations for economic growth and honest government, not dependent on under-the-table money. The attitude of tolerance of corruption is spelled out in Robert E. Hartley's book, "The Dealmakers of Downstate Illinois: Paul Powell, Clyde L. Choate, John H. Stelle." He describes the "wink-and-grin" attitude in Powell's own words at an appreciation dinner: "My brother Hartwell and I put 50 cents in the plate each Sunday, but they never let me pass the collection plate."[63] In politics, though, Powell took charge of the collection plate, not just to feather his own nest, or to bring home the bacon, but to spread the bacon around in a complex web of job buying, vote-buying and influence peddling that became endemic.

Some did not "wink and grin." Instead their stomach was turned. They were embarrassed by those who knew of it and tolerated it, and they saw the Dan Walker campaign as an opportunity to rid themselves of a corrupt system and replace it with one that honestly served a broader interest in southern Illinois. My role in the Walker campaign gave me direct observation of this contrasting view with many opportunities to see it with stark clarity. My vantage point was focused in part by the desire of campaign leaders in Chicago to keep both sides pulling Walker to an election victory against an incumbent Republican Governor.

David Cleverdon and Vic deGrazia made clear to me that my job was to pull these disparate Walker supporters together, adding in the hard-core Simon supporters from the primary. Addition, not subtraction is the way to win general elections. If I had any problems with Einar Dyhrkopp and Tony Castellano, deGrazia said to call him and he would work it out. I was not to cause trouble with them.

I quickly learned there was plenty of trouble all by itself in Steve McCurdy's county, because Steve's uncle, Vallie West, was fighting on the county board with Paul Simon supporter and Perry County Democratic Chairman, John Rednour, a member of the Democratic National Committee. Before long, Doris Bertrand, in the county north of Betty Ison, let me know she had her own problems with Paul Simon's friend, and President of the Salem National Bank, Jerry

Sinclair. Nearly every person I began to call on had a similar tale of conflict along the lines of the Walker/Simon or the Powell/reformers divide.

My saving grace was that I liked all these people in southern Illinois and felt myself one of them. They all shared my common purpose of winning with Dan Walker as Governor. Our solid workers kept signing up new recruits, and we counted them and added them to our citizens committee file boxes. I also had a recalcitrant Simon supporter of my own close to home in Pud Williams, who had helped Paul Simon carry White County. He was still smarting from his own unsuccessful efforts in backing a loser in the Democratic primary for governor.

Dan Walker had not walked in White County. A year before, I had driven south into the next county to meet him. This became Pud Williams' opportunity. I told him he needed to redeem himself, and I could help him do it. A big fundraiser, where people all over the county could come meet the now-famous new candidate for governor, was what we needed and right away.

I could only remember one Governor in my lifetime having visited the county. That was when over half the county was under water in 1961, in the great flood, where the Skillet Fork, Little Wabash and Big Wabash rivers all rose in unison. Governor Otto Kerner came in to inspect the damage and offer to help out. His helicopter landed at the high school football field and he walked over to shake hands with a few of State Senator "Fat" Ziegler's friends. He quickly disappeared back into the helicopter, viewed the flood and was soon gone. I didn't know it at the time but Vic deGrazia was then serving as Governor Kerner's Director of the Department of Business and Economic Development. No one in White County had ever heard of deGrazia, but now they had heard of Walkin' Dan. He had become a celebrity candidate for governor downstate, and his folksy, friendly, listening style was drawing people to him. People had never seen anything like that from a potential governor of Illinois.

I lobbied David Cleverdon and the campaign scheduler for an early date with our candidate, and with that commitment we printed tickets which sold for $25 each. I told Pud his goal was 300 people and a packed house at the American Legion. In the meantime, I learned that Walker's family members could also campaign. I scheduled his wife Roberta for a White County tour to further solidify interest in the campaign. She came with her daughter, Robbie, met Pud's Williams' wife, Dorothy, and gave nice talks about her family at coffees and receptions around the area. She was charming, everybody liked her and I watched her connect in a personal way. Very few people from the Chicago metropolitan area ever visited southern Illinois, but now a potential Governor's family was making friends there. Their talks were not promising patronage jobs, but instead advocated a better way of doing things. I asked for more family visits throughout my 28-county area.

Dan Walker, with his daughter Kathleen, arrived on time by plane from Chicago and walked into the American Legion hall with a presence and demeanor that was compelling. He didn't pass by anyone looking for the big shots. Instead he locked on with his firm handshake, looked every person in the eye, complimented them, thanked them for coming, and then listened, his glaring blue eyes focusing right on them and every word they said. He blew people away with his personal magnetism. Immediately on his arrival he moved not to the head table Pud Williams had set up, but throughout the crowd, to shake hands with everyone present, including those in the kitchen cooking the food. He paused only briefly to say hello to me, and I could tell from his brief thanks that he was pleased that he now had a southern Illinois organizer who could put a good event together.

He didn't eat a bite at the dinner, though everyone else had the same good meal the American Legion could crank out. After working the crowd, he went to the podium, was quickly introduced by Williams, and gave a stirring speech, thanking the people of southern Illinois for propelling him to victory over Daley. He was going to continue the fight and he needed our help. He was combative, brave and on his quest. He didn't engage in long-winded pandering, but made clear that he owned a shotgun and loved to hunt, that he had grown up on a tomato farm in San Diego in the Depression, and that he loved being in southern Illinois. It wasn't long and he was gone. The local press magnified his presence, both in the paper and on the radio. I just wanted him to come and blow people away like that in all my counties.

Just north of Betty and Troy Ison, Doris Bertrand was working away in Salem, in a county Walker walked through and carried in the primary. Three-time candidate for president, William Jennings Bryan, was born in Salem and the son of a devout Baptist. As a judge, Bryan prayed for God's assistance before every judicial decision. His statue stands now in Salem after being displaced by a new bridge from its original placement in Washington, D. C.

Bertrand was the hardest working and most effective individual campaign vote getter I met on the campaign. Her goal was 800 absentee votes for Dan Walker from voters who otherwise would not have voted. She found them in nursing homes mostly, and she bird-dogged the process from ballot application to when the ballots were mailed directly from the county clerk's office, to their arrival at the nursing home where she made sure they got to the voter. Most generally voted for the candidate she supported. She had other rivals at this process in both parties, one of whom had worked for Paul Simon in the primary. She now wanted to get enough votes for Dan Walker to beat her Republican absentee vote rival working in the county for Richard Ogilvie the incumbent Governor. Bertrand was old school enough to want that woman's patronage job in state government, a beauty shop inspector.

But Jerry Sinclair, leader of the local Democrats, President of the Salem National Bank, and close friend of Paul Simon, stood in the way. deGrazia wanted him on board and directly set out to schedule a meeting between Sinclair and Walker. Bertrand and her friends got wind of this in the rumor mill immediately. They feared that once

Sinclair sat down with Walker he would effectively cut them out of the campaign and run things his way, as a centralized county power broker, in the general election and thereafter. My phone was ringing off the wall with this fear, and the callers wanted something done about it.

I called headquarters and asked about arrangements for a meeting between the gubernatorial candidate and Sinclair. It was on, at the bank and private. "No," I said to the scheduler. "You can't do that and undercut what we are doing organizationally with the primary supporters. Walker said no backroom deals, and he must stay out of any back rooms in Salem." My message got through, and they changed the meeting to a public dining room at the Salem Holiday Inn.

The two men sat down at a table in the center of the restaurant. Many of the primary supporters found tables around the edges of the dining room, where they could see, but politely out of hearing range of the conversation between Walker and Sinclair. What they witnessed was a short chat, and Walker quite openly and abruptly walking out, leaving Sinclair sitting alone. The volunteers were ecstatic at witnessing Walker's independence. Sinclair was livid at this public rebuke.

Later I learned from Walker that he intended to win Sinclair over, but that their conversation had been bizarre. Quite quickly, Sinclair informed Walker that "the Democratic candidate for governor" (Paul Simon) had promised him he could be his Director of Personnel. "Now that you are the Democratic candidate for governor," Jerry continued, "I expect you to honor the Democratic candidate for governor's promise." Dan had never heard something so absurd. This strange continuity of commitment from the unelected political machine endorsed party candidate to the elected party candidate after the primary confounded his view of democracy. He wanted to win Marion County in the general election but agreeing to Jerry's offer to take charge of personnel issues statewide was no way to do it. He simply and quickly told Jerry no and walked out, quite openly and defiantly.

Walker's opponents routinely called him arrogant. His supporters loved it as he stood firmly with the voters and the people, not the politicians and their machine.

Einar Dyhrkopp called a meeting at Tony's Steakhouse in Marion, where Tony Castellano had a larger-than-life oil painting of his friend, Paul Powell, hanging in his office. He assembled Walker volunteers from all over southern Illinois to help sell tickets to an upcoming large fundraiser at Carbondale. Dyhrkopp was skilled at leading fundraisers in this time before campaign disclosure, and he wanted a large, successful event at $50 a person with involvement and buy-in from all the counties in southern Illinois. Week after week most of the volunteers gathered and shared stories of success and prospects we needed to add to the event.

At one point a couple weeks before the event, Dyhrkopp, who was good at counting, too, made it clear that we had met our $50,000 goal so we could relax the fundraising pitch and make sure everyone who had already bought a ticket showed up. Russell Dawe, who was new to all this and working his first campaign after meeting Walker on the walk, questioned why the slow down. He thought we could raise much more money in the last couple weeks. Dyhrkopp told him that's not the way we do it. We pledge all we can raise, and due to the weakness of the southern Illinois economy, that's only $50,000. For that, we want help, and if the campaign needs more, we'll ask them for something more in return. We all rested on our goal for the next two weeks, as he had instructed.

The campaign strategists in Chicago wanted a different style of fundraising that emphasized Walker's grassroots appeal. If we could take a small group raising small amounts and turn them into a chain-letter style movement growing exponentially, that could make a huge difference. "$2 for Dan" they called it. With great enthusiasm in Chicago, it was planned and ready with plenty of "$2 for Dan" buttons and pre-printed worksheets. They wanted each organizer statewide to pick the most talented volunteer who would then invite seven more volunteers to a coffee at their home, pledging each to donate $2 at the event and then to invite six more to a coffee at their home, who would each give their $2 and then invite five people to their own coffee and so on. As seven became 42, and then 210, the numbers across the state would get big as the chain progressed.

Betty Ison took to this like a true multi-level marketer. I helped her carefully pick her seven, distributed not just from her county but from around the region, so our chain could spread out and grow.

She followed up and found that by the time the five attendees at the second level were trying to invite four people to another coffee, they were inviting many of the same people the other five attendees were inviting. The chains tended to operate on top of each other in a concentrating, not a blossoming fashion. She called and cajoled and helped recruit, until her husband, Troy, began to complain that her phone bill was bigger than the money they were raising. Her chain gave out at about $4,000, but it was the largest one by far in the state. We gained another 2,000 volunteers into the southern Illinois campaign, most of them continuing to proudly wear their "$2 for Dan" buttons like badges of honor.

Governor Ogilvie was behind in the polls as Dan Walker's fame from his walk and upset victory continued his momentum after the primary. Ogilvie looked for a model re-election strategy for an incumbent who had raised the income tax. He found it in Governor Nelson Rockefeller, the only known Governor who had raised the income tax in his state and then been re-elected. Rockefeller's people had a simple answer: throw lots of money at it; overwhelm your challenger in a flood of dollars. Ogilvie did just that, raising record amounts from road contractors and Republican big shots in the era before campaign contributions were disclosed. His television campaign began in July, an unheard of five months before the election. His "Ogilvie is a Good Governor," spots were working, and Dan Walker's lead was steadily eroding in the polls. His record of spending more than $4 million dollars sounds small in today's money-dominated politics, but he was outspending Dan by 4 to 1, and we could feel its effects.

We continued counting volunteers and their activity, building toward the November election. We worked voter registration drives, canvassing to identify and persuade voters by plus minus zero, combining forces with other candidates on the ballot, and preparing for election day efforts to safeguard and get out our vote. As we identified those who said they would vote for Walker, we wrote them down as a plus, with Ogilvie supporters becoming a minus. The undecideds were zeros and marked as potentials for more persuasion closer to the election. We counted and reported on it all. I learned my own set of distinctions between the bullshitters, the workers and the organizers. Some of the talkers worked through their networks and gossipy chains that were endemic to the culture of southern Illinois, like putting something on the local radio. They didn't produce many numbers you could count, however. Some were effective talkers while others were just self-serving bullshitters deluxe. More effective workers, such as Doris Bertrand, generated real numbers leading to real votes. Others, including Betty Ison, were the cream of the crop organizers, who had a talent for seeing what needed to be done, successfully recruiting others to help, and achieving accountable and growing results.

Others had a real talent for seeing what we were up against. As president of the local chapter of the NAACP, Ruby Jackson, in Metropolis, knew her opposition. To hear her tell it, the McAfee machine had been delivering minority voters to Republicans in Massac County since Lincoln. Slaves from Kentucky had made it across the Ohio River to freedom in Metropolis, and that's as far as they got. Since then, the local Republicans organized the minority voters with the local township welfare system, and the local slum lords and grocery stores. You voted, you signed your welfare check over to Garland McAfee who paid your rent directly for you, and your groceries were delivered regularly from his store under his "grocery plan." That was all. Cash left over? No, you had to do things extra for cash. Voting was one of those extras.

Ruby Jackson alerted me the day even more cash arrived from up north, and it came in a private corporate twin engine plane landing at the local airport where Republican Senator Chuck Percy stepped off the plane to fund their election day operation. She said we could work and count and organize until the cows came home, but if we didn't have a strategy for dealing with that cash on election day, all four Black precincts in Metropolis would come in almost unanimously against us.

In most other counties, our new volunteers faced the old expectations of the patronage machine. If volunteers were working just to gain jobs, and there were only so many patronage jobs to go around, then the competition became internal for that limited number of possible jobs. The effort narrowed to those who wanted or were promised the jobs, leaving everyone else out, and misdirected us from the reform objective Dan Walker was advocating. Our best organizers rose to this occasion with the hope of changing this old system for the better. They wanted to do more than just count or look for jobs; they wanted to follow through and be part of the change to help all of southern Illinois, politically, economically and governmentally.

This was a basic change from the corruption and "me too ism" of the wink-and-grin Powellite approach. It had different motivations, objectives and approaches to building a broader election victory. Walker had inspired this group and helped it grow and become more active. Was this kind of change driven by the American Dream? Or was it changing the ideals of the American Dream in a new and positive way through grassroots politics?

The reality of the Ogilvie TV surge was that the Dan Walker for Governor campaign needed to not just raise more money but focus time and resources on a media response to the "Good Governor" ads with its own paid television throughout Illinois. Television advertising with money was becoming a dominant political tool and in the summer there was no paid television from Dan Walker countering Ogilvie's message. There would not be until much closer to the election.

We had to cut spending on everything else, and in Chicago we learned that our salaries were on the chopping block. Just two months into the summer, I had to face the choice of becoming a volunteer organizer without salary or returning to law school in New York after Labor Day. Every other organizer faced this same challenge of this unilateral change in working conditions.

It was a hot meeting in the Chicago headquarters that summer. Were the schedulers and advance men still getting paid? What about their expense allowances that we didn't receive? How do we put gas in our cars and pay our phone bills? Out of this disputed meeting came a proposal to let us fund our own operations by raising our own campaign contributions in local bank accounts, spending it locally in support of our own organizing activity. This internal dispute also was essentially one of control, and in my view, Vic deGrazia lost this argument and part of his control of the campaign. Significant responsibility was delegated to the campaign staff that stayed the course. Now we had a new duty of raising our own funds over and above what Einar Dyhrkopp or the central campaign was doing. We would then decide how best to spend it to elect Dan Walker.

We also learned that in most of downstate, from there on out, we wouldn't be seeing the candidate. Travel was expensive and most of the votes were in the Chicago media market, where the campaign had to make sure the Daley machine stayed loyal to the entire Democratic ticket.

In other words, we were on our own. I stopped into the scheduling office before I headed south that day and asked the family scheduler how many family campaigning visits could I get to keep the troops going when they couldn't see the candidate himself, whose walk and personal campaigning had drawn them to the cause in the first place. I received a positive response. I went back to my local organizers and let them know that we would need to do local fundraisers and events built around campaign visits from Walker family members.

The local organizers rose to the occasion. We were in the battle now and committed. We raised enough money to pay for some of my cash needs, but we put most of it into headquarters rent, phone lines, and some local radio ads, especially at stations on the Indiana, Kentucky and Missouri border. The Chicago campaign didn't want to buy much or any TV advertising there because of the inefficiency at stations located out of state with only part of their audience in Illinois.

A grassroots group taking charge of their own local politics was part of the reform Dan Walker was advocating. Down from Chicago came Dan's four oldest children, Dan, Jr., Robbie, Julie and Kathleen, who got to know volunteers from all over Illinois as they applied their father's lessons, talking, listening and loving southern Illinois and its campaign volunteers. As Dan, Jr. and Robbie went back to college, Kathleen, Dan's oldest, became the mainstay of this effort.

As we became better at this new effort at rallying and motivating our volunteers, Kathleen would come down even more, often staying for two to three day road trips across the 28 counties. She had graduated college from Santa Clara in California and was working in corporate lending at the Bank of America in San Francisco before the campaign. Her enthusiastic support of what her father was doing came through as she left her good job on the west coast and returned to Illinois as a volunteer. She had helped in the past in the Adlai Stevenson campaigns for state treasurer and senator that her father helped lead, and she added smiles, laughter, experience and solid communication to the skills of her younger brothers and sisters. She was the best surrogate campaigner we could ask for, and folks all over southern Illinois responded favorably to her efforts.

So did I. We were fast friends in a hurry, talking between stops on the road about the campaign. Motivation and a sense of common purpose were driving results far more than just counting and listening to Chicago for direction. Breaking the grip of Chicago domination was much of what the campaign was about downstate. Kathy and I plotted along the route, trying to fill out the organization, keep the other volunteers happy with the efforts of Einar Dyhrkopp and Tony Castellano, and driving it all forward with everybody on the same page. Kathy and I were increasingly writing the content of those campaign planning pages together.

That approach worked better because it was local and attuned to what our volunteers wanted to achieve. As we crisscrossed our organizing region, 160 miles from north to south and 80 from east to west, we had plenty of time to talk about everything else that came to mind, too. I played country music on the road, and Kathy learned all I knew about Waylon Jennings, Merle Haggard and Tammy Wynette. As the miles passed and events stretched late into the night, our conversations became continuous and more personal. Working hard with a common purpose creates its own sense of adventure and a powerful attraction.

Einar Dyhrkopp was working hard, too. I tried to meet with him at his Gold Hill Ranch from time to time to stay on top of where he was finding strength or where we needed to address weakness. He showed me his calendar, and it was filled with night meetings at veteran's clubs and Elks clubs all over the map. He said support from those private clubs was a key to a broader appeal, and he had something to offer them. He held up his letter signed by Dan Walker on campaign stationery, telling me he made clear to the clubs that as governor, Dan Walker would make sure the state police didn't raid their clubs.

The clubs all had illegal slot machines in the back rooms of their bars, and it meant a lot to them to be assured they could keep them. He told me he held up the letter for all to see in his speeches, and those who ran the clubs were coming on board. I was fascinated at his approach but wondered if that letter was going to cause Dan Walker trouble. I read it while talking to Dyhrkopp at his desk and noticed that it said nothing at all about protecting the clubs from slot machine raids. What an interesting campaign deception, I thought, but what, too, were its long-term consequences?

Einar Dyhrkopp also was excited about figuring out Ogilvie's fundraising methods. With Clyde Choate, Dyhrkopp had found a small road contractor who was willing to share information with them, encouraging the contractor to spread his story with local Republicans involved in fundraising. He told them that his construction company was in trouble and badly needed a new and lucrative state contract to stay afloat.

After a bidding notice was published for road contracts in the area, he got a call asking him which contract he was interested in. He let the caller know what he had in mind, and the caller suggested that he go to the Statehouse Inn in Springfield the next week with a briefcase filled with a substantial amount of cash. The expectation was about 10 percent of the total contract price, and Dyhrkopp loved that his source was willing to fill him in on these details. The contractor didn't know the identity of his caller, and he asked how he would know who to talk to at the Statehouse Inn. The caller told him he didn't need to know that. He was told to simply wait in the lobby with his briefcase and they would meet him there.

He did as he was told and was met by two men he did not know personally who asked him to join them in their car parked outside. They went on a quick ride through Springfield with little conversation. They then asked that he leave his briefcase in the car as they dropped him back off at the hotel. "How do I know I'll get my contract?" he asked. "You'll know when your bid is accepted," they replied.

I asked Dyhrkopp if he was going to turn this information over to law enforcement or the press to expose how Ogilvie was raising so much money from road contractors. "No, that's not the idea at all. We just want to know how to duplicate that procedure to raise our own money when we win." I had a hard time keeping a straight face on that one. Following Vic deGrazia's instructions, I called him to let him know what had been shared with me. "I'll take care of it," deGrazia said.

CHAPTER 16

FROM THE SOUTHERN ILLINOIS GOVERNOR'S OFFICE TO THE CLYDE CHOATE CHALLENGE

I was exhausted as November arrived. Miles and miles on the road, late nights, and the constant flow of phone calls and problems, though, were coming together with a motivated group of volunteers. Incomplete reports of various indicators we were to count were not always liked at the Chicago headquarters. Greater local control attuned to southern Illinois as we funded our own efforts left me satisfied we were getting the job done in a more effective way. As it turned out, voters, too, were motivated and ran up good margins in southern Illinois to help elect Dan Walker. That was the number that really counted, and it was one of the best in the state. We were all happy with that.

We only broke the Metropolis paper ballot chain voting fraud Ruby Jackson had told us about in one of the four Metropolis precincts. Our volunteers there, however, saw the picture of how hard work, motivated by the prospect of further reform, could make a difference.

I thought the results were spectacular. In the 28 downstate counties I worked, Walker carried 22 of them. In the key inverted

"T" area running down Interstate 57 from Salem to Marion, and then crossed with the inverted "T" from Murphysboro east to Harrisburg, he carried all the counties, running up substantial margins in Franklin and Jackson counties. In Jackson County, home of Southern Illinois University, our teamwork even helped make it the only county McGovern carried in any state for miles around. Walker beat Ogilvie by just under 2% statewide, about 80,000 votes in the midst of the Nixon 1972 landslide victory nationwide. Illinois stood out because of Walker's leadership, and southern Illinois stood out in his victory.

The Chicago campaign honchos noticed our good results, and David Cleverdon asked me for two follow-ups. He wanted a list of the names of good volunteers with good qualifications to serve in state government. He also asked for any reform ideas about programs or policies that were well suited to southern Illinois. He didn't ask for my unreimbursed travel or phone expenses that exceeded what we raised while the Chicago campaign was spending its funds on TV. The big campaign ignored my substantial submission of those that they never really wanted to even see.

I received some good recommendations. Frank Kirk, on the Southern Illinois University faculty, had led much of our effort in our largest county. In Jackson County, party unity meant the presidential, gubernatorial, and local campaigns all worked together and all shared in an outstanding result. Governor-elect Walker accepted my recommendation on Frank Kirk and appointed him Director of Local Government Affairs.

Nolan Jones had done an excellent job in Cairo, Dan Walker knew him from years past, and I included him on my list. Jones, not Jerry Sinclair, was appointed Director of Personnel. Pud Williams, whose political skill and reputation grew during the campaign, was a natural choice for Director of Agriculture, and he was at the top of my list. I had helped Pud move from the farm and his role as chairman of a small rural county board, to a bigger stage in Illinois government.

A few others got appointed assistant directors, or ultimately served in key positions in state government. I learned later that the appointment of the Director of Mines and Minerals, a key one for the predominant southern Illinois coal mining community, had been delayed.

My most creative recommendation was for the creation of a new approach to implementing southern Illinois priorities. Governor Ogilvie had built a new office building in Marion, filled with patronage employees. I recommended, in a written policy paper I drafted, that Dan Walker establish there instead a Southern Illinois Governor's Office. It would use a relatively new communications capability that had not yet been adopted by state governments, a toll-free line, so ordinary citizens could easily air their problems and seek assistance directly from the chief executive. A staff would handle the calls, but on a regular basis, the Governor would spend a day in his southern Illinois office, meeting directly with those with the most complex or pressing problems, and taking individual executive action to address those concerns.

When he was there, the Governor would personally answer some calls on the toll-free line, opening up a problem-solving channel, not a patronage channel, into state government. Southern Illinois citizens no longer would have to rely on people in Chicago, or travel nearly 200 miles to Springfield, or work their way through the Powell era patronage focus of the local party leaders to draw attention to their concerns. Instead the Governor would come to them, and his office would be there listening and working every day. For the Governor, this would also provide a direct, strong feedback mechanism on what was actually going on in his executive agencies of state government. I proposed, too, that some of the staff of the office would work on coordination of economic development, to facilitate real progress helping the entire region.

My dream was that I would be able to head up that Southern Illinois Governor's office, which I saw as advancing in a straight line from taking the opportunity to meet Walker and join him on the walk. It also reinforced being on the right side of my argument with Pud Williams about reform of Illinois politics. It would add a substantive role to my detour from law school onto the Dan Walker for Governor paid campaign staff, adapting "$2 for Dan" to be the best in the state, and contributing creatively to an excellent electoral victory in my region of the campaign. I had advocated for more key appointments of department directors from my area than any other region, and I wanted to cap that off with my own new role to work with them and our new Governor to creatively solve problems and implement our resulting reforms for the next four years.

My developing relationship with Kathleen made that ambitious plan more complicated than I anticipated. Kathy quickly scheduled a return trip to southern Illinois just days after the election. She wanted to do a victory tour of sorts with me, and we personally visited with every key volunteer over the next few days. We also decided what we were going to do.

The personal side seemed so very easy to us. We were getting married, as simple as we saw that. We both came to that mutual conclusion without much hesitation, and it was a wonderful decision after knowing each other just a few months. Were we returning to New York, where I was ready to end my leave of absence, or did we prefer California where Kathy had graduated from college and had worked in San Francisco?

Kathy wanted to go to law school, too, but she had a problem. Her father had told her that as a well-paid corporate executive with plenty of personal resources, he could afford to pay for and send all his seven children to colleges of their choice, but he would only send his sons to graduate school. Her younger brother, Dan, Jr. already was in law school at Northwestern at his father's expense, and she didn't think returning to her job at the Bank of America offered much possibility of advancement for women.

Law school was important to both of us, but where, when and how was quickly at issue. It wasn't hard for us to reach a conclusion that staying in Illinois, where a new Governor was going to make change that we were already a part of, might be a better approach to what's next than heading off to either coast.

Kathy told her parents we were going to be married and the sooner the better. I scheduled an appointment with her father in the campaign headquarters to talk to him about our plans and to ask his support. I had known Dan Walker as a candidate for Governor for a little over 18 months; I had known Kathleen for only four.

I worked for his campaign on his paid staff, helped raise money for his campaign, and helped pull together the disparate political elements in southern Illinois after his bruising primary victory. I was part of his political team. He had recruited me personally for that role beginning in the early days of his walk in Shawneetown. But now I was not talking to him about simply continuing in his political operation while he was Governor. I was instead talking to him about the daughter he openly called his "Princess." That was a different thing altogether.

He let me know he considered me a rebel, and one from the southern Illinois culture as well. He was a bit of a rebel himself, of course, having led the greatest political revolt in Illinois history in writing the "Rights in Conflict" report on the 1968 Democratic convention and running to defeat Boss Daley's political machine, followed by deposing the Republican's favorite "good Governor." He wanted to know how well his daughter understood that about me and why she was in such a hurry to marry.

Our conversation was straightforward, a bit blunt at times and longer than I expected, as though we were addressing an unresolved issue that Kathy and I considered already resolved. He invited me to spend Thanksgiving with his family in Deerfield, so Kathy and I could help Dan and Roberta better understand what we were proposing to do. Our meeting in the Governor's campaign office had not been a congratulations, 'I am glad you want to marry my daughter' meeting.

Kathy was ready to do a December wedding, and Roberta was appalled at her haste. Roberta had her hands more than full with plans for a Governor's inauguration in January and rearranging the schooling of her youngest of seven children, Margaret and Will. Her daughter, Julie, had been formally engaged to be married for about a year, and her wedding wasn't scheduled until April. How could Kathleen suddenly cut in front of her sister's plans? Roberta saw this as neither fair nor appropriate.

Kathy and I spent more time together before Thanksgiving and prepared to deal with her family dynamic. There was no slowing us down, and our emotional connection continued to grow even more deeply. She worked with her mother and sister Julie on a January wedding date. When Dan told us that President Nixon was planning a spectacle at his inauguration that required all state governors to act as a color guard personally carrying in their state's flag, he felt pressured with negative consequences for his state if he refused. We suggested he tell the President that he was sorry, but his daughter was getting married on January 20 and he must decline attending the President's inauguration.

Thanksgiving was fun in Deerfield, and I got to know Kathy's family even more. Dan was busy with the transition, and in the midst of the family talk, he had one main political issue he wanted to discuss with me. "Did I know Russell Dawe very well?" he asked. I had worked closely with Russell who was from Valier in Franklin County. He, along with George and Agnes Michalic in West Frankfort, and Sy and Irene Schwartz in Benton, were the key Walker volunteers in the most solidly Democratic county in my area. I knew he had met Dan on the walk and was a loyalist to the core.

Dan wondered why Clyde Choate and Einar Dyhrkopp were backing him for Director of Mines and Minerals. He knew they were unhappy with him for passing over their earlier conventional political recommendations for other cabinet posts, and he thought it a bit strange that they would now back an independent Dan Walker supporter with no prior political connections. I quickly asked Dan for the other alternative, because I thought I knew the answer to his question. Dan told me it was someone from around Harrisburg, but he was unsure of the name. "Clarence Crick," I said, and he said, "Yes that's it."

I told him Crick was close to the coal industry, and I knew he was involved with Dyhrkopp's fundraising efforts. He's their guy I told him. "They are playing a game of double switch, hoping you'll turn down their recommendation again and go on to the second choice." The Governor told me he expected something like that from those two. "It's going to be fun to call Clyde Choate and Einar Dyhrkopp to tell them I have appointed their recommended candidate, Russell Dawe, for Director of Mines and Minerals."

Were we at a family gathering to work out the family issues about an upcoming wedding? Or were we sitting in front of Dan's fireplace, just the two of us, comparing political notes? It was both, for sure. This conversation, like many others to come, cemented Dan's role as my political and personal mentor. I was a young, arrogant and rebellious political advisor who was more than willing to debate or contest issues with other political leaders and those on Dan's team, whether it was Clyde Choate, the Minority Leader of the Illinois House of Representatives, or Vic deGrazia, who was to be Deputy Governor. This role was a lot more interesting and enticing to me than heading back to New York to finish law school.

In December 1972, the mandatory chapel case reached finality. Everyone involved in the case had known it might go all the way to the Supreme Court and on December 18, we found out that the highest court in the nation had denied certiorari. In other words, they would not review the opinion of the D. C. Circuit Court of Appeals in its decision abolishing compulsory chapel at the service academies. That decision would stand as the final order. There would be no more establishment of religion at the service academies in open violation of the First Amendment.

The Supreme Court receives many petitions for review every year, and it normally denies most of them in a two-word statement, "certiorari denied." That's it. No reasons. No explanations, and not even a kind word to the lower court decision it leaves standing as the authoritative and final word on that case. On the chapel case, they added "8-0," making it very clear by issuing its denial differently than usual. There was no desire by the Justices of the highest court to return to the world of official religions and required participation, or to step back toward the unification of church and state.

To have done so would have been to turn back toward a deadly and terrible precedent that American immigrants had rejected formally in the American Revolution. The American people had formally codified, in the Constitution and Bill of Rights, their political and religious beliefs on freedom, the issue at the heart of their revolutionary break from a bad and violent history of coercion.

This victory also was a victory for the American Dream. My grandmother stood torn in that cattle pasture, finally deciding that the danger of John Kennedy's unification of his Presidency with the Pope was no longer her concern. Her internal debate, and the stance of those of us who stood up persistently as "troublemakers" for religious freedom at the service academies, are part of the ongoing process of re-making the American Dream. So was Dan Walker who stood up against Boss Daley and the protestors who were beaten by police in Grant Park and on the streets of Chicago in 1968. These individual actions, and many others over the decades since the American Revolution, have continued to progress, solidify and reinforce the values that drive the American Dream. Its reinforcement, reform and resilience gives hope to all who aspire to it.

What we learned in the Circuit Court of Appeals decision of Anderson v. Laird, 466 F2d 283 (DC Cir., 1972), *cert. denied*, 93 S. Ct. 690 (1972) is that those precedents, going all the way back to the Virginia Declaration of Rights, mattered in a tangible sense. From that point, the mandatory chapel military formations every Sunday morning at West Point, at which attendance was required, simply ended.

Free exercise of religion continued, as the First Amendment requires. However, establishment of religion in the military by our government abruptly ended upon the written order of the circuit court of appeals. The "troublemakers" had won, and the coercion of a powerful military chain of command in open defiance of the First Amendment was swept away.

Requiring attendance and participation at a religious service was in reality a throwback to an earlier era. The unification of church and state traces its roots to about 400 A. D. when the Romans made Christianity their official state religion. They sought to use religion as a means of social harmony. The emperors and the popes were part of the same structure to keep their people in line. Religion backed up by violence, or its threat, kept the empire alive. In this merger, the Roman Empire became Christendom, and Christendom continued beyond the fall of the Roman Empire.[63]

Horrible, bloody history resulted through the crusades and early pogroms persecuting non-Christian Jews, led by a top down system of popes and bishops overseeing a religious hierarchy. Religious leaders defined and identified heretics so that state power and violence could curtail the spread of their differing religious beliefs. After a thousand years, Luther and the reformation, armed with the printing press and Bibles printed in native languages, challenged this powerful structure. The crackdowns on heresy intensified, however, with burnings at the stake, warring Protestant and Catholic provinces, and other coercions to continue the dogmas of Christendom into more recent history.

The free will and religious teachings of the Bible that condemned violence led slowly toward toleration of differing religions and to the even more vibrant seeds of religious freedom. Distant from the shackles of the aristocracy, the kings, and the hierarchies of priests, bishops, popes and archbishops of Canterbury, the American colonists pursued their own freedom.

Over time they turned freedom of religion and thought into economic freedom with democratic ideals. William Penn, Roger Williams, and large groups of Baptist and Methodist ministers sought not just toleration of their beliefs, but true freedom to exercise them without official tipping of the scales of choice toward coercion in official churches. Some early states modeled the English system of an official church. But when Virginians, at the urging of Baptists, successfully campaigned to cut off taxpayer support of an official church, James Madison and Thomas Jefferson found themselves courting the votes of those who sought full religious freedom. They listened to their pleas, applied their own enlightenment ideas of natural law, and drafted the cornerstone documents of American religious freedom.[64]

The American Dream, based on values and freedom, was propelled forward as they took their skillful expressions in statutes and amendments through development in Virginia, whose model was then insisted on by the ratifying debates of the U. S. Constitution, to become the Bill of Rights.

Citing this historical as well as legal precedent, Judge Bazelon, the Circuit Judge of the D. C. Circuit Court of Appeals, wrote in the mandatory chapel decision that the purpose of the establishment clause of the First Amendment was to "protect absolutely the core values of religious liberty." He quoted the specifics first written and advocated by Thomas Jefferson and James Madison in Virginia in 1786:[65]

> That no man shall be compelled to frequent or support any religious worship, place, or ministry whatsoever, nor shall be enforced, restrained, molested, or burthened in his body or goods, nor shall otherwise suffer on account of his religious opinions or belief . . . 12 Hening, Statutes of Virginia (1823) 84.

Bazelon ruled that this made clear that attendance at religious services may never be compelled because the First Amendment generalized this language without losing its meaning. It provided for "freedom from governmental imposition of religious activity." He pointed out that the religious neutrality policies articulated in later Supreme Court interpretations did not mean that the rules banning a religious establishment by the government must bend if they conflicted with military interests, saying:

> When the power, prestige, and financial support of government is placed on a particular religious belief, the indirect coercive pressure upon religious minorities to conform to the prevailing officially approved religion is plain.[66]

What was more meaningful to me personally was the shifting of the trial court's reliance on senior military officers on the effects of compulsory chapel to a specific reliance on the better qualified students who testified on its effects:

> This casts serious doubt on the validity of the court's findings, since those upon whom the regulations have an impact—the students and their religious advisors—are uniquely qualified to testify as to their effect.[67]

This not only made clear that those in military service retained their constitutional rights, but it confirmed that the testimony Lieutenant Leslie and I gave under oath had meaning to the court. Judge Levanthal, who joined in the majority ruling, pointed out that the *amicus curiae* were shocked at the military's claim of secular effect of compulsory attendance at chapel, saying such a claim was "to debase and manipulate religious worship as a mere instructional tool."[68]

Besides the Baptist Joint Committee, those who submitted *amicus* briefs included the organization representing 35-member denominations in the General Commission on Chaplains. The Commission plays a key role in recruiting chaplains to serve in the military. In 1964 they had found that compulsory chapel at the service academies had an adverse effect on recruiting chaplains, and petitioned the Department of Defense to end the practice. Their brief, as well as their court testimony in the case, made clear that most religious denominations supported free will in religious matters and the legal guarantees that protect it.[69]

Judge Leventhal also noted that cadet testimony demonstrated the "development of resentment, hostility and cynicism toward religion in cadets." This counter-productive effect cast doubt on the senior military witnesses' claims, and he specifically cited the experience of the four cadets at West Point who were denied relief from compulsory chapel and called "troublemakers" as a result.[70]

To read that language in the court's final ruling specifically about me, when I remembered so well walking the area during June Week while Lieutenant General Koster, in a speech to all my classmates, pointed to the area and called me a "troublemaker," was significant closure to me. My appeals for change to the military chain of command and in testimony in federal court, in such an important legal but contested precedent, had borne fruit. That high court decision went a long way to remedying my sense of disillusionment based on my experience with the Army and provided finality. At the same time, I was elated at our political victory with a leader I believed in and saw as a solid and wise mentor, and whose daughter was about to join me in marriage, where she would motivate and teach me much more than I yet knew.

"Let government step back. Let people step forward." That was my favorite line from Dan Walker's January 1973 inaugural speech. He broke precedent and moved his inauguration ceremony from inside to out in front of the Lincoln statue on the east side of the Illinois Capitol. Instead of legislative leaders or other politicians, Governor-elect Walker invited all the campaign organizers to each designate one volunteer to sit with him on the inaugural stage. I selected Betty Ison who joined him there, as did his family and father. I had a seat in the front row of the audience, sitting directly facing Mayor Daley, who came from Chicago to sit as a dignitary with the new governor.

After the swearing in and speech, Kathy wanted me to meet her grandfather, who I knew only by his alcoholic reputation and the fortuitous timing of retiring after a long career in the Navy to start a tomato farm in San Diego in 1929. He was a man of a few words, at least to me. "I've got a long shotgun, boy," he snarled at me on the steps of the Illinois Capitol. "And if you mess with my princess, you'll be staring down its business end." He had no more to say. Kathy expected a more friendly reception but was not surprised at her grandfather, who had been idolized in family lore.

I was surprised to meet and talk to Mayor Daley at the inaugural reception in the Executive Mansion. In my view, whatever his past successes, Daley was on the wrong side of the divide in the country over the Vietnam War, and his belligerence toward the legitimate criticism in the Walker report on the 1968 Chicago Democratic Convention was beyond the pale.[71] Yet on this day, he was ebullient, smiling and friendly, his big blue eyes lighting him up. He was not the ogre or bully I expected in person. His friendly gesture to Dan Walker's victories seemed authentic enough that day.

Despite Bishop O'Connor's insistence that the Governor's daughter be married in the Springfield cathedral, Roberta and Kathy informed him of a different choice. She wanted a little church in a town where she had campaigned, so we assembled in Chatham just outside of Springfield for a marriage ceremony presided over jointly by her family parish Catholic priest from Deerfield and my Baptist minister, Reverend Huff, from Carmi.

The reception at the Executive Mansion was large, with people from the campaign, my southern Illinois relatives, Kathy's Deerfield and California family and friends, along with mine from West Point. The mansion butler served champagne in stemmed glasses as the long reception line wound up the circular stairway to the ballroom upstairs. Mildred Barbre, my mother's cousin and a member of the Georgia General Baptist Church, my grandmother Inie's church near Maunie, asked if there was any cold Coke to drink in those nice glasses. She was one of many Baptists who never drank, not even champagne or wine at weddings. Many joined her and kept the butler busy. Standing in the reception line at the top of the stairs with the

Governor, Roberta and my mother Darcy could see people as they approached. Glasses filled with clear liquid were the people from Lake County. Those with glasses containing dark liquid were my Baptist relatives from southern Illinois. Lots of Coke got consumed at that party.

One of that group thought it was fine to enjoy some of the peach pie laid out near the wedding cake, not knowing Kathy wanted no cake, but instead planned to cut the pie with the Walker family pie spoon. When Kathy and I approached for the ceremonial "not cake but pie" cutting, she found only crumbs and a single slice of peach at the bottom of the pan. She ran upstairs from the reception crying, convinced her brother Charles had played a very dirty trick on her at her wedding. It took me a while to convince her to come back down and enjoy the reception in this first crisis of our marriage. Charles suffered Kathy's ire for decades until at my cousin Darcy Ackerman's wedding another cousin, Bernice Bingman, laughed and admitted she was the first to dip into that peach pie.

Kathy and I soon drove south on a long, circuitous drive toward New Orleans on a honeymoon that did not quite meet her standards for a relaxing Caribbean beach resort in total luxury. Our challenges continued as we returned to Illinois.

CHAPTER 17

FROM ASPIRATION TO RETALIATION

Vic deGrazia did not think I should work in state government as the new son-in-law of the Governor. Making excuses for nepotism in Chicago was not in the game plan for the new reform administration. I watched as the campaign organizers took on good roles helping out, from Tony Dean as Director of Conservation to Pat Quinn as a Governor's aide next door to Dan's office. Dan used the small office he had used as an aide to Governor Stevenson in 1948, with most of those I worked with on the campaign staff clustered around him on the second floor of the Capitol, ready to continue the fights for political reform in Illinois. Others from the campaign served as deputies to directors of the cabinet departments, reporting directly back to deGrazia if any director dared to defy any of Deputy Governor Vic deGrazia's orders.

deGrazia didn't want anyone indigenous from southern Illinois to lead the Southern Illinois Governor's office in Marion, and I learned his hand-picked leader for that slot was being shipped in from western Illinois. Kathy had applied to the new law school at Southern Illinois University in Carbondale for the first fall class. My plan to work in government temporarily to help pay her way until she completed her first year so we could then finish together was not working.

I knew that Vic deGrazia's recommendation that I not join my fellow campaign staffers working closely with the Governor in state government would prevail. I also knew that Dan Walker liked the plan for his daughter and I to pursue law school together. However, Kathy and I also worked hard and successfully on the campaign before our marriage and did not accept a complete banishment from the political victory in which we shared. Our law school plan was a good one, and we, like Einar Dyhrkopp and his slot machine raid exemption promises, had our own promises to keep.

I wanted my proposal for a Southern Illinois Governor's office to work and work well to implement reform in our region. I urged hiring Dorothy Hughes, whose husband John worked at the Ziegler No. 4 coal mine near Johnson City. Dorothy and John met Dan Walker on his walk, and Dorothy could fill her home to standing room only in her famous campaign coffees where the candidate would listen to the coal miners, looking each in the eye and shaking every hand. There was no budget to pay Steve McCurdy, still a student at Southern Illinois University, so he worked every week as a volunteer. The toll-free phone line went in, ringing off the wall. Steve McCurdy and Dorothy Hughes responded to every call. Governor Walker came down and regularly took calls, too, and met with those having plans for a better southern Illinois.

The compromise put into effect for me was that before returning to law school I would work locally in the Department of Business and Economic Development with an office across the foyer from the Southern Illinois Governor's office. I kept watch and made sure it was carrying out its mission while learning how governmental assistance to economic development actually worked. deGrazia cringed as the press reported that the governor's son-in-law was at work in state government 180 miles south of Springfield.

Meanwhile, the state police raided their first slot machine club in southern Illinois. I had informed the governor about Einar

Dyhrkopp's campaign of promises holding up Dan's signed letter. It wasn't Vic deGrazia, who told me he could take care of it, who ordered that raid, but the governor himself. Dyhrkopp was incensed and asked for a personal meeting with the governor in his Springfield office. Much like the Jerry Sinclair meeting, but in private in the governor's office in the Capitol building, the meeting ended quickly and Einar Dyhrkopp was handed his coat, ending his support of Governor Dan Walker.

Governor Dan's reception in the Illinois legislature was not warm. He brought in qualified appointees, some from out of state, not the usual political suspects. This was a major change in how things were done. Seeking merit in top cabinet positions instead of just rewarding political supporters put a new emphasis on delivering quality to the taxpayers.

Some appointees had played key political roles in the victory. Mary Lee Leahy was an excellent litigator and reformer who had worked in federal court to repeal the 23-month rule in Illinois primaries, which boosted Walker's suburban turnout of crossover voters in the 1972 primary. Before a federal court struck down this rule in Pontikes v. Kusper, 347 F. Supp. 1104 (1972), a Republican could not change and vote in the next Democratic primary. The existing law prohibited voting in the primary of one party if the voter had voted in the primary of another party within the preceding 23 months. One of the plaintiffs had voted in a Republican primary in 1971, and even those who had not would be restricted on changing primaries for 23 months into the future. Independent voters and ticket splitters were thus discouraged from their free ballot exercise, and primary turnout was depressed in an effectively closed primary system.

When Governor Walker nominated Mary Lee Leahy to head the Environmental Protection Agency, the Illinois Senate balked at the required confirmation vote, effectively clamoring to the argument that the reformer Dan Walker was being as political as anyone in his choice. She had worked constructively with other delegates in the 1970 Constitutional Convention to establish the environmental article to the Illinois Constitution, but she also had legally opposed and prevented the seating of the Daley delegates to the 1972 Democratic National Convention. Her legal work in support of independent Democratic causes, the same type of reforms Dan Walker was leading, outweighed her substantive qualifications in the Senate's eyes.

What Dan Walker's campaign had fought to change was now even more clear to his supporters, though a bit muddy to those receptive to his attackers. The merits of Dan Walker's appointments were discounted to stymie any further momentum for political reform. The battle line on fundamental reform was drawn and held. Those who supported Governor Walker became even more motivated to seek further political reform.

In southern Illinois this battle line revolved around Clyde Choate, the minority leader of the Illinois House of Representatives. From Anna, Choate was Paul Powell's successor to a leadership role in the House. He carried out the transactional politics where part of the transaction resulted in personal profit. It was well known that he was among those who, while as a legislator, voted for and led the effort to expand gambling on horse racing, lining his own hip pocket with racetrack stock whose value was enhanced while paying him substantial cash dividends.

Rumor had it, and rumor was its own version of truth in southern Illinois politics, that Choate was effective at the use of cash to whip together a voting majority when needed. He now sought to work with deGrazia and claimed to be the key counter-balance to Mayor Daley's forces in Springfield.

I saw

- illegal gambling in veterans' clubs,
- legal gambling at race tracks owned by politicians, and
- a closed political patronage system for jobs

as indicative of Choate's approach. What I didn't see is how a reform Governor could ally himself with this.

Daley controlled about a third of the Illinois General Assembly by keeping the Chicago legislators on two payrolls, one their legislative pay by the state and another paid by the city of Chicago. If a legislator dared to vote against Daley's wishes, their pay could be cut in half the next day as they quickly lost their city job.

Downstate Democrats could offset that to some extent, but Republicans held the majorities in both the House and Senate and preferred to vote with the Daley legislators to oppose the new Democratic Governor Dan Walker. These power realities in a co-equal branch of government made it difficult for a Governor of a different stripe. Political efforts already were under way to recruit more reform-minded legislative candidates who would support the Walker administration, but the 1974 election was a couple years away. It was a rocky time in Springfield. Trying to make the new Governor look bad was the favored political sport of the day.

I was dismayed that Vic deGrazia so easily bought into Choate's web of deceit instead of standing firm against it. This did not represent the Dan Walker I knew, and in any battle one is only as strong as the weakest link in the team.

Paul Powell's demise drove home and publicized the reality of Powell's corrupt money machine. It didn't just support illegal slot machines in civic and veterans' clubs and contest control of road building contracts through pay to play but ran a job-selling and intimidation network that made their closed patronage system a dominant political force. When a changing post-war economy demanded a strengthened economic force instead, why didn't the successor to its leadership respond to changing circumstances? Why did Choate's actions emphasize the crumbs of a state's economy, one large enough to place it in the top twenty economies in the world if the Illinois economy was compared to other countries?

Were jobs at the Vienna prison or Anna State Hospital more important than lifting the strength of an economy just south of the international economic powerhouse in Chicago, or the leading agricultural economy in the Corn Belt throughout downstate Illinois? Why was it not agriculture, or economic development, or the international trade infrastructure than ran through southern Illinois as the dominant political issue? How did just hundreds of patronage jobs in state institutions trump that? I thought Powell and Choate had missed the big picture with their narrow transactional and personally motivated focus. They were distracted by everyday minutiae, not focused on the big picture. Increasingly, people whose eyes had been opened by a reform Governor wanted to do something about it. The attitude of "they may be crooks, but they are our crooks," was fading.

A Johnson County Democratic leader unaligned with Clyde Choate thought he should have some say about job applicants at the Vienna prison. He advised a woman who needed a job to support her children to seek a cook's job at the prison. They didn't pay Clyde Choate the 5 percent of salary or any amount of front money, and skirted the network watching these things closely. She instead passed a state Department of Personnel test, with the agency run by Nolan Jones instead of Jerry Sinclair. To the surprise of many, she received a notice to report for work in the kitchen of the prison. Little did she know how unwelcome she would be. She just wanted honest work to support her family.

Informally in the prison she was told that there had been a mistake, and she should cease showing up for work. Her violation of the unwritten rules of patronage required that she forfeit this new job which she valued. Instead it belonged to another who had paid for it and was backed by Clyde Choate. She responded that she was willing to work hard and needed the job.

The pressure built in the prison for her to leave. It culminated as she washed dishes in the kitchen while the prisoners refused to leave their dining room tables and instead pounded their spoons on the tables chanting her name. It was such a clear threat in a world new to her that she retreated to the safety of her family home, giving up the job she needed. A loyal Choate supporter who had paid in cash for that job then took her "rightful" place in the political patronage machine, cooking at the Vienna prison.

Such people did not come forward to the press. They were afraid to chronicle intimidation to state's attorneys or law enforcement. The political culture of southern Illinois was set by long tradition, and they only whispered such stories with caution. The rumor networks were traditional, too, and they spread this truth of corruption, intimidation and money into a common understanding of how the system really worked. Defy it at your own risk was the unwritten rule, and most quietly acquiesced.

Clyde Choate was disliked by the reform-minded supporters I had worked with on the Walker campaign. They felt how deeply the corruption ran. Increasingly they also resented Vic deGrazia, whose Chicago credentials stood out in a region distrustful of Chicago's urban ways. Combined with his tendencies as a keen political manipulator, deGrazia often was seemingly at odds with the governor's reformist message, which quickly caused confusion and resentment. Sending in one of his "yes men" from elsewhere in the state to head the Southern Illinois Governor's office did not help deGrazia's standing in the south.

Steve McCurdy volunteered regularly in the Marion Governor's office to help solve citizen problems that came in over the toll-free line. One of McCurdy's college friends was from Anna, Choate's hometown, knew him from up close and greatly disliked Choate. His anti-Choate group from Union County thought some bumper stickers would help lead to change and after printing them up began their efforts to spread them around Choate's district. One of those bumper stickers was put on McCurdy's car before he drove away for his honeymoon.

Before he returned from the honeymoon, pictures of McCurdy's bumper, along with a picture of his Illinois license plate and a verification from the Secretary of State's office of the plate's owner, arrived in Deputy Governor's deGrazia's office early Monday morning.

Choate was incensed and demanded that McCurdy be removed from the governor's payroll before any legislation could be moved that week in Springfield. The Minority Leader of the Illinois House of Representatives, Choate was on strike over a bumper sticker at a wedding.

It turned out that the friend also had applied a bumper sticker to a car of a strong Walker supporter from Randolph County, Janet Wolff. An active Democrat and Frances Dyhrkopp's deputy as state central committeewoman, Wolff had attended a women's luncheon in Shawneetown hosted by Frances Dyhrkopp and attended by dozens of women from all over southern Illinois. The featured speaker at the luncheon was Clyde Choate.

Word quickly spread among the women who had seen Wolff's bumper sticker in the parking lot. Choate lost his temper and screamed at Wolff, who did not know the bumper sticker was placed on her car while at McCurdy's wedding. She responded with her honest excuse, and before the sun set, McCurdy's Democratic Precinct Committeeman in Pinckneyville, Roger Knapp, was enlisted to take a picture of McCurdy's car, which was parked while the newlyweds honeymooned. By Monday, that Polaroid photo was on deGrazia's desk, and later that morning he instructed the Southern Illinois Governor's office to fire Steve McCurdy, who had only recently been hired on a part-time state payroll after months as a free-to-the-state volunteer.

McCurdy returned from his honeymoon a few days later and took up his place in the Southern Illinois Governor's office answering the phones. Everyone was too embarrassed to tell him he had been fired by the Deputy Governor while he was away. deGrazia's office manager was hiding from this controversy while McCurdy worked away. I went across the hall and let him know the bad news. Storming out of the building waving his arms, McCurdy exclaimed they never fired him when he met Dan Walker on the walk, or distributed his primary literature across the whole county, or worked for weeks without pay to help Dan Walker carry out his reforms promised in the campaign.

I went to lunch with him to help calm him down. The lunch, of course, turned into a plan to respond. Not long thereafter, Steve came over to the place Kathy and I lived in Marion, and my sister, Donna, was down for dinner there as well. She had accepted a legislative liaison slot in Springfield working with John Filan and Roland Burris in the General Services Department.

We knew that Barbara O'Connor, a close friend of Vic deGrazia's, was in town, scouting out what was going on in southern Illinois. She drove by our house that night and reported back to deGrazia the names of everyone in attendance at our dinner.

My sister Donna was back in Springfield after her trip south and was promptly told that she, too, was fired from her job in the Walker administration. She was accused of attending an anti-Clyde Choate meeting at her brother's home in Marion.

Donna had turned down a different job offer outside state government to move to Springfield and work for Dan Walker. She retreated in tears to Pud Williams' office as Director of Agriculture at the state fairgrounds.

Aghast, Williams immediately put her on the agriculture payroll and called Vic deGrazia to inform him he had done so. deGrazia threatened his job as well, but Williams retorted that he worked for the governor, not the deputy governor. He told deGrazia that if the governor wanted

My sister, Donna, with my cousin, Tom Vaught and his wife, Faith, flanking Pud Williams

him gone as Director of Agriculture he would be happy to take his call personally.

CHAPTER 18

FROM VIC DEGRAZIA TO
THE FRONT PORCH

The governor didn't call, and Donna continued to work at the Department of Agriculture for the rest of his term. He did, however, call me about our opposition to Clyde Choate. I made clear that the alliance Vic sought with Choate was antithetical to Dan Walker's campaign and governorship. Choate was a dishonest schemer who would only degrade the governor's objectives. Someone needed to stand up to him, not ally with him.

The governor made a persuasive case that me running for the legislature, even if I could win in Choate's district, was a bad idea. He didn't see any long-term merit in it for me or Kathy, and he thought our plan to finish law school was too good a plan to delay. He knew his own campaign had already distracted me from staying in law school in New York. He told me how after graduating from the Naval Academy but deciding not to make the Navy a career, he had chosen to leave California and move to Chicago, where it was easier to rise in the legal profession by your own merit, not through family or business connections. We both were service academy graduates, liked the law and were attracted to politics. It was easy to understand each other, and it was a thoughtful, persuasive and personal call that Kathy and

I both appreciated given the controversies and complications he was facing every day.

Vic deGrazia, of course, also called and played the bully. Threats and bluster only more greatly exposed his faulty plan to work with the unreliable Clyde Choate in a way that I believed was contrary to Dan Walker's purpose and mission in state government. Like many, deGrazia was willing to accept the dirty underbelly of politics and try to work with it. I was not.

Why was I more persuaded to counter his sinister purposes than to agree with the governor's convincing positive argument in keeping with my own long-term interest? When one achieves a great victory, such as the chapel case, or contributes to a greater cause, such as in Dan Walker's reform win as governor, the flaw one should watch for with humility is arrogance. The positive momentum from winning does not automatically continue.

Nevertheless, I played the arrogant momentum card and decided to publicly challenge Clyde Choate in the 1974 Democratic primary. I could articulate clearly my criticism of Choate's leadership, and the press loved the story. "Governor's son-in-law challenges party leader Clyde Choate," made for good headlines. My anti-Clyde Choate quotes resonated, and people called and pledged to help.

The *Southern Illinoisan* reported on March 12, 1974, that I raised the ethics issue right away:

> ". . . Vaught fired the opening shot when he listed his personal income details at a press conference. Vaught also made a file of campaign contributions open to the press. He challenged the other candidates to do so—mentioning race track holdings, which Choate has listed in his Illinois disclosure form. . ."

At that time Illinois was still stuck with a century-old system of electing three members from each representative district. Choate was famous, a Medal of Honor winner from World War II, a former acolyte for the powerful Paul Powell, and a 25-year incumbent with a patronage army who knew his district like the back of his hand. Under that system, he could seek bullet votes, so when his supporters voted only for him, that counted as three votes. The second Democratic representative in the district came from the largest of the 12 counties. Dick Hart was a coal industry lawyer and their internal lobbyist in the legislature. His conflict of interest was virtually his campaign slogan because he was standing up for southern Illinois coal mining. His largest county in the district gave their bullet votes to him. The primary would nominate two Democratic candidates for the fall ballot, where three of four from the two parties in the general election race would then be elected.

My only strategy against this stacked deck was to campaign hard, outwork them, and hope the new blood of a reform that sought to work closely with the new governor for the good of southern Illinois would bring change. I was 25 years old and jumping in as an amateur into my first race for political office. Bob Ellis, the editor of the *West Frankfort Daily American*, later told me that when he interviewed me about my campaign, he had never seen such an arrogant approach to seeking political office. I had not yet fully absorbed that in order to be accepted by enough voters a good campaign required much listening, compassion, excellent communication skills and a common purpose.

Dan Walker did not give up on me, though. He respected those who stood up to power, as he had done. He called and told me he didn't like what I was doing, but since it had become real, he needed a plan to work it to his advantage. He told me deGrazia would be calling with that plan.

Still angry at me, deGrazia said he could bail me out of my predicament. He would set this up as a test for Clyde Choate. If Choate wanted to have a working relationship with the governor as a future Speaker of the House he would have to use his political skill to work together. Choate could direct enough of his bullet votes to me so that the two of us would win, leaving Dick Hart to come in third. When a voter cast two votes in the primary for his favorite two candidates, each of them got one and a half votes in the cumulative voting system. So instead of Choate running his bullet vote way up like he usually did, deGrazia believed he could split enough votes with me to prove his reliability and working relationship with the new governor.

deGrazia made it clear to me that I was not to continue my criticism of Clyde Choate in the campaign, because my winning the election depended on him and the arrangement deGrazia was putting into place. He told me I might as well get used to it because if I won I would only be a back bencher anyway. No one would listen to me in Springfield. I would still have to work with Speaker Choate and his ally in the governor's office, Vic deGrazia. His message was to shut up and get with it if I wanted the governor's support in the campaign.[72]

Dan Walker told me he would come down and campaign for me after he had convinced deGrazia to calm down about my rebellious streak. Instead they would use it to test Choate. If deGrazia thought Choate could be a good ally, let him prove himself.

Steve McCurdy showed up at my house in the morning darkness day after day during the winter of 1974, ready to drive me to campaign and shake hands at coal mines, factory gates and in cafes and small towns all over southern Illinois. We drove and we talked and called on the phone. We wanted to win on our own by working it hard. We raised all the money we could while visiting Mound City, Metropolis, West Frankfort, Herrin and towns all over the 12 counties of the district. We went to Springfield and cut TV and radio ads and spent every dime we raised running them at the stations in adjoining states that covered southern Illinois. We went down in deep coal mine shafts with miners, walked precincts, went to party meetings in townships and counties, and campaigned all over the district. We worked and traveled every day rallying hundreds of volunteers who joined the campaign. The governor came down and campaigned with us, urging change in the Illinois legislature that was blocking his leadership. It was fun and positive. We met thousands of people, and it was a huge learning exercise.

We carried two of the 12 counties over Clyde Choate and most of the rest against Dick Hart. But Hart ran up his bullet vote in Franklin County, and Choate did the same with his bullets, openly defying deGrazia's prescription for working with the new governor's candidate for a victory. I was not surprised Choate remained his slippery self, but I was disappointed we couldn't overcome it.

Choate won this battle in a longer war for reform, just as he had temporarily won the battle deposing Steve McCurdy from the governor's payroll. He didn't yet know that we had set him up for a larger strategic loss that would end his leadership in the Illinois House.

CHAPTER 19

FROM LAW SCHOOL TO THE VICTORY OVER CLYDE CHOATE

I headed back for law school as Kathy was finishing her first year at Southern Illinois University at Carbondale. The law school was brand new and the second public law school in Illinois. Dean Hiram Lesar and Associate Dean Tom Roady saw it as an opportunity to recruit an excellent faculty. They built fresh the kind of law school that has served our region and the state of Illinois well. It was smaller and more personal than New York University School of Law, and I liked it better.

It was Kathy who really liked and worked hard at law school, and we were one of only a few married couples going to law school simultaneously. Governor Walker came down one weekend that summer to visit at our place in Marion while we cooked hamburgers on the grill. We sat on the front porch and reminisced about the people in southern Illinois we had met on our campaigns. He liked it there and always liked to talk about farmers and coal miners and the friendly people in downstate Illinois who reminded him of his days working on his father's Depression-era tomato farm on the outskirts of San Diego.

He continued to believe I was better off having lost the election and was heading back to law school, but he thanked me for making clear that Vic deGrazia was wrong about Clyde Choate. He said he needed "honest brokers" as allies in the legislature, and Choate was too much of a schemer to ever fill that bill. He said he expected real Democratic gains after Watergate. He planned to help campaign as governor for those new candidates, and that could result in majorities he could work with in the legislature.

He knew it was unprecedented, but he intended to also publicly intervene in the internal campaign within the Illinois House of Representatives to elect a new Democratic speaker after the election in early 1975. He believed he could block Clyde Choate in the House even if Mayor Daley supported him.

He said his problem, though, was that no one would believe him. Governors never openly interfered in such an internal vote in the legislative branch of government. Daley would have his solid block of votes, and they would rally new legislators by reciting the old rules on legislative independence in electing a speaker. They would argue that the governor had no role in the choice. He needed a way to rally his own supporters, many of whom he had recruited and was backing in the election, as well as those on the fence. He had to create confidence that the weight of a determined governor could block an unacceptable candidate for speaker. Otherwise, his effort would be dismissed early on as just more folderol from a new and inexperienced governor.

He asked if I had any ideas on how to help do that. He wanted to use the personal, family affront of Choate's running up his bullet vote in the primary to the detriment of the governor's son-in-law as something other legislators would understand. They knew how the bullet voting system was manipulated, and if he could convince them Choate had crossed the line by personally insulting the Governor of his own party, then he thought he could block Choate. It was worth it to create a new more positive dynamic of legislative interaction and support. But would the legislators believe he was serious?

I told him I thought he should begin now by spreading that message early on the floor of the House. Why wait until the speaker's election in January? Each of his departments had a legislative liaison with floor privileges and could go onto the House floor to lobby in support of their department's budget or legislation.

Why not make Steve McCurdy one of those legislative liaisons? Choate had demonstrated his power by having him fired from the Southern Illinois Governor's office. Putting him back right on the floor to begin spreading the word that the governor was going to stop Clyde Choate from becoming speaker would demonstrate Governor Dan Walker's power.

It would be a clear and visible statement of his determination to stop Choate. Legislators would understand and believe that because Steve McCurdy would remind them of it daily. He would tell them how Choate got him fired, but the governor put him back to work against Choate. The governor's credibility and McCurdy's personally delivered guerilla tactics on the floor would demonstrate the strong leadership and determination it would take to stop Choate in his own bailiwick once and for all. McCurdy was called to report to work in Springfield the very next week.

The 1974 general election was successful in electing more Democrats supporting Governor Dan Walker. Harold Byers and Bill O'Daniel were both elected in southern Illinois. They joined a growing number of independent-minded legislators willing to ally with the governor to stop Clyde Choate, despite Daley's delegation remaining solid pro-Choate.

The speakership battle lasted throughout January with a deadlock that prevented the House from organizing by electing a speaker. Choate peaked at 61 of the 89 votes needed for election. John Matijevich of Lake County, Bill Redmond of DuPage County, Rolland Tipsword of Christian County, Gerald Bradley from McLean County, and Harold Washington, the future Mayor of Chicago, were among those who rallied the opponents, and Walker actively backed the Choate opposition.

In a watershed phone call Major Daley conceded to Walker that he had won this one and asked for his compromise candidate.

Governor Walker suggested Bill Redmond of DuPage County, and Daley readily agreed. Daley also commented in that phone call to Walker that he had learned that Clyde Choate was a liar, since he had misled Daley into supporting him.

This compromise set the stage for a productive working relationship among Democrats, who in 1975 controlled the House, Senate and the governor's office for the first time in three decades. Labor was able to gain improvements in unemployment compensation and worker's compensation. Mass transit gained in the Chicago suburbs with the Regional Transportation Authority and its improved funding. The working relationship of Governor Walker and Mayor Daley along with the newly strengthened downstate Democrats such as Senator Vince Demuzio, with help from the independents including Senator Bill Morris of Waukegan, Representative Mike Holewinski or Representative Harold Washington from Chicago, created a new momentum for Democratic legislative accomplishments.

This new legislative team made major changes to assist working people through improvements in unemployment compensation and workmen's compensation. Labor pushed for and received enhancements to the widow's pension for teachers, police and firemen. They made heart attacks while on duty as a police officer a cause for a disability pension. They raised the cost of living adjustment for pensions from 2 percent annually to 3 percent annually. They passed legislation to strengthen organized labor by prohibiting the use of professional strikebreakers.

For downstate farmers they created an exemption from the sales tax on farm inputs, particularly farm chemicals applied to improve the production of farm crops. In southern Illinois, where I had worked the campaign, they loaned the smallest county in the state, Pope County, $140,000 interest free to pay its bills when they came up short amid the financial pressures of recession and oil embargoes. They made reforms to the mental health code and improved services for people with disabilities in state facilities. They reformed access to mortgages and escrow policies associated with those mortgages.

They created penalties for delayed payment of insurance claims, created a right to cancel a new life insurance policy within 10 days of its sale, limited credit insurance to the total unpaid outstanding loan amounts it covered, and limited the ability of insurance companies to cancel existing fire insurance policies. None of these consumer and labor protections could have passed in a divided government without the political victories led by Governor Walker in Illinois in the 1974 elections.[73]

Governor Walker's main objective, however, was not substantive legislation. His main objective was to be a strong executive while changing priorities. He didn't see state government's purpose as servicing the patronage armies and personal conflicts of interest of politicians. He took his own name off the welcome signs at the state's borders, saying instead "The People of Illinois Welcome You." Putting people and taxpayers first was his mantra, and he was constantly challenging the wink-and-nod politics that made excuses for our crooks, just because they are our crooks. His executive order that eliminated the practice of requiring approval from your local county party chairman to take a job in state government galled those who pretended that getting your share of patronage jobs was a sign of success for your region.

He changed the priorities with management practices like zero based budgeting to create efficiencies in the administration of his state departments and the 50,000 or so employees reporting to the governor. He used the enhanced budgetary powers, including the line item and reduction vetoes of the 1970 Constitution, to hold down spending and pledging not to raise taxes.

He issued executive orders to prohibit state employees from giving him campaign contributions[74] and against pay-to-play for state contractors. His Executive Order No. 5 required retroactive disclosure of campaign contributions by suppliers and regulated businesses but was struck down by the courts as violating separation of powers. Executive Order No. 4, however, involved disclosure by employees under the Governor's control in the Constitution and created a precedent for further ethics regulation in the management of state government.

To further curtail the patronage machine hold on state government employees, Governor Walker granted collective bargaining rights to state employees through another executive order. These rights extended to teachers and when a Cook County Judge sentenced a teacher's union leader to jail for contempt in leading a strike, Walker pardoned him so that he was released from jail. It was another decade before legislation cemented this ground-breaking step to extend collective bargaining rights to Illinois public employees.

When the state's economy was threatened by the oil embargo, he focused his team of department heads on obtaining necessary fuel and the nitrogen fertilizers made from it. He insisted on a government that served people and their needs. By his leadership and victories, he cemented the shift in the political view of the state from a Cook County/Downstate focus to a more realistic view of the state's political map by thirds: one-third Chicago, another third for Cook County suburbs and collar counties, and the remaining third downstate. This gave new focus to the needs of the entire state.

By addressing the missing highway infrastructure in the national interstate highway plan for that part of western Illinois known as Forgotonia, he built an interstate highway west from Springfield to Quincy on the Missouri border. Likewise, when St. Louis built a loop around that city that didn't include Illinois, he took the steps necessary to connect the loop by getting early approval of the environmental impact statements through Frank Holten State Park, just east of East St. Louis, through which it had to pass. These were administrative and competency actions by those directors he appointed who were chosen as best qualified to do the job. His actions emphasized executive action, not legislative debate.

By 1975, the new revenue stream from the 1969 income tax and the efficiencies achieved through his successful work on the state budget was used to increase state funding for education to 48 percent of the total. His efficiency efforts throughout state government, and his use of line item and reduction vetoes, backed up this fiscal priority on education. It also implemented the education article of the new Constitution requiring the state assume the primary role of funding elementary and secondary education and eased pressures on local property taxes. He was able to increase state reimbursements to school districts for special education, especially for those who needed extraordinary services which local districts could not provide from their local resources. Existing law only provided $600 per child per year of state money for such purposes, but Walker more than tripled it to $2,000 or more per child, depending on where the additional services were performed.

Forty-eight percent of total elementary and secondary school funding in Illinois coming from state sources was the high-water mark in state history. Republican Governor Thompson later reversed this high point of state support, lowering it while he was governor to about 33 percent of the total, shifting billions of expense from the fairer state sources primarily funded by the income tax and sales tax to the less fair and more unequal property tax, crippling the efforts of schools in poorer districts throughout the state to improve their education for their children.

Unfortunately, the compromise between Walker and Daley fell apart. Some believe that Vic deGrazia purposely maneuvered to create a further confrontation with Daley in the 1976 primary. According to deGrazia's thinking, a second victory in a Daley confrontation in a primary would launch Dan Walker as a 1976 presidential candidate, making Walker, instead of Jimmy Carter, the independent reform Democrat to pick up the pieces in Washington after Watergate.

Walker huddled regularly with deGrazia, Dave Green, his numbers strategist and pollster, Norton Kay, his press secretary, and Bill Goldberg, his general counsel, to set political strategy. Kathy and I would hear about these meetings in our regular family weekend visits to the Executive Mansion in Springfield. We often flew there in the White County Flying Club Cessna, returning back to law school on Monday. Our flights were based out of the new Carmi airport, prioritized by Walker's Secretary of Transportation to replace the outdated, short and dangerous strip near the Little Wabash River. Nearly every weekend the governor flew to community events where he would march in a parade, shake hands and listen to voters. His regular "accountability sessions," a forerunner to today's political town halls, put him front and center with only a microphone to respond to any and all questions coming from the crowd. As he relaxed during weekend family dinners we were able to hear what he had learned about political communication, the use of television, face-to-face listening, and his role in leading the fight for political reforms and standing up for everyday people.

CHAPTER 20

CONCLUSION: AS THE AMERICAN DREAM IS RE-MADE

By the time the 1976 re-election campaign rolled around, Kathy and I were about to finish law school. We had moved to a rental property John McCarty had built for himself on 80 acres surrounded on three sides by the Crab Orchard National Wildlife Refuge. When he decided he could have built an even better place, he moved to the next ridge and built it, renting us his first home. We drove the 20 or so miles daily into the law school, skirting the wildlife refuge and Devil's Kitchen Lake through the beauty and peaceful surroundings of the heart of southern Illinois. It was a great beginning to our marriage and a great way to finish law school.

We also kept in touch with Walker supporters all over southern Illinois and often fielded their phone calls or visited with them on weekends. We were prepared to work southern Illinois again in Dan Walker's re-election campaign. Einar Dyhrkopp was no longer Chairman of the Southern Illinois Dan Walker for Governor Committee, but Tony Castellano and most of the original Walker supporters stayed loyal. Troy and Betty Ison helped fill the fundraising void left by his desertion from the cause.

Troy Ison thought we needed a rousing fundraiser, attuned to the culture of southern Illinois and packed with even more attendees than the largest Dyhrkopp had ever organized. He made a deal with the Oak Ridge Boys to sing at the fundraiser, and drawing a larger attendance than ever, we netted more than Dyhrkopp's $50,000 limit. The rousing and emotional singing and the political speech by Dan Walker fired up the region for his re-election.

Pat Quinn, who worked as a governor's aide throughout most of the term, also was not a political rubber stamp for Vic deGrazia, the re-election campaign manager. Instead of taking a role in the re-election campaign he broke off to lead the effort for a Constitutional amendment petition drive on legislative ethics, banning advance pay for legislators, adding mandatory prohibitions on conflict of interest voting, and eliminating the double dipping on multiple payrolls that Mayor Daley used as a compliance tool with his voting block in the General Assembly. As we prepared for more than a thousand from southern Illinois to attend our Oak Ridge Boys fundraiser, deGrazia, ever the hand of coercion, made very clear that we were not to circulate Pat Quinn's petition among those who attended that event.

Instead, at the event entrance we lined up tables where circulators and petitions were laid out ready for signatures to make sure every attendee had the opportunity to sign the Political Honesty Initiative at our successful event. A thousand more voluntary signatures for Pat Quinn's crusade resulted.

Later we told deGrazia that we were not raising the money for him to control in the re-election campaign and would not send him the $50,000+ check. Tony Castellano, Troy and Betty Ison, Kathy and I had agreed in advance to this symbolic protest against his schemes. We thought we were justified in not trusting him, despite his official leadership role approved by Governor Walker. Kathy took the irate phone call from her father and politely asked that he furnish the account information for Dave Green's TV expenditures so that our efforts could be sent directly through Green to bolster the statewide TV message statewide, not to deGrazia's organizational antics. We wired those funds to Green and patted ourselves on the back for standing up for an appropriate use of the funds we worked successfully to raise and support Dan Walker's re-election.

The re-election campaign, though, was not effective at communicating Governor Walker's successes in bolstering the education funding improvements that was such a high priority for parents raising their children in the Cook County suburbs. Mayor Daley was ready and going all out in his last hurrah to turn out his vote and take revenge for Walker's refusal to build the crosstown expressway and otherwise kowtow to Chairman Daley. Downstate and southern Illinois improved their 1972 results but the weaknesses in the suburbs were not sufficient to offset Daley's effective campaign in Chicago. In southern Illinois, Governor Dan carried more than two-thirds of the counties, indicating more permanent support for his political reforms.

I lightened my load in what would have been my last semester in law school to work as much as I could in that re-election campaign. Kathy kept her normal load and campaigned with us at night. All over southern Illinois, groups of Democratic supporters and workers would gather nightly in township buildings, union halls, bingo halls and other community buildings for "meet the candidate nights" where everyone on the ballot would have a chance to meet people and say a few words in support of their candidacy. Kathy was that spokesman for the governor's re-election night after tiring night.

Tyrone Township was in western Franklin County, the largest county in Clyde Choate's representative district and home county to Dick Hart, the other Democratic state representative, and they met on Kathy's birthday. Those two were not supporting Dan Walker for re-election. Instead, before a packed house of volunteers and loyal Democrats that night in Christopher, they gave their usual vindictive and venomous anti-Dan Walker speeches. With rancor, they listed every slight, every mistake, every policy with which they disagreed, and they had a long and insulting list. Dick Hart went even further that night and continued his tirade against Walker for over half an hour. Kathy was sitting in the front row with the other speakers. There were no kind words or respectful or polite references to her representing her father. There was only one nasty side to his speech, and it demanded revenge. I worked the back of the room with other volunteers and saw many of the people present cringe at the impolite nature of it. That was just a warmup for Choate, who took it all one step further, as he paced back and forth and raised his voice and spewed even deeper anger and resentment.

Next was Kathy's time to speak. She had lived in southern Illinois for more than three years, had adopted its university law school as her own, and personally knew nearly every Walker supporter in the room. Her "I'm one of your now," smiling and friendly approach relating personal family stories about her father was such a stark contrast to what the group had just heard. She didn't have to talk long because her refusal to respond to anger and resentment with the same said it all. As the meeting closed, nearly every woman in the room huddled with her, some near sympathetic tears responding to the emotional exchange they just witnessed. They were hugging her and apologizing for the discourtesies she just faced with politeness and composure. Clyde Choate had lost this evening's battle for votes, and Governor Dan carried Franklin County by a wide margin.

Working with these people personally, knowing that people in southern Illinois were mostly kind and friendly, was a great experience in this campaign. They knew who stood for what. It wasn't exactly deGrazia's Saul Alinsky strategy, but it spread through the political networks to the culture of southern Illinois, which continued to support the governor's re-election campaign.

We finished that evening with a surprise birthday party for Kathy. Steve McCurdy had a cake ready at a little restaurant in Sesser, but the long speeches went too long, and it was beyond their closing time. McCurdy explained what had happened, and the owner readily kept his lights on and his door open. He was polite and friendly and was honored to help the governor's daughter celebrate her birthday.

Others didn't know it yet, but she was pregnant with our first child, and the end of law school and the Dan Walker term as governor marked the end of this chapter in our lives.

A winding path of victories and losses, learning the lessons of humility despite arrogance, and making our own mistakes had taken us here. We had continued down the road to the American Dream and were ready to remake it even more in a new robust phase of raising a family and learning to independently survive and prosper in the economy of southern Illinois.

Thomas Jefferson said:

> Truth can stand by itself. Subject opinion to coercion: who will you make your inquisitors? Fallible men; men governed by bad passions, by private as well as public reasons. Notes on Virginia (1784) at 476 in Religious Freedom.

This has been a story filled with standing up to fallible men. Those stands amid controversies are part of a re-shaping of the American Dream that continues. Colonel Al Haig, in his threats and retaliation for simply asking that First Amendment rights of freedom of religion be restored to young, aspiring Army officers at West Point, ignored that we had all sworn to uphold the Constitution. Truth stood by itself and lies and coercion did not prevail against that. The American Dream was strengthened.

Those standing to defend racial discrimination in housing at Fort Bragg, whose overall mission is to protect freedom, stoked bad passions. They subjected Cornelius Cooper and other soldiers to disrespect and provoked his distraction from the truth of his inquiry into the morality of war. These, too, were also fallible men. They were Army officers steeped in a bureaucracy that made huge mistakes: pretended that body counts were valid measures of victory, believed that tactical military victories through firepower in the Vietnam War were strategic ones, and claimed that peace with honor could only be achieved by massive bombing and killing of millions of people in the highlands, jungles and rice paddies of Vietnam. The American Dream was eroded.

Clyde Choate and those who stood with him were dishonest brokers, pretending that patronage armies and their own personal and profitable corruption justified marching in lockstep with a top-down political machine. They were just as fallible, standing in the way of good government in Illinois. This has been a story of standing up to them as well. I believe the victory in defeating Clyde Choate as Speaker of the Illinois House was a victory for the American Dream. The ideals of the American Dream stand taller today as a result.

The American Dream is about those ideals, chief among them freedom of religion, from which flows freedom of thought and inquiry as well as economic freedom to build a better life grounded in those ideals. When fallible men or women, as we all are, challenge this dream with dishonesty, corruption, careerism or coercion, the miracle of the freedom in the American Dream is that others can stand against them. It is these small and cumulative victories that both protect the American Dream from disintegration and bolster it with new ideals, challenges and progress.

EPILOGUE

- A Whores' Game
- The Humility of Listening
- Efficient Markets
- Refuge

The Whores' Game

Farewell, Governor Dan

I kept listening to Governor Dan Walker. He lost the 1976 primary in Illinois because of revenge, arrogance, and his inability to deliver his message on education to crucial voters.

The revenge belonged to Mayor Richard "Boss" Daley, a political dictator who Walker had knocked off his throne four years earlier. On the second time around, Daley would suffer no surprise defeat and utilized political division as his saber.

The arrogance was enhanced by Deputy Governor and Campaign Manager Vic deGrazia, who used his narrow band of schemers to foment an unnecessary strategy. He wanted a confrontation with Daley to finally slay the Boss. Their hope was to use that victory to famously rocket Governor Walker into Presidential contention in the post-Watergate vacuum.

Walker's inability to deliver on his fiscal message was crucial in the 1976 primary vote in the Chicago suburbs. He had achieved during his term the 1970 state constitutional goal of funding elementary and secondary education primarily with state sources of revenue. By reforming the inequities of the uneven, outdated and inadequate property tax system, Walker knew this crowning achievement was his key to winning the primary. The Chicago big media refused his television advertisements of explanation, backed by a Federal Communications Commission restriction on issues ads too long before the election. Such a suppression of political speech was the key to his loss. It was also a forerunner of today's corporate control of the self-

Governor Dan Walker campaigning with me in the beginning of my challenge to Clyde Choate at a southern Illinois coal mine in 1974. This was the first step toward defeating Clyde Choate as Speaker of the Illinois House in 1975.

aggrandizing media propaganda machine that haunts us still.

Yet Governor Dan was my mentor, and I studied his every lecture, self-reproach, and *mia culpa*. Sitting with him in the Executive Mansion private family dining room, or on weekends upstairs in the Governor's quarters, or on the road after a day of campaigning, I heard so much of his pride, regret, and lament. He struggled with the gap between competence and loyalty in his appointments. He was proud of his natural ability to reach voters directly, face-to-face, listening and communicating over the top of the political commentators, reporters, TV anchors, and editors who he believed distorted his message. He studied the demographics of change, expounding on the diversity, regional differences, and motivations in the different regions and sub-cultures of Illinois. His trial attorney style of cross-examination, hypothesis, and focus could break into his relaxed and professorial style of reflection, and in those moments his wisdom shined brightly. I enjoyed this unique opportunity to witness his history during his times of triumph, and later in times of tragedy.

The gap as a lame duck between a primary defeat in March and gubernatorial succession the following January was an agonizing period for my hero. His reflection could be both enlightening and lamentable. In one of those moments he warned me pointedly about my inclination to engage in future political warfare. "Never forget, it's a whore's game," was his admonition.

He had followed and dealt against organized crime, political self-interest, greed, disloyalty, and incompetence as he rallied and led the first crusade for political reform in our state in decades. The obstructionists were strong, skilled and capable. He welcomed that challenge, but the whores were those who either blatantly or deceivingly put self-interest above their oath of office, their duty to those they represented, or basic ethical standards. Their relentlessness colored the whole enterprise, creating a necessity to both understand and seek to counter the ethical distortion of the whores as they wielded their deceitful charms. I had never heard that analogy before.[1]

Political Honesty

My experiences in southern Illinois confirmed his strong words. I thought practicing law in a small law office created the flexibility to continue working the political reform Governor Dan had launched. The first

Through all his initiative petition drives, primary and general elections, Pat Quinn liked to campaign with me in my red pickup truck.

opportunity was to work with my friend Pat Quinn on his Political Honesty Initiative petition drive. Quinn began the drive before Walker's 1976 primary campaign. He left Vic deGrazia and rowed his own boat into the political maelstrom with enthusiasm, skill and luck.

It wasn't hard to find signers to a petition that sought a vote on ending advance pay, double-dipping and conflict of interest voting in the Illinois General Assembly. Powered by many from the "Greatest Generation," thousands of grassroots people joined in circulating that petition.

This power for ordinary citizens was new to Illinois in the 1970 Constitution, though, and that left the Illinois Supreme Court to define its limits. With tortured legal reasoning about the meaning of the word "and," they found the proposed amendment stretched too far and forbid the Political Honesty Initiative access to the ballot, despite more than 600,000 valid signatures.

The silver lining was that the General Assembly itself backed down and ended advance pay under the political pressure the petition drive created. This mixed victory and defeat led to much discussion and strategizing among those of us who had joined with Pat Quinn. The status quo politicians thought this was only a clownish charade, led by a gadfly, yet dangerous demagogue, whose mob-like petition drives could possibly upset their apple cart.

We were determined to make real this new initiative power, which was limited to reforming the General Assembly. We saw it as a safety valve when the politicians failed to reform themselves, but we knew from our experiences with Governor Walker that the entrenched powers would fight back. It wouldn't be a fair fight.

A recently elected state representative's work made clearer to us that the General Assembly had no interest in reforming itself. Harold Byers would introduce bills in the Illinois House seeking simple but meaningful reforms to clean up the House's ethical lapses. He became known in whispered conversations on the House floor, and as the whispering grew louder on third reading for a floor vote, other legislators heard the chant: "Bad Bill Byers, Bad Bill Byers!" His bills were chanted down by the other legislators as the green buttons on the board indicating a yes vote turned to red as the chants grew in volume. Byers, a book salesman to schools by trade, elected to his first public office as a state representative in the 1974 post-Watergate elections, had a saying about it: "I never met anyone under indictment before I was elected to the legislature, but then I met many among my seatmates, both indicted and convicted for corruption."

Many other legislators lobbied internally, and legally, for their own private sector employers, or for companies they owned a stake in, in both apparent and real conflicts of interest. Others served on two payrolls, one paid in advance on their first day in office as a legislator, and a second patronage job in Cook County. If they voted the wrong way when Boss Daley directed them, then the next day their pay would be cut in half as they lost their patronage job in Chicago. Others required a sort of toll payment, with their hand held behind their back seeking campaign money for a vote. If the lobbyists or favor seekers didn't pay the toll, their legislation didn't pass.

The corruption, for the gambling thugs, or real estate cartels renting property to the state, or the regulated utilities seeking to bypass a more uniform and open rate regulation by the Illinois Commerce Commission, was creative in its ways to manipulate and win in its own self-interest. The voters' tools, on the other hand, were too weak in application to completely change the political paradigm. Voters knew it, lamented about it, were ashamed of it, and yearned for a chance to rein it in.

Some of those motivations had led to a vote for the Governor who walked the state, listening as he walked for 1,197 miles in the summer months of 1971. Those voters then witnessed the obstruction and opposition to the changes he sought, and they were disillusioned when many of his reforms were politically impossible to carry out. Pat Quinn's petition drive captured this frustration with the hope for a direct tool of change, but the Illinois Supreme Court, an elected body partly political and partly legal, put the knife to that hope.

Pat Quinn and his more than 10,000 petition passers were not deterred, their energy and potential power apparent. In 1978, Governor Jim Thompson sought to capture that spirit of reform and bottle it into an advisory referendum on limiting taxes that was fueled after California voters in their Proposition 13 limited property taxes in their state. The petition drive Thompson led also garnered more than 600,000 signatures, but the staying power of advisory votes was limited.

Pat Quinn and I exchanged drafts of potential new petition drives and considered the widespread frustration with property taxes, utility rates and pay raises for elected officials. We looked in more depth at the history and constitutional intent of the 1970 Constitutional Convention and its statewide ratification vote.

There we found the footprints of Sam Witwer, a Republican attorney from Chicago who had been elected President of the 1970 Illinois Constitutional Convention. Witwer's book on his reminiscences of the convention laid out the history that led to its many compromises, including the limited initiative power in the proposed constitution.[2] It was not a general initiative, like those in effect in 26 states, including Missouri, Michigan, and Ohio in the Midwest. Instead, it was a compromise to allow only changes in structural and procedural subjects in Article IV, which concerns the General Assembly.

Early in the deliberations of the 1970 Illinois Constitutional Convention, the Chicago Democratic delegates brought up a minority committee report on cumulative voting in multi-member districts. This cumbersome device had been included in the 1870 Constitution intending to make sure both parties were spread geographically throughout the state after the Civil War. In practice, it had become a status quo tool of political deception and control, which most politicians did not want to lose.

Faced with this floor action on first reading, however, the convention turned away this effort to preserve multi-member districts, and by a floor vote, single member districts made it into the initial draft of the proposed constitution. Witwer's diary commented that Chicago politicians wanted to retain cumulative voting "because this gave to the Machine complete control over who that third person would be . . . that person would be a weak Republican under the domination of the Democratic organization."[3]

Witwer, as convention president, recognized that losing cumulative voting "could be disastrous for them and they cannot stand it."[4] He recognized that the convention would have to reverse single member districts for the new constitution to be approved by voters in the ratification referendum. Delegate Thomas G. Lyons, leading the Chicago Democratic delegates, said "he wouldn't buy any 'single-member' districts."[5]

Eventually the downstate Republican delegates suggested a separate ratification vote on cumulative voting or single member districts in the approval referendum by voters.

Elsewhere in the deliberations, a complete initiative power as a means of amending the constitution after its enactment was only included in a minority report. This idea surfaced later in Article XIV, Section 3, which provided for only a limited initiative power concerning only structural and procedural subjects in the Legislative Article.

Sam Witwer had a specific change in mind for the delegates who preferred single member districts. If they could not prevail in the separate question on initial ratification, they could later use the legislative initiative in Article XIV to seek its adoption by petition and referendum by the voters.

Despite the opposition by the Chicago Democrats, Witwer saw the need to change the cumbersome multi-member district system of electing the Illinois House. In the system then in effect, two candidates from each of the two major parties ran in the general election for three seats, and the voter could cast their three votes for one, two, or all three candidates, dividing their three votes among them. Only one of the four candidates would lose the election, guaranteeing that at least one representative was elected from each party in each multi-member district.

Eliminating the confusion of cumulative voting, in which each voter could assign their three votes to one, two or three candidates on the ballot, would lead to replacing it with a simpler single member district system. Each voter would then cast one vote to elect a single representative for their single member district. Witwer joined the effort to use the constitutional initiative in 1974 to put a single member district draft amendment on the ballot, but it failed to garner enough signatures.

Witwer's 1974 draft, though, was solid. Drawn up and supported by the President Witwer of the Constitutional Convention, a respected Republican attorney, its drafting was aimed directly through the initiative compromise from the constitutional convention. Would the Illinois Supreme Court find that more difficult to strike from the ballot? Quinn thought blocking it from the voters would be tougher for the court, if enough valid signatures could be gathered.

That assumed a fair fight after the long, difficult process of gathering hundreds of thousands of signatures from voters all over the state. Would the 10,000 petition passers, who were discouraged that their prior 1976 effort in the Political Honesty Initiative was quashed, put in the work to gather that many signatures once again? It appeared so in 1980, but as soon as the petition drive was gathering steam and 100,000 signatures had been gathered, the General Assembly decided to play dirty.

This proposed amendment, known as the Cutback Amendment, ended multi-member districts, and in doing so reduced the number of members of the House from 177 to 118. Facing voter anger over legislative pay raises, 59 elected officials would be retired from the Illinois House if this amendment passed.

The Illinois General Assembly passed a retroactive law changing the rules of petition passing to make it harder to do. In a completely new rule, they required the petition circulator who solicited and witnessed the signatures to be from the same county as the signers on the circulator's petition.

If that petition passer was working in a mall, like I did at St. Clair Square in Fairview Heights, then the customers at that mall drove in from many counties. With the new rules requiring the petition passer to be a registered voter in the same county as the petition signers, the ability to collect valid signatures was thwarted. If the shoppers came there from 10 counties, 10 petition passers from those counties would have to be present to collect all the possible signatures without mixing them up on a petition page circulated by someone from a different county.

This retroactive law sought to apply its new restrictions to the 100,000 signatures already gathered. Compliance with such a standard before anyone knew the new rules, especially before the new rules were even passed, would be most difficult. Fortunately, the Illinois Supreme Court validated sufficient signatures to allow the Cutback Amendment on the ballot, and it was approved by the voters by a large margin in the general election in 1980.

It was also important that this new rule not discourage the use of the constitutional initiative in the future. In a federal court challenge where I joined as a plaintiff, the Federal District Court for the Northern District of Illinois found these unduly restrictive petition laws a violation of the First Amendment to the U. S. Constitution. The court upheld the right to freely associate with others in petitioning for a redress of grievances. In Coalition for Political Honesty v. Illinois State Bd. of Elections, No. 81 C 2718, 1982 U.S. Dist. LEXIS 12411 at 7 (N.D. Ill. Apr. 23, 1982), that right was upheld.

Citing a West Virginia case that struck down similar "magisterial district restrictions," Federal District Judge George N. Leighton found the Illinois restrictions even worse because they also added a requirement to "investigate circulators they encounter to determine that they share the same residence if they wish their signatures to be valid."[6] This created a substantial burden on the petition process without a compelling reason. His order declared this single jurisdiction requirement unconstitutional.

This threw cold water on any subsequent dirty tricks by the General Assembly to restrain petition passing under Article XIV, but two subsequent petition drives, a broadening of the initiative power in 1982 and a term limits constitutional amendment in 1994, were not allowed on the ballot for voter approval despite gathering the required signatures. The narrow definition of both structural and procedural subjects remained an obstacle to using the safety valve delegates to the 1970 Constitutional Convention adopted after their debates and reports.

Is the freedom of association, free speech, and the right to petition government for a redress of grievances essential to the American Dream? Can a system based on the value of self-government adjust and reform if its citizens are denied such a fundamental right?

Is the answer to these questions dependent on how much the American Dream is dependent on broadly held values that citizens can assert, defend, and live by? Do they wish to see those values reflected in their government, implementing the principles of self-government articulated in the Declaration of Independence and the Constitution?

Is the American Dream only about material advancement in the economy? Can top-down directed large businesses and institutions simply achieve enough material welfare for citizens by making the economy grow and prosper? If so, and the American Dream is that narrow, then I think not.

On the other hand, if self-government is a valued part of the American Dream, then grassroots citizens can stand solidly for that value. They will need to work at it, believe in it, and shove aside the dirty tricks set up as obstacles in their way. In the end, though, the cumulative effect of individual assertion of those values advances, matures and reflects those values. The hope for the ever-growing advancement of those commonly held values becomes self-sustaining.

An initiative power was not included in the U. S. Constitution adopted late in the 18th century, nor in the state constitutions throughout the United States at that time. It came more than a hundred years later as citizens asserted their own rights to control their state governments. Those who stood up and demanded and achieved this right were leading fundamental change. Their improvement on the American Dream extended the power of self-government to the ballot box in about half our states.

Not long after other states adopted initiatives, an Illinois proposed initiative amendment in 1919 failed by one vote in the Illinois General Assembly, despite support from Illinois Governor Frank Lowden. Illinois waited instead until the 1970 Constitutional Convention for a limited safety valve to change the General Assembly by initiative, since it quite obviously was unlikely to adequately reform itself.

With the Cutback Amendment this limited change became real. The Illinois Supreme Court finally approved the use of this constitutional initiative after thousands of petition passers gathered signatures, and hundreds of thousands signed the petition. The voters provided the required 60% approval at the ballot box in 1980.

Since the adoption of the first state initiative powers around the beginning of the 20th century, initiatives in other states have addressed many subjects, including civil rights, abortion, capital punishment, nuclear power, tax policies, handgun control, the environment and bilingual education.

Citizens have passed initiatives to directly limit campaign finance contributions and expenditures of candidates as well as to require public financing of candidates. They have altered the institutions of representative government by approving term limits on elected officials and requiring a supermajority of the legislature to raise taxes. State ballot initiatives have been used to adopt conservative policies, such as tax limitations, as well as liberal policies, such as legalization of medical marijuana. Some have addressed governance policies, including provisions for direct democracy, direct election of

U. S. senators, direct primaries, home rule for municipalities, secret ballot, women's suffrage, nonpartisan primaries, voting by mail and legislative redistricting.

These initiative petition drives and campaigns raise a debate, and often a decision, on the application of values to our political system. They seek to improve on a political status quo too often driven by self-interest, deception and manipulation. How the power of initiative will continue or decline in importance will be one of the factors in the gradual re-making of the American Dream, for better or for worse.

The Humility of Listening

The Clash of Fiscal Stability

It is quite apparent today that voters' desire for government spending does not match their willingness to pay for it in taxes. I experienced this dilemma personally as an elected school board member when I saw the need for more revenues in my children's school.

I experienced it even more directly through my long-term friendship and work with Pat Quinn, who was serving as an elected Lieutenant Governor of Illinois in the crucial year of 2008. When I moved from downstate to Naperville in 1990, then newly elected Treasurer Pat Quinn asked me to help him manage the Treasurer's Office. I signed up and spent four years helping improve the investment of state funds. Treasurer Quinn also took steps to make those investments do double duty in helping taxpayers also achieve economic growth, efficiency in financing Illinois agriculture, and improved affordable housing. This experience convinced me that a political leader could apply the values of the American Dream to produce real positive results.

Pat Quinn was willing to repeatedly take on difficult political campaigns, some of which he won for higher office. After a couple losses, I remember talking to him on the phone about the merits of running for Lieutenant Governor. He did and lost again in the 1998 primary.

In 2002, Quinn won without the support of the winning candidate for Governor since the Lieutenant Governor was nominated in a separate primary election but then matched on the ballot with the Governor only in the general election. Pat Quinn became the Lieutenant Governor with Governor Rod Blagojevich, whether Governor Blagojevich liked it or not.

He didn't. That didn't discourage Lieutenant Governor Quinn. He worked every day, just as I had seen him do as Treasurer, to accomplish something for all the people of the state, especially those who worked from paycheck to paycheck. I worked for him on a part-time contract early in his Lieutenant Governor's term. When it was becoming clear that Governor Blagojevich might not be allowed to finish his full second term, I applied and was hired to work as a Deputy Director of the Illinois Department of Central Management Services. There I learned a great deal about the day-to-day operations of state government.

The Non-Transition Transition to Governor Quinn

In late 2008, Lieutenant Governor Quinn called wanting to get together for lunch. We talked about the possibility, growing more likely, that the Governor would be either convicted of taking bribes or impeached by the General Assembly.

In that scenario, how does a Lieutenant Governor prepare to assume the duties of Governor after the incumbent Governor is removed from office? Not only that, but how does that occur without a normal transition that lasts a couple months after an election, where the new office holder and the retiring office holder collaborate on that transfer of power. During an impeachment of a Governor, or a federal criminal conviction, that kind of transition simply does not happen.

I agreed to help and was ready on January 29, 2009, when the Illinois Senate voted unanimously to remove Governor Blagojevich from office.

Late that afternoon, an hour or so after that Senate vote, Lieutenant Governor Quinn was sworn in as Governor. The group of us joining to help him walked with him from the House chamber to the Governor's Office in the Capitol, where the aides for the former Governor were awaiting their fate, wondering if they would be off the payroll the following day. Governor Quinn sent word to them to return to work in the morning, when he would address the next steps.

We then walked to the Executive Mansion for dinner. Having never seen the Governor's quarters, and knowing my knowledge of the quarters having been there many times during the Governor Walker term in office, Governor Quinn asked me for a tour.

This kind of tentative beginning, simply responding to the immediate issue at hand, marked a non-transition transition. It was hardly sufficient to prepare for an office of overwhelming and near impossible challenges as Governor of a major state. The non-transition was quickly over as the Governor's budget speech was due to a joint session of the General Assembly a matter of days after his swearing in. The draft budget had been prepared through months of work by the former Governor's staff. There was little time to change it, and the General Assembly viewed it with disdain and distrust.

A triple crisis was underway. The economy was in the midst of the Great Recession with revenues dropping off precipitously and somewhat unpredictably. At the same time, automatic spending mechanisms designed to counter a recession increased outlays.

Former Republican Governor George Ryan was in prison and former Governor Blagojevich was headed that way. The corrupt misconduct of two consecutive Governors had distracted them from minding the store, and the problems of a structural fiscal deficit had ballooned.

The corruption of a pay-to-play mentality, combined with smoke-and-mirrors budgeting, had created an ethical crisis that fostered distrust and confusion. How does a new Governor, with a new staff and a weaker political mandate as a caretaker Governor, deal with compounding and accelerating fiscal problems?

Since the General Assembly had no confidence in the budgetary numbers presented in the Governor's budget speech, what should be the beginning point on finalizing an annual budget during the spring legislative session? If there was no trust in the accuracy or validity of the Governor's budget numbers, how would working through the appropriations process over the following few weeks and months result in a real budget for the next fiscal year that could create stability in the midst of the Great Recession?

Governor Quinn asked me, and other members of his staff, to work with the former Governor's budgetary staff to remedy this cascading crisis and growing fiscal instability. As we undertook this difficult task, Jerry Stermer, Governor's Quinn's chief of staff reminded us: "This is the big leagues, and here they throw at your head." The mood for collaboration and solving problems was not good.

The Dysfunctional 50% Budget

Many legislators were not inclined to engage in a process they no longer trusted. The give and take, debate and lobbying, and final resolution could not proceed effectively if no one believed the numbers being discussed. Such credibility was necessary to any successful discussion or negotiation. The absence of credibility was real and endemic. The smell of corruption and stench remained in the smoky halls of the Illinois Capitol.

The General Assembly disregarded the Governor's budget numbers. They polled their members, surveyed their caucus, and funded their top five priorities 100%.

That left about $10 billion of the prior year spending priorities unfunded. They appropriated those low priority items without much further consideration at 50% of the prior year. Nearly $5 billion of the normally expected spending was out the window.

When the word of this final action in the legislative session reached those who were funded at 50%, the phones in the Governor's Office were ringing off the hook. How could groups normally receiving grants for social safety net spending, for probation officers in our court system, and many other grant areas, operate on only 50% of last year's spending? Neither had anyone seen any legitimate or reassuring process arrive at such an incomplete and distasteful result.

The Governor quickly vetoed what was called the 50% budget. With no budget approved, no one gets funded. A total government shutdown loomed on July 1, 2009. Local governments, non-profit grantees, entire departments of state government, social safety net spending, law enforcement, education, and all the other priorities of Illinois' government were kaput.

The veto was not a solution, but it was a sure-fire way to get the leaders and members of the General Assembly to talk to the Governor about how to reach a real solution.

Governor Quinn liked to invite key members of his staff to dinner in the Executive Mansion. As the Sun went down we gathered with the Governor in the well-appointed family dining room for a great meal prepared by the mansion chef and his staff. This more private dining room was downstairs next to the commercial type kitchen used to serve much larger numbers at parties and receptions held upstairs in the more ceremonial and ornate part of the mansion. The discussion, though, was anything but nice and fun, and extended into the late evening hours. The conversation was serious, harsh, difficult, frustrating, excruciating and long.

Who could recommend to the Governor a solution to this budgetary dilemma? He sat with us for hours listening and asking for help in finding an answer. There was plenty of hemming and hawing and much talk, but the discussion was going nowhere. There were no immediate answers, and the meeting could not be continued to next month, next week, or tomorrow. There had to be a plan now. The pressure was immediate, and it was palpable in our moods.

I found it easier to let the mind wander and pretend I was not even there. I remember thinking that I had learned to do math in my head while working in the hot Sun on the farm in Burnt Prairie. Sitting in the Executive Mansion family dining room, I found an envelope and on the back of it wrote out ten minus five equals five, the size in billions of the deficit under the flawed, but vetoed, budget. With state revenues going down every day in the worst recession since the Great Depression, what could fill the increasing $5 billion deficit?

There had to be a bridge to fiscal recovery of the economy, and the most functional bridge could only be medium-term borrowing, to be repaid in a few years when the economy recovered. But with the state's bond rating diving toward the bottom, how could this be done? How would the required 60% of the General Assembly ever vote to approve it?

Doing math in my head, an idea slowly became less a daydream as the key numbers I knew from working on the budget draft jarred me from this inattention. The vetoed budget fully funded the actuarially required pension payment. No one wanted to compound the state's rating agency problems or ability to issue state bonds by not funding the pension.

Putting these two seemingly unrelated elements together, the pension funding requirement and the medium-term bridge loan concept, suddenly created a doorway to a solution. It simply popped into my mind like waking up from a bad dream. I began to join the talk at the table.

If we could borrow the approximately $3.5 billion dollars required to fully fund the pension and pay those borrowed funds into the pension, then the pensions were still fully funded. That freed the funds from existing revenues that the flawed budget had planned to spend on the pension to fill the budget hole.

The 50% budget quickly became more like an 80% budget, which was not nearly as dire. It could create a modicum of fiscal stability on the way out of the Great Recession. The numbers didn't completely add up, but daydreaming about math had put an alternative on the dinner table in the mansion.

With lots of follow-up work, this idea came to pass, and in effect, led to me becoming the next official Director of the Office of Management and Budget for Governor Quinn. I worked on four difficult budgets during his term as Governor.

This seed of an idea was only possible if a key value of the American Dream was in place. It takes a dream based in values to survive a crisis atmosphere of a state spiraling into disarray. That primary value was teamwork, learned through generations of building a new country on the North American continent despite recurrent crises. It was passed on by families in their individual struggles and was demonstrated year-after-year on the fields of friendly strife on our sports teams. In many ways, we already knew how to do this.

The dream was fueled even more by a Governor courageous enough to veto a bad idea and by a Governor immediately ready go back to its authors to develop something better. Such leadership, armed with a new idea of how to do it, began to take hold.

The initial idea drew wide support because no one wanted to strip funding of the pension and do further harm to the state's bond rating while utilizing large capital borrowings to carry out an infrastructure program that created real jobs in the recession. This led to working out a repayment schedule to repay that new debt from future general revenues over a short number of years, leaving all the pension funding intact.

With help from the Chicago financial community and their Republican friends in the General Assembly, details were crafted and votes assured to approve the plan. Bond underwriters in Chicago and New York helped sell the bonds despite bad bond ratings. They achieved a workable interest rate and repayment schedule the state could pay.

Teamwork made it come together. We lobbied hard to get 60% approval in the General Assembly, negotiated with the legislative leaders and appropriation chairs on how to spend the extra funds, and created the credibility and momentum that had been absent. Governor Quinn began to become not a caretaker, but a respected Governor. He would become known as a man to work through a problem despite its difficulty or political downsides.

These established values of the American Dream enabled taking on the confusion of conflicting priorities, political constraints, and the distrust of presumably false numbers. They built a stable base where we could address the remaining longer-term difficult issues on the road forward.

The bond authorization passed, the bonds were sold at reasonable, low and single-digit interest rates to be paid back in only four years, and the spending holes at least partially filled. The budget impasse was solved in a matter of weeks, not months. We were ready for the next set of looming problems.

Tax Increases or Draconian Cuts

As we approached the next budget year, the state operating budget remained greatly out of whack. The pension borrowing technique would need to be used a second year in a row while we struggled with the longer-term solutions in an election year.

Facing two difficult elections, both the primary and the general in 2010, Governor Quinn asked me to become the permanent Director of the Governor's Office of Management and Budget

(GOMB), a position requiring more than just the spreadsheets and planning of an annual budget. It was also weighted down with the responsibility for issuing and seeing to the sale of state bonds and the implementation of budgetary plans to reduce spending with agencies constantly on the lookout for ways to do more, spend more, and appeal to every possible ally for more money. The job required saying no over and over to the lobbyists and political interests who supported excessive spending, a very unpopular and draining undertaking. I both supported the Governor's policy goals and recommended difficult choices for budget cuts to keep the ship afloat.

Governor Quinn was very specific in his instructions: "You must communicate to everyone, the legislators, the interest groups and the general public, because they don't fully understand the budget." He was seeking not just communication, but honesty in building the credibility necessary to forge consensus.

I immediately asked for Kelly Kraft to help me, since the Governor had hired her to join his press team of mostly print reporters. A talented and perceptive television anchor, I needed her as a member of a team willing to forge strong alternatives and defend them. I asked Malcolm Weems, who had worked well in the prior administration in Central Management Services, to join me as my Chief of Staff. I recruited Emily Monk, knowing her skills from her prior work at my investment firm. Sheila Henretta, with substantial financial experience at Jones Day, was hired as our General Counsel. John Sinsheimer, who had proved his worth in the bond market while working at the Illinois Student Assistance Commission, also was hired. This core group, plus many others in the budget office, were indispensable to facing the daily challenges of saying no to the big spenders, yes to the Governor's priorities, and listening to the legislative staff, leaders and appropriations chairs on how to get this done.

The elephant in the room was what to do about raising taxes, while we whittled away to reduce spending based on robust analysis and real cuts to the bone on the lower spending priorities.

How do you raise taxes in an election year when the incumbent Governor, who stepped up after an impeachment, must face the voters? Governor Quinn did not duck this question and made clear a tax increase was going to be required.

What was not answered was how much? Some political advisors to the Governor cautioned him not to shoot himself in the foot by asking for too much. Many had an alternative small number, but I knew that wouldn't work. A leader cannot promise an unpopular tax increase as a solution only to not solve the fiscal problem.

As we worked through the budgetary scenarios in GOMB, I saw an ongoing imbalance in the operating budget. The revenues were perpetually less than the spending, plus longer-term the spending was growing faster than the revenues.

Already the number of state employees had been reduced by the prior administration by more than 10,000. The Department of Corrections could not replace its attrition and its mandatory and expensive overtime was ballooning. The Illinois State Police were having difficulty filling their patrols on the interstate, and no one wanted to witness accidents or attempted crimes in the middle of the night with no state police officer available to respond. State parks were being closed. Education was floundering under increased property taxes and tuition payments. Some saw a looming nightmare if we were going to face a complete permanent closure of one of our state public universities for lack of funds. Token cuts were not going to do it, and the cuts of fat, muscle and bone were already taking their toll on services, the social safety net and public safety.

I was obligated by the Governor's explicit instructions to explain this and build credibility about the numbers. To communicate with the public in a state as large as Illinois, one of the top five in population in the country, required working with the press. Many asked good questions. Some disagreed editorially with what we were doing. Others seemed to play a "gotcha" game to create snappy headlines. We needed the press as allies to explain and let our message get through in a straightforward way. We also needed them for feedback when we made mistakes or were losing our way. The role of the press is challenging, necessary, and a part of the open approach to involving our citizens in public decisions.

Bloomberg News was expanding its operations, with greater attention to the problems of state government in the Great Recession. They requested a detailed interview in my office with a small contingent of their reporters. As was common, they brought a small television camera with them and set it on our conference room table to record the entire meeting.

Much of the discussion in the press was about our accumulated unpaid bills and how many years of unbalanced budgets had resulted in a large accumulated deficit. Bloomberg's main question was different and simple: how much is the annual operating deficit in Illinois government? I told them approximately $6 billion a year. That's a huge number, and it begins with a B, not an M.

Then came the follow-up question: "How much of an increase in the state income tax would it take to balance that annual deficit?"

I have seen plenty of public officials duck, change the subject, filibuster and simply not answer a question like that. I would not do that, so I fairly quickly answered: "2%."

Bingo. They had their story. It was all over the front pages of every newspaper I saw the next day. The TV had the story, and they played it up by seeking to attribute my statement to Governor Quinn. After all, the Director of GOMB works only for the Governor and is a hand-picked member of his senior staff. Why would I say something the Governor had not authorized?

Those were not follow-up questions. They were simply in the news stories. Emily Monk entered my office and suggested I get my head down because an entire cohort of political advisors were upstairs in the Governor's Office. Some suggested that I be fired immediately. Why was I speaking where it was only the Governor's prerogative to go?

My phone went silent. Others working for the Governor remained mute. I didn't know what would happen next, and the

Governor had to explain his position time and time again. Governor Quinn didn't call, but at a Saturday meeting in Springfield he walked into a room, not expecting to see me there. Most eyes in the room froze and followed us closely as he suggested we step into a side room for a private chat.

I didn't know what he would say, but soon recognized it was the Pat Quinn I had known for years. Speaking to me calmly, he let me know this would be OK, but that we should keep quiet about it for a while. I sensed he thought airing this question in the press would probably help us long-term in getting the income tax passed, but I would have to cool it for a while. I also knew he was the one who had to ride the big waves in the storms, not me. The least I could do to support the Governor was to keep my mouth shut for a while.

Governor Quinn asked me to serve as his Director of the Governor's Office of Management and Budget, not just to work up the numbers but more importantly to communicate honestly about the budget. Candor was required to make the case, but controversy often followed as we faced the need to raise taxes to address the fiscal crisis in Illinois.

As the plan for passing a large increase in the income tax evolved, it became clear that it could only happen when the votes could come from the General Assembly after the 2010 election. Voters don't like lame duck tax increases, but it was not Governor Quinn who was ducking. The legislators were afraid to expose a tough vote just before voters could send them home.

As December progressed, Emily Monk, Malcolm Weems and others worked up the budget numbers with current data and turned it into one-page budgetary projection spreadsheets we could discuss with the Democratic legislative leaders. No Republicans were even close to supporting this idea. Getting every necessary Democratic vote in the House and Senate was crucial or the tax increase would not pass.

Those meetings followed a common agenda by practice. The Governor would welcome Speaker of the House Mike Madigan and Senate President John Cullerton into his large, ceremonial office where oil paintings of Abraham Lincoln were prominently displayed on the wall. They would all sit around the large conference table, usually joined by Jack Lavin, Jerry Stermer and I. The Governor would call on each of us to introduce a topic advocating his views on it. In the income tax meetings, the legislative leaders brought their budgetary or other key staff members, who joined in a ring of chairs around the table.

After a few questions from our staff presentations, the meeting would move into direct back-and-forth conversations between the Governor and the legislative leaders about what the precise content of the proposed bill would be and how it would affect future budgets. I answered as many questions as I could and often went back to prepare more specific answers for the next meeting. The legislative staff members also asked some questions or expressed reservations about our approach.

The meetings continued through December. As the holidays approached, some of the meetings moved to the phone but always with a need for a revised and updated spreadsheet. Emily Monk named her spreadsheet drafts, going through the normal lettered spreadsheets until she ran out of letters. She then creatively went to names of precious metals, or colors, or other names so we could go back to discuss earlier alternatives and try to keep the discussion and the agreements on the final numbers straight.

It became clear that some legislators wanted other provisions added, such as spending limits, to make sure fiscal balance, not great increases in spending, was the goal. The numbers troubled some because $6 or $7 billion is a lot of money, and its impact on families, businesses, and the state's economy were combined with specific concerns about its impact in their legislative districts.

As January began, Governor Quinn was sworn into his new full term and we celebrated at the Inaugural Ball and after parties. The lame duck General Assembly was still in session, with just a few days before their terms expired and a new group of legislators took office.

Throughout the inauguration and celebratory events, the budgetary discussions and legislation drafts continued, were reviewed, discussed and revised. During the celebrations, I was summoned to meet with Speaker Madigan in the Capitol. Some spending limits were being added to the tax increase draft, but the Speaker wanted certainty on the numbers in those limits. He understood the numbers, but he wanted my hard and fast commitment that the final number was both acceptable and workable. After a brief discussion, he put me right on the spot with those in attendance, asking me for a final number., Then, like an auctioneer, he stared down at me saying, "Going once, going twice, sold as the final number in the bill draft."

We were all committed to the draft and turned our undivided attention to making sure we could get 60 votes in the House before sending the bill to the Senate for final passage. Some legislators didn't want to vote for it at all, but others said they would vote for it only if they were needed for the 60th vote. They made it clear that if they were only the 59th vote, or the 61st vote, they would vote no. The Governor, the Speaker and all the bill supporters were engaged in counting heads and making sure the 58th, 59th and 60th votes were cast without the need for anyone to be the 61st vote. There didn't seem to be many profiles in courage in this process, though many cast a tough vote. In reality, every yes vote put their position as a legislator on the line.

It became clear to me in this negotiation and vote counting process leading up to a large tax increase that the downside risk to the legislators loomed much more strongly than any positive credit for solving a long-standing problem. The political calculation was that that those in the public who were offended would demand a pound of flesh. There was no expectation that would be offset by gratitude or support from tax increase supporters. Courageous legislators would bear that uneven burden largely alone.

When the 60 votes were on the board in the House, and just a few hours before the General Assembly's term ended according to the Illinois Constitution, the bill went to the Senate. Thirty votes were required there, and just as in the House, they all had to be Democrats. Not a single Republican would cast a bi-partisan vote for this needed revenue. As the debate raged, no televised picture of the debate was available to us so we listened over the remote speakers in the Governor's office. As we heard the debate continue, and knowing there were no votes to spare, we heard the sound of a gasp over the speaker followed by a call for medical assistance. Had one of our votes collapsed, suffered a heart attack, or become incapacitated and unable to vote? Was someone in physical jeopardy amidst the stress of this unpopular and difficult process? We heard only silence.

In a few minutes, we were reassured when we learned that a House member Rep. David Miller, who had come over to help lobby for the income tax, had collapsed under the stress of the evening. He soon recovered and everyone took a deep breath, awaiting the somewhat delayed final passage of the largest income tax increase in the state's history. The $6 billion was on the way from the taxpayers as soon as Governor Quinn signed the bill passed by the General Assembly in its final hours.

In a state government with a constant clamor for priority in spending decisions, a lingering structural deficit due mostly to unfunded pension liabilities, and an economy slowly recovering from the worst recession since the Great Depression, this was a huge deal. More than $6 billion a year in new revenue can solve a great host of problems. It also clarified the fact that no more fiscal help would be on the way. We would have to learn to live within the limits of this hard-fought result.

Does it Require Being "Brutal" to Make Deep Budget Cuts?

As the Governor's appointed Director of the Governor's Office of Management and Budget, I was as hard-nosed as I had to be to make difficult recommendations to the Governor on cutting the budget.[7]

A governmental budget that repeatedly faces a "structural deficit," means that built-in expenditures due to changing demographics, increased demands for services, or growing unmet needs are increasing at a rate higher than the rate of increase in revenues generated from the state's economy. Those budget-busting structural deficits were at the heart of the controversy on how to achieve fiscal responsibility yet also implement important spending priorities.

I didn't shrink from making hard decisions or imposing realistic limits on hiring, delayed implementation of new programs in the budget, or facility closures and outright reduction in services in lower priority areas. Efficiency changes, too, were needed, such as reducing leased office space, moving away from paper to electronic records, or shifting away from large, inefficient state hospitals to community-based care for the disabled.

In months of meetings with GOMB staffers, agency directors and deputy directors, we worked up budget proposals for the Governor's approval and budget speech. I often pushed back hard in these internal meetings to arrive at the recommendations

Hard decisions on budget cuts took their toll on consensus and personally as Illinois adjusted to living within its enhanced revenues after the 2011 tax increase.

presented to the Governor for his annual state budget.

Sometimes the enthusiasm for spending by those who believed strongly in what they were doing overwhelmed their responsibility to work with the Governor to help him set priorities. In the end, it was his decision to make those priority assessments in his budget draft. He then presented recommendations to the General Assembly for their debate, consideration, amendment, or approval in the appropriations process. This post-budget address phase also lasted months and entailed working with appropriation chairs, legislative leaders, and working groups to finalize the adopted state budget for the next fiscal year.

I got pushback from those appointed by the Governor as department heads, and sometimes from his other staff members. I didn't hesitate to remind them that states don't have a Federal Reserve System and can't print more money on paper like the federal government does.

Instead, Illinois government had to operate on existing revenues, cut lower priority programs and reduce inefficiency, or find ways to borrow the money under the scrutiny of rating agencies and bond investors. Our long-term pension deficits were already huge, and most of our borrowing was to pay for infrastructure projects that created thousands of jobs in our state during a recession. Especially after the income tax increase passed, deficit spending, or smoke-and-mirrors to cover it up, was simply not an option.

My facetious references, asking those in our internal budget preparation meetings if they saw a money printing press in the corner of my office like the federal government has, were just the beginning. I fiercely advocated phased implementations of personnel hiring, insisted on closing inefficient offices or facilities, and minimized my meetings with lobbyists seeking additional funding. I had learned at West Point that achieving the mission required sacrifice, hard work and determination. With the largest tax increase in the state's history in place, there was little choice left but to live within its capabilities.

All this caused some to refer to me as a "tyrant." My allies in Central Management Services, who implemented some of these cost savings initiatives, were deemed "terrorists" in the halls of the executive administration. These hard feelings would sometimes run so strong that peace conference lunches would have to be arranged so the cabinet secretaries or directors and I could sit down together informally and get back on the same page of supporting the Governor's priorities.

We had a small reprieve on Medicaid funding since, under the Great Recession federal stimulus law, the federal government temporarily raised the federal match to 62%, instead of the normal 50%. Medicaid spending in Illinois in FY 2012 of more than $14 billion served 2.7 million recipients. A 12% reduction in federal funding loomed as the stimulus expired--more than $1.6 billion annually in the state's share. Added to the larger growth in Medicaid expenditures from structural factors, which had been constantly growing for years, if not decades, and despite the tax increase, a new fiscal crisis was arriving.

According to the projections of the Civic Federation, in a report GOMB assisted to prepare, the annual increase in unpaid Medicaid bills would approach $4 billion by the end of Governor Quinn's term. The cumulative backlog of unpaid bills would build to nearly $12 billion.[8] These conclusions, prepared by a non-partisan, research-oriented and well-respected group in Illinois, were impossible to ignore. In my mind, it was clearly time to dig in and insist in internal meetings preparing the budget that this disastrous result be addressed.

In meetings of the National Association of State Budget Officials I listened to what other states were doing. Arizona impressed me because they simply reduced the Medicaid reimbursement rates to providers by 10%. Their budget director said the gloom and doom predictions of hospital closings, bankruptcies, and system failures presented by hospitals, doctors, nurses, dentists and other medical providers was completely overblown. They raised doubts that medical care could be delivered with such cuts in one of the largest segments of that state's economy. Arizona passed the 10% reimbursement cut anyway. Not one of the gloom and doom predictions occurred. The next year they cut the reimbursement rate by another 10%.

I knew from my discussions with the Illinois Department of Healthcare and Family Services, this would never fly. The medical lobbies were simply too strong and the political costs too high, despite the proven feasibility of this approach in other states. Instead, I proposed in budget drafts for discussion with the Governor that we cut Medicaid spending by $2 billion, with the details to be worked out in a joint legislative/executive working group.

The Governor and the legislative leaders were open to this discussion because unpaid Medicaid bills to providers were a political stone around their necks. They knew something had to be done. Legislative liaisons broached the $2 billion amount to the lobbies, especially the Illinois Hospital Association. They countered with a proposal for only $40 million in cuts.

At this point I repeated my often-expressed statement on the M's and B's. Too often budgetary discussions were about millions of dollars, and a cut of millions in double digits can contain a lot of pain for those losing those services or funds. However, the continuing state fiscal crisis with the Medicaid structural deficit was in billions with a B. It takes a hundred $10 million painful cuts to save a billion dollars. The health care lobbies were only willing to offer four of the needed 100 small cuts.

The climax of this mostly internal discussion was reached in a meeting in the Governor's formal office on the second floor of the Capitol. Sitting at the end of the table, to the right of the Governor, were those who advocated small cuts to Medicaid and continued deficits. Their arguments were all over the place about future changes in demand, the effectiveness of management, and help from the lobbyists in holding down costs. Every key aide to the Governor, and all the affected cabinet secretaries and legislative liaison staff, were on that side of the table, all to the Governor's right. I sat alone on the Governor's left, listening to their spending pleas. They talked for what seemed like hours as dinner time approached.

They finally concluded and expressed to the Governor that there was a consensus among them to not proceed with the big cuts. Up to that time, I had only listened and asked a few clarifying questions, as though I had nothing else to say.

As they sought to smugly close the discussion and walk away from this problem, I interjected that there was another view. I had not yet had my say on my recommendations. The Governor was willing to listen to that different view.

My argument was simple but harsh. I recommended that he read the Civic Federation report, which is accurate, and then let me know how doing nothing will prevent the multi-billion dollar deficits in state spending as this problem festers. I asked they consider how every other category of state spending, elementary and secondary education, higher education, college scholarships for low and middle income students, public safety, corrections, state parks, regulatory agencies, and other human services will suffer. I pointed out that literally every other aspect of state spending will be hurt if this continues.

Finally, I asked how a Governor who was brave enough to advocate the largest income tax increase in state history, will face the voters in 2014 and answer the question of how that did not solve our fiscal problems. The accumulated deficits would literally be higher, not lower, after an infusion of more than $6 billion a year from the taxpayers.

Stark differences sat on the two sides of the table. Governor Quinn listened. Then he concluded the meeting with a tongue-in-cheek remark along the lines of 'now that everyone is in agreement, let's go over to the mansion for dinner.' At least that comment changed the mood to a few smiles.

Julie Hamos, Secretary of Healthcare and Family Services in charge of the state Medicaid program, had a long history of service as a state representative and was a well-respected and hard-working leader. Joining me in the buffet line for dinner in the mansion private dining room, she had just one question for me: "I understand the fiscal argument, but how could you be so brutal?" Being confronted face-to-face in such a personal way by a knowledgeable and respected member of the Governor's team was hard to swallow. I sluffed it off by stating that I had a reputation for being tough on fiscal matters, and I had to live up to that reputation.

That answer was truly insufficient given the circumstances, but the Governor soon decided to accept my proposed number of a $2 billion cut. He even held up the Civic Federation report that had been so helpful in summarizing and documenting the need for this change in his annual budget speech.

The legislative leaders convened a four-person working group, with two legislators each from the Senate and House, two Democrats and two Republicans total, to work with the Governor on achieving this tough cut in the appropriation process. Julie Hamos was in the key seat constructively pulling together the detailed possibilities of what could be cut, line by line. It turned out that many of the spending programs were not a required part of federal Medicaid at all. They were simply optional programs that allowed state additions to qualify for the federal Medicaid match. Over time, they had crept into the program as non-mandatory add-ons, and had become the centerpiece of the cuts. In a hard negotiation, the working group's possible cuts approached $1.3 billion.

I urged the Governor to add enough of a rate decrease to achieve the $2 billion target, but he instead advocated a large cigarette tax increase, which would do double duty in long-term reductions in Medicaid medical costs due to reductions in respiratory illnesses and cancer. It also provided revenues that could be spent to achieve Medicaid match. The new total was quite close to the $2 billion target. It was implemented that year by the General Assembly and signed by the Governor.

Harsh cuts though lead to hard realities. Thousands of Illinois citizens were going to lose medical benefits they had been previously receiving. On a personal side, my drumbeat of fiscal restraint was wearing thin on those committed to improving the delivery of necessary services in Illinois. I had learned being elected three different times to two different school boards that successful school superintendents who take on hard problems generally have only a limited lifetime as a superintendent. Their effectiveness as a leader begins to wane as the hard feelings and pain of tough decisions builds on them. I was in that same position.

Continuous political or leadership conflict also takes a personal toll. My children with their own children reminded me that even on holidays visiting them, I was not really there. They said my mind, attention, and constant phone and email responses meant I was not really present. My doctor told me to retire or the stress would kill me. I stayed with it because I knew the harder toll was in the Governor himself, and I resisted moving on.

Governors, though, are also better served with some rotation of staff so new energy takes on the new problems. As we hit the bottom on cutting expenses, we faced a rebound in revenues as the recession waned. The budget needed leadership attuned to this reality to build the programs back up, not to be locked into the opposite downward spiral.

I faced the reality that I needed to return to family and my investment business and began my own transition to move on. I had finally achieved what I had missed by being unable to work during his term with Governor Walker. My work for Governor Quinn had turned out to be an even more productive four years. I was thankful and eternally grateful to Governor Quinn for that opportunity.

I learned, too, that state governments are in a perpetual fiscal crunch. The federal government has seized control of all the best revenue sources, and then delegates the tough domestic needs to states through mandates but without funding. When the federal government mandated special education services for all children in our educational system, it improved the lives of millions of people. But it didn't send the money to pay for it. Limited state revenues were stretched, local property taxes increased and the federal government looked the other way.

The American Dream and its values have more aspects than just those visible in open government debate. Spending is not everything that state government does, and leadership is not always in high profile positions. The everyday activity within our families, businesses, and private lives, and what we learn and do there, carries great long-term influence. From the midst of the clash on public spending in Illinois, I was now returning to those other aspects of the American Dream.

Efficient Markets

For decades, I had mused on the question of what parts of professional service were most productive. Raising cattle attracted me as a teenager, as did flying airplanes. In choosing military service at West Point, I encountered how leadership could make a difference in achieving the mission, be it military or civilian. My encounter with law professor Wynne Morriss led me to believe in the legal system. Despite the fact that the wheels of justice turn slowly they also grind very finely. It achieved results. My clash with the military chain of command over the First Amendment and compulsory chapel at West Point led me to law school and to the practice of law. Joining Dan Walker in his campaign of Illinois political reform led me into the world of politics and what it could accomplish.

Along the way, though, I begin to see that the fields of law and politics had their limitations and failures. Within the controversies around those failures, it was the values at stake that really influenced the ultimate outcomes. I practiced law in the 1980s for longer than I originally intended and saw the frustrations and short-comings of an inefficient legal system that emphasized combat by dollars instead of justice. I gravitated away from the courthouses and found myself instead more productive when helping businesses solve problems.

Profitable and nimble businesses often created their own problems, while seeking to be unimpeded by regulatory, legal or litigious hurdles. These businesses sought to avoid the constraint of law or regulation. They were so anxious to stay away from the courthouse that I identified with their efforts for a more efficient and profitable path.

They had to run the gauntlet of risk from all sorts of threats-- tax, regulatory, competitive, financial, and personnel failures. Their way through this morass was often evasive, or down and dirty. This meant they generated enormous need for legal help to unsnarl their own blindsided collisions with these risks. Helping them extricate from the meat grinder of a legal system that moved slowly was challenging, fun and productive. At the heart of the solution was efficiency, plain and simple. Getting it done with minimal costs and risk mitigation was a real approach that worked.

Where could this efficiency play out in the most effective way? As opposed to drafting hundreds of words in trusts and estate planning documents, what if the emphasis was on efficiently building up the investments to implement such plans? Instead of protecting the title to real estate with abstracts and title insurance, what if the emphasis was on using the appropriate leverage to reinvest and acquire more profits? Instead of traveling to the courthouse to file and litigate disputed rights, the travel that counted was to places of opportunity to build a small business.

Decisions like that are made every day by business people, lawyers, financial planners, investment advisors, tax planners, accountants, and hard-working people trying to utilize their time well. In which decisions is there more productivity and promise? What kind of help do people need to make such good choices?

It seemed to me that the idea of asset management made more sense than the practice of law. While practicing law I enrolled in the DePaul University Master of Law in Tax program, and then the Certified Financial Planner program. Finally, while working in Treasurer Quinn's office, I enrolled in the Chartered Financial Analyst educational and licensing program to learn the nuts and bolts of managing investments and tailoring them to client objectives.

As I completed my time in the Treasurer's Office, I was ready to head out and find employment with a large financial institution where I could participate in an investment management process that would enable me to later begin my own investment management practice for clients.

It wasn't to be. Transitioning from practicing law with a law degree is not the same as making financial decisions backed up with an MBA. Spending time in politics is not considered efficient in the business community. Why would a high-level financial institution want my help instead of the financial types they were training and fostering in their own organizational development efforts?

One high level bank interviewer asked me at the final interview how he could justify hiring me, when my father-in-law, former Governor Dan Walker, was in trouble with the savings and loan regulators and being prosecuted for violating their regulations in managing his (not mine) savings and loan association. He didn't find my answer satisfying.

A friend who was advocating my hiring at a large bond firm told me I had come across as a risk taker, like Xenophon the Greek who backed his small army with a cliff to their rear, leaving them no choice but to fight to the death and defeat their attackers. Bonds are for safety, not risk takers.

My idea to seek out a large firm to learn investment techniques and approaches was foundering on these excuses for not welcoming my talents. But I had worked in a large organization in helping the Illinois Treasurer manage a multi-billion-dollar short term portfolio of government funds. We had enhanced return, hired outside professional investment managers to achieve better objectives, and defended against a run on our publicly held money market fund, IPTIP, after a similar fund collapsed in Orange County, California.

I decided that was enough, and advocated that a partner join me in moving from large institutions to the small and nimble investment management approach we could do on our own. Together we gained the confidence and trust of investors and produced results that exceeded those of competing larger firms.

Technology, trust and teamwork made us successful, and we grew and attracted younger employees who made us more competent as we learned the business helping our clients together. Today, four of us (three of whom are women) from that experience have spun out into our own smaller and more nimble women-owned firm based on teamwork and willingness to learn new skills to add value to our client accounts.

Managing other people's or institutions' money creates great opportunity to study and understand the economy and how other managers add value to their investments. My favorite oracle through years of this activity has been Warren Buffet. Listening to him take all questions from the floor for five hours on a Saturday afternoon, year after year at his annual meetings, provides a window into how he allocates capital. His talent at building Berkshire Hathaway, and the way he brought on key managers and successors as he grows older, applies to so many issues within the investment management business.

One of my many favorite Buffet quotes is the following:

> *The best way to think about investments is to be in a room with no one else and to just think. If that doesn't work, nothing else is going to work.*

The confidence to trust one's analytical strengths and do the work it takes while you are at it is a key to investment success. I look forward to his every annual meeting more each year.

My partners and I have now been at it for a couple decades. As long as the clients appreciate what we do, we won't be stepping aside any time soon.

Refuge

Stepping aside from the investment business for four years to help Governor Quinn placed me squarely in the maelstrom of the deception, manipulation and controversy of Illinois politics. It was different from the greed and fear that underlies much of the investment world. Not long after I left state government I told my Pastor, Tim Wilkins, that I needed to hear the gospel preached to counter these everyday assaults in my work.

Besides helping me take on hiking the Grand Canyon rim to rim, which Tim and his wife, Kellyann, had done, Tim found time for conversations with me at Panera about Paul's letter to the Romans. Romans' expounding of Christian theology is well known and flows from the nature of God as follows:

> For what can be known about God is plain to them, because God has shown it to them. For his invisible attributes, namely, his eternal power and divine nature, have been clearly perceived, ever since the creation of the world, in the things that have been made. Romans 1:19-20, English Standard Version of the Bible.

The message further resonates in my favorite verse:

> Do not be conformed to this world, but be transformed by the renewal of your mind, that by testing you may discern what is the will of God, what is good and acceptable and perfect. Romans 12:2, English Standard Version of the Bible.

About this same time, Jay Boyd started showing up at my door in Naperville. I was working in downtown Chicago at our investment firm, and I at first had no idea who he was. It turned out he had accepted a job to raise money in northern Illinois for the Carmi Baptist Children's' Home and Family Services. This was quite a job for a recent graduate who had moved from his home in Alabama to work in Baptist missions.

I agreed to meet with him at the Starbucks in the downtown Chicago Loop. He got right to the point, saying I was a sporadic contributor to the children's home, which I had been familiar with since going to high school with its residents in Carmi. Jay suggested I do a monthly credit card contribution of $85, and give the children's home $1,000 a year, which I quite quickly told him I was OK with. He wasn't done. He said I needed to go with them on their mission trip to Uganda.

A group of recent college graduates had met Pastor Goffrey, a local Ugandan Baptist preacher, who was trying to put together funds to build an orphanage in a rural area on the south side of Lake Victoria. Pastor Goffrey could handle the construction labor but needed $40,000 for materials. The young graduates all had families involved with the Baptist Children's Home in Carmi, and upon returning to Illinois they enlisted them in a new mission for other orphan children in the world who needed help. Within a few months they had raised $80,000 to begin the orphanage. The Baptist Children's Home continued to support this effort in Africa and planned to undertake mission trips every few years. Jay Boyd said I should sign up.

In Mt. Vernon doing mission trip preparation with a

The posted notice of my lost baggage at Entebbe International Airport in Uganda. Helping out on the Baptist Childrens' Home mission trip to the orphanage it helps there turned out to help me even more as we helped the orphans there.

half dozen volunteers from southern Illinois, I found these trips to help others ended up helping me more. Laurie Ingram and I helped solve the largest problem of our trip. Laurie had served as a missionary in South Africa for a decade or so and understood how culture can retard progress. She described a situation where a young mother had died in childbirth not long after the father drowned. The local police helped the baby survive temporarily but were stymied by the African custom that allows only family members to name a baby. None were there. The local police, though, would not let the child be taken to the orphanage without a birth certificate, and they were culturally helpless to name this baby on the birth certificate themselves.

Laurie thought she knew an answer. She said all of us on the mission trip should search our memories for a family name common to at least two of us. We would then, in effect, welcome this baby into our extended families by allowing the baby to accept our family name on her birth certificate. Laurie and I had a common family name, Elise, which was my mother's middle name. The next day, baby Elise was accepted at the orphanage with her name recorded on her birth certificate.

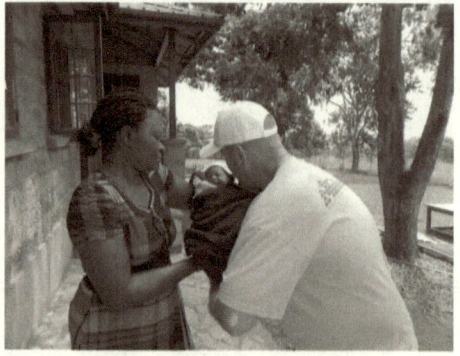

Baby Elise being accepted into the orphanage in Uganda.

Haiti, our neighbor in the Caribbean, is a much poorer country than Uganda. Ostracized and excluded from the international economy through reparations and discriminatory trade because of its successful slave revolt a couple centuries ago, Haiti never recovered. I had responded to Pastor Russell Howard's call at McGregor Baptist Church in Fort Myers to sponsor a child there. Seeing Dawn Shoemaker at the Haiti booth at the Global Impact Conference piqued my curiosity. To me, Dawn looked to be a recent college graduate filling in at the Haiti booth while the missionaries were on coffee break. She looked much more like a recent college volleyball player than someone I could associate with a Haiti mission.

Dawn's answer to my point blank question of what she had to do with Haiti was unexpected. She was raising her initial funding to become a full-time missionary in Haiti. Like Jay Boyd, after telling me about sister church relationships and schools for children in Haiti, she suggested I join the Haiti mission trip later that year. Dawn signed me up for the mission trip training classes, which were much more elaborate than our one preparation meeting for Uganda. Haiti is just tough, full of violence, poverty, disease and stark living conditions. Many find it hard to take on.

Because of the ongoing sister church relationship, most of the training team had been to Cotes de Fer, a fishing village on the south coast of Haiti. They assured the few rookies that they would look out for us, and not to worry. Our mission was to bring Creole Bibles to build on the entire church's single Bible, give goats for families to raise. and to collaborate with the local pastor and deacons on projects for the church. One part of our group would build and equip new classrooms for the school and the other would conduct medical clinics at the church and its outlying branches in the mountains.

Giving goats to the families we sponsored in the McGregor Baptist Church's sister church in Cotes de Fer, Haiti.

The pastor's wife had meager food supplies but every morning fixed a well-prepared breakfast for our team and the local missionaries. Becky Thompson, a resident missionary living for nearly a decade and raising her family in Haiti, was a pharmacist by trade and helped lead the medical mission. I was assigned as a pill counter and guarantor that the children would really swallow their de-worming medicine. One morning a disagreement arose at the breakfast on priorities between building classrooms, evangelizing, and providing medical clinics. Becky spoke up and prayed that we continue the medical clinics. I had never heard such an articulate explanation of Matthew 25 in such a real and immediate context:

> 'For I was hungry and you gave me food, I was thirsty and you gave me drink, I was a stranger and you welcomed me, I was naked and you clothed me.' Then the righteous will answer him, saying, 'Lord, when did we see you hungry and feed you, or thirsty and give your drink? And when did we see you a stranger and welcome you, or naked and clothe you? And when did we see you sick or in prison and visit you?' And the King will answer them, 'Truly, I say to you, as you did it to one of the least of these my brothers, you did it to me.' Matthew 25:35-40. English Standard Version of the Bible.

There in our humble surroundings, being fed and cared for by poor people in one of the poorest countries in the world, just 600 miles off the Florida coast, the importance of caring for the least of these rang loud and true. Becky's articulate and heart felt words of pleading urged that we not cancel a medical clinic for other priorities. She read the verses, explaining every word in a calm, deliberate and patient manner, appealing for us to be glad in implementing this Biblical direction. It wasn't near the same as hearing these verses preached in an air-conditioned church filled with well-fed and healthy people.

Into the mountains we went, meeting local friendly people who had walked for hours to attend our medical clinics. We administered de-worming and other medicines, did our best to care for a Zika baby and her mother, and celebrated our common bonds as people on Earth who lived just a few hundred miles apart.

Tom Miller and I were the rookies, but we returned looking for more to do, choosing the Stephen Ministry to help others in crisis.

There is refuge in these words and truths. There is also refuge in carrying them out daily with a grateful heart. They represent just some of the values that underlie the American Dream. Our freedom of religion to pursue, understand, and think through, both with gratitude and a spirit of service, is a wonderful legacy that the American Dream represents. It allows us to be not conformed to the world and at the same time to find refuge from its turmoil. May we do our best to make it better.

NOTES

Introduction

1 Colley, David P. *Decision at Strasbourg: Ike's Mistake to Halt the Sixth Army Group at the Rhine in 1944.* Annapolis, Maryland: Naval Institute Press, 2008.

2 Whiting, Charles. *America's Forgotten Army: the True Story of the U. S. Seventh Army in WWII—and an Unknown Battle that Changed History.* New York, New York: St. Martin's Press, 1999.

3 Brokaw, Tom. *The Greatest Generation.* New York: Random House, 1998. For other examples of the attitudes of this generation.

Chapter 1: From Burnt Prairie to West Point

4 Adams, James Truslow, *The Epic of America.* New Brunswick: Transaction Publishers, 2012, originally published in 1931 by Little, Brown, and Company.

5 Ibid, 405.

6 Swamp & Overflowed Lands in the United States, Issued October 7, 1908 by the United States Department of Agriculture at www.brittlebooks.library.illinois.edu.

7 Federico, Giovanni, *Not Guilty? Agriculture in the 1920's and the Great Depression.* Cambridge University Press, Journal of Economic History, vol. 65, no. 4, 2005, pp 949-976. *JSTOR,*

www.jstor.org/stable/3874910. See also Iowa Public Television, *Hard Times.* 1979 at www.iptv.org.

8   Transcript from the John F Kennedy Presidential Library, as quoted on www.NPR.org on December 5, 2007.

9   Adams, James Truslow, *The Epic of America.* New Brunswick: Transaction Publishers, 2012, originally published in 1931 by Little, Brown, and Company, 404.

Chapter 2: From the Liberty Baptist Church to the Cadet Chapel

10   Truscott IV, Lucian K. *Dress Gray.* Garden City, New York: Doubleday & Company, Inc., 1978.

11   Spieth, Susan I. *Gray Girl.* Create Space Independent Publishing Platform, 2013, and *Area Bird.* Create Space Independent Publishing Platform, 2015, and *Witch Heart*, Create Space Independent Publishing Platform, 2016.

12   *"Together Again,"* by Buck Owens, Capitol Records, April 4, 1964.

13   Burns, Ken, Lynn Novick and Geoffrey Ward. *The Vietnam War*, Episode 5, PBS, 2017. For the circumstances of Rich Hood's combat death in Vietnam in 1967. When watching this documentary series at home on my TV, I saw Rich Hood's face fill my TV screen, as his classmate explained his death. The feeling of shock and dismay was palpable nearly 50 years after those events occurred.

14   *"We Gotta Get Out of This Place,"* written by Barry Mann and Cynthia Weil, recorded by the Animals, MGM, June 15, 1965.

15   All Biblical references are to the King James Version.

16   From the Catechism of the Catholic Church, paragraph 2309: The strict conditions for *legitimate defense by military force* require rigorous consideration. The gravity of such a decision makes it subject to rigorous conditions of moral legitimacy. At one and the same time: - the damage inflicted by the aggressor on the nation or community of nations must be lasting, grave, and certain; - all

other means of putting an end to it must have been shown to be impractical or ineffective, as quoted at www.scborromeo.org.

17 O God, our Father, Thou Searcher of human hearts, help us to draw near to Thee in sincerity and truth. May our religion be filled with gladness and may our worship of Thee be natural. Strengthen and increase our admiration for honest dealing and clean thinking, and suffer not our hatred of hypocrisy and pretence ever to diminish. Encourage us in our endeavor to live above the common level of life. Make us to choose the harder right instead of the easier wrong, and never to be content with a half truth when the whole can be won. Endow us with courage that is born of loyalty to all that is noble and worthy, that scorns to compromise with vice and injustice and knows no fear when truth and right are in jeopardy. Guard us against flippancy and irreverence in the sacred things of life. Grant us new ties of friendship and new opportunities of service. Kindle our hearts in fellowship with those of a cheerful countenance, and soften our hearts with sympathy for those who sorrow and suffer. Help us to maintain the honor of the Corps untarnished and unsullied and to show forth in our lives the ideals of West Point in doing our duty to Thee and to our Country. All of which we ask in the name of the Great Friend and Master of all. Quoted from the Chaplain section of the usma.edu website, 2018.

18 Clark, General Wesley K. Clark. *Winning Modern Wars: Iraq, Terrorism, and the American Empire.* New York: Perseus Books Group, 2003. On the Iraq War, Clark said in his Introduction at page xiv: "It has thus far been a perfect example of dominating an enemy force but failing to secure the victory."

Chapter 3: From Grandma Vaught's Concept of Religious Freedom to Alexander Haig

19 Mote, Edward. *My Hope is Built on Nothing Less.* The Lutheran Hymnal, Hymn # 370, 1834.

20 Gelfand, H. Michael. *Sea Change at Annapolis: the United States Naval Academy 1949-2000.* Chapel Hill, North Carolina: The University of North Carolina Press, 2006.

21 Fred Van Atta was a classmate in Company D-3 and H-3. In his third year at West Point, he had conducted this study as part of a class requirement for a paper.

22 Major Bruce Dalgleish was one of our better tactical officers in the Third Regiment. In the USMA Class of 1961, he had served as a Cadet Regimental Commander. He did two tours in Vietnam and retired as a Colonel after many years of service in the Army. See http://www.usma1961.org/Class%20Memorial%20 Pages/A-1%20Bruce%20Dalgleish.pdf.

23 See https://en.wikipedia.org/wiki/M._Collier_Ross.

24 A short obituary at http://www.west-point.org/users/usmafriends/ 20111206/ provides some detail of Bob Berry's career as a lobbyist, Army officer and inter-related political career.

25 One mistake that resulted in walking the most hours on the area was rooted in accepting help to pay the larger phone bills we were encountering as we sought some outside support and advice. Lucian accepted the use of a phone credit card from a friend in New York and shared it with us. The phone company soon determined the card was fraudulent causing our phone bills using it to be unpaid. Upon learning of this we promptly paid the bills ourselves. When West Point learned of this mistake, they called it "gross lack of judgment." For that Lucian and I spent much of the spring of 1969 walking off 88 hours of punishment tours on the area.

26 See https://en.wikipedia.org/wiki/M._Collier_Ross.

27 A short obituary at http://www.west-point.org/users/usmafriends/ 20111206/ provides some detail of Bob Berry's career as a lobbyist, Army officer, and inter-related political career.

Chapter 4: From Chapel Donations to the Area

28 This recent book on My Lai not only describes "Pinkville," but lays out in detail, after decades of research, the appalling and embarrassing story of My Lai, including Koster's role in its initial cover-up, for which he was demoted and retired from the Army. See also "Report of the Department of the Army Review of the Preliminary Investigation into the My Lai Incident." Peers, Lieutenant General W. R., 14 March 1970, especially at pages 12-9 to 12-12 for specifications of Koster's failures of command.

Chapter 5: From Duty, Honor, Country to Disillusionment

29 In his famous speech, Martin Luther King, Jr., considered his dream rooted in the American Dream: "I say to you today, my friends, though, even though we face the difficulties of today and tomorrow, I still have a dream. It is a dream deeply rooted in the American dream. I have a dream that one day this nation will rise up, live out the true meaning of its creed: 'We hold these truths to be self-evident, that all men are created equal.'" Martin Luther King, Jr., speech copyright 1963, on record at archives. gov.

30 Chris Gray, "The Forgotten Festival," *Houston Press*, September 2, 2009.

Chapter 6: From Airborne School to Federal District Court: *Anderson v. Laird*, 316 F. Supp. 1081 (D.D.C. 1970)

31 "The Horse Solders," directed by John Ford, theatrical movie, United Artists, June 17, 1959. https://en.wikipedia.org/wiki/The_Horse_Soldiers

32 Hackworth, David H. and Eilhys England. *Steel My Soldiers' Hearts*. New York: Simon & Schuster, 2002, page 8. See also www.currahee3-506.org/history.

33 See *Washington Post* obituary of Joseph Hannon, Assistant U S Attorney and chief of the civil division from 1955 to 1972, when he became Superior Court Judge in Washington, D. C. He was a graduate of Catholic University School of Law and had served as B-17 pilot in World War II. https://www.washingtonpost.com/archive/local/1990/03/21/joseph-hannon-superior-court-judge-here-dies/8f462307-0ce1-4379-8c16-6d6b602bba4e/?utm_term=.f5123857aabe

34 Timberg, Robert. *Blue Eyed Boy*, New York: The Penguin Press, 2014, 118-121. Timberg recounts his interview with Billy Graham after a Naval Academy chapel service. See also Appelquist, A. Ray, editor. *Church State and Chaplaincy*, Washington, D. C.: The General Commission on Chaplains and Armed Forces Personnel, 1969.

35 Ibid., 121.

36 *Trust and Obey*, by John H. Sammis, traditional hymn, 1887.

37 Noonan, Jr., John T. and Edward McGlynn Gaffney, Jr. *Religious Freedom: History, Cases, and Other Materials on the Interaction of Religion and Government*, Foundation Press, Third Edition 2011. For an extensively documented history of the progress toward religious freedom. Noonan is both a law professor at the University of California at Berkeley and a Circuit Judge on the Ninth Circuit. Gaffney is a professor of law at Valparaiso University School of Law. Having developed their text over decades of legal scholarship, they added hundreds of pages to their third edition on the earlier history of religious toleration and freedom from ancient times through the American Revolution.

38 Noonan and Gaffney, 160.

39 Metaxas, Eric. *Martin Luther: The Man Who Rediscovered God and Changed the World*, New York: Penguin Books, 2017.

40 Noonan and Gaffney, 416-420.

41 Noonan and Gaffney, 473.

42 Armstrong, O. K. and Marjorie Armstrong. *The Baptists in America,* Garden City, New York, Doubleday & Company, Inc., 1979. See also Noonan and Gaffney, 470-476.

Chapter 7: From Anderson v. Laird to Retaliation

43 https://en.wikipedia.org/wiki/United_States_Armed_Forces #Personnel.
44 www.AUSA.org. The author's Article 138 complaint about AUSA activities at Fort Bragg in 1970 also documents AUSA's activities and positions.
45 www.AUSA.org.

Chapter 8: From Carrying a Rifle and Binoculars as a Forward Observer to Political Resistance

46 The author's and Cornelius Cooper's Article 138 official complaint about racial discrimination in housing at Fort Bragg in 1970 documents these events.

Chapter 9: From an Alert to 1LT Cornelius Cooper, West Point's First Conscientious Objector

47 Mobley, Richard A. *U.S. Joint Military Contributions to Countering Syria's 1970 Invasion of Jordan,* www.ndupress.ndu. edu, Issue 55, 4th Quarter, 2009.
48 Martin, Douglas. "Rev. Dr. Roger L. Shinn, Theologian, Dies at 96". *New York Times,* June 2, 2013.
49 Konvitz, Milton R. *Religious Liberty and Conscience,* New York: The Viking Press, 1968, especially at pages 88-98.
50 Peace Education Division of the American Friends Service Committee. *The Draft?* New York: Hill and Wang, 1968, 1-9.
51 United States v. Seeger, 380 U.S. 163 (1965) and Welsh v. United States, 398 U.S. 333, 1970.

52 https://en.wikipedia.org/wiki/Ike_Atkinson for details on convicted Army Master Sergeant Atkinson, concerning drug smuggling from Vietnam involving U. S. military personnel.

53 Heinl, Jr., Colonel Robert D. *Vietnam: The collapse of the armed forces,* www.libcom.org, August 23, 2009, originally published in Armed Forces Journal, June 7, 1971.

54 Ibid.

55 Gillette v United States, 401 U.S. 437 (1971) on selective conscientious objection and United States v. O'Brien, 391 U.S. 367 (1968) on draft card burning.

56 Army Regulation 604-5 covers procedures for security clearances.

Chapter 10: From the Army to Law School

57 Notes from the desk of Harry Vaught, handwritten letter dated October 15,1970.

Chapter 11: From Fort Bragg to Pud's Farm

58 Vaught, David, "Music to Plow By," *The Village Voice*, July 22, 1971, citing the lyrics of "After the Fire is Gone," written by L. E. White, recorded by Conway Twitty and Loretta Lynn, Decca Records, January 4,1971.

Chapter 13: From New York City to the Political Field

59 The film *9 1/2 Weeks*, directed by Adrian Lyne, Metro-Goldwyn-Mayer (MGM), theatrical movie, released February 21,1986 used our neighbor's much improved barge as a location in the movie with Kim Basinger and Mickey Rourke.

60 I ultimately did more than a dozen country music columns for the *Village Voice* between February 26, 1970, and November 18, 1971, plus one other piece Diane Fisher referred to *Country Music Magazine* on Waylon Jennings.

Chapter 14: From Recovery to a New Mission

61 Possley, Maurice, and Patrick Reardon, "U. S. Moves in on Woodlawn Housing," *Chicago Tribune*, September 21, 1986.
62 Alinsky, Saul D. *Rules for Radicals*, New York: Random House, 1971.

Chapter 15: From the Grassroots to the Executive Mansion and Mayor Daley

63 Hartley, Robert E, *The Dealmakers of Downstate Illinois: Paul Powell, Clyde L Choate, John H Stelle*, Southern Illinois University Press, 2017, 13.

Chapter 16: From the Southern Illinois Governor's Office to the Clyde Choate Challenge

63 Noonan, Jr., John T. and Edward McGlynn Gaffney, Jr. *Religious Freedom: History, Cases, and Other Materials on the Interaction of Religion and Government,* Foundation Press, Third Edition 2011. For an extensively documented history of the progress toward religious freedom. Noonan is both a law professor at the University of California at Berkeley and a Circuit Judge on the Ninth Circuit. Gaffney is a professor of law at Valparaiso University School of Law. Having developed their text over decades of legal scholarship, they added hundreds of pages to their third edition on the earlier history of religious toleration and freedom from ancient times through the American Revolution.
64 Armstrong, O. K. and Marjorie Armstrong. *The Baptists in America,* Garden City, New York: Doubleday & Company, Inc., 1979, Chapter 1, "John Leland and the Bill of Rights," 1-17.65 466 F2d 283, 286.
66 466 F2d 283, 295.
67 466 F2d 283, 290.

68 466 F2d 283, 298.
69 466 F2d 283, 300.
70 466 F2d 283, 299.
71 Royko, Mike. *Boss: Richard J. Daley of Chicago*, New York: E. P. Dutton & Company, 1971.

Chapter 18: From Vic deGrazia to the Front Porch

72 Karen Rothe and Henry deFiebre, "DeGrazia slips in, sees party chairmen about Vaught," *Southern Illinoisan*, March 14, 1974, detailing DeGrazia's and Walker's visit to southern Illinois indicating support of both Choate and the author in the primary election a few days later.

Chapter 19: From Law School to the Victory Over Clyde Choate

73 Laws of the State of Illinois Enacted by the 79th General Assembly, Illinois Legislative Reference Bureau, 1976.
74 Executive Order Number 3, February 8, 1973, included in paragraph 2 this prohibition, "No employee shall ask or require any other employee, whether in an exempt or non-exempt position, to make a political contribution."

Footnotes
Epilogue

1 PJ O'Rourke's book Parliament of Whores, 2003. https://www.amazon.com/Parliament-Whores-Humorist-Attempts-Government/dp/0802139701
2 Samuel Witwer, Con Con Diary: Reflections of Samuel W. Witwer, Wichita State University, 1996.

3   See Witwer's conclusion of the Chicago Democratic organization's rationale for holding onto multi-member districts in Con Con Diary.

4   Ibid.

5   See Thomas Lyons quote confirming the Chicago Democratic organization's position on single versus multi-member districts in Witwer's Con Con Diary.

6   Coalition for Political Honesty v. Illinois State Bd. of Elections, No. 81 C 2718, 1982 U.S. Dist. LEXIS 12411 at 7 (N.D. Ill. Apr. 23, 1982).

7   "During his time as Governor, Pat Quinn signed six state budgets into law, cutting state spending by more than $5 billion while providing sufficient revenue for vital public services such as education, healthcare, public safety, and human services." Quoted from http://governorquinnportrait.org/budgeting-for-results.html, the portal Governor utilized to specify his record as Governor at the time his official portrait was hung in the hall of the Capitol.

8   **Five-Year Medicaid Projections Show Growth in Unpaid Bills** *February 3, 2012,* a report by the Civic Federation, at Five-Year Medicaid Projection Shows Growth in Unpaid Bills | The Civic Federation https://www.civicfed.org/. The Civic Federation is a non-partisan government research organization working to maximize the quality and cost-effectiveness of government services in the Chicago region and State of Illinois.

The author at a medical clinic in the mountains of Haiti.

www.ingramcontent.com/pod-product-compliance
Lightning Source LLC
Chambersburg PA
CBHW021710120626
46545CB00004B/1494